Where

Have All

the Flowers Gone?

Where Have All the Flowers Gone?

THE FALL AND RISE OF THE WOODSTOCK GENERATION

Anthony M. Casale
and Philip Lerman

Andrews and McMeel
A Universal Press Syndicate Company
KANSAS CITY • NEW YORK

Library of Congress Cataloging in Publication Data

Casale, Anthony M.
    Where have all the flowers gone? : the fall and rise of the
Woodstock generation / Anthony M. Casale and Philip Lerman.
        p.   cm.
    Bibliography: p.
    Includes index.
    ISBN 0-8362-1847-7 : $16.95
    1. Baby boom generation—United States. 2. United States—Social
conditions—1960-1980. 3. United States—Social conditions—1980-
I. Lerman, Philip. II. Title.
    HN59.C37   1989
    306'.09'09046—dc20   89-14926
                                                              CIP

ATTENTION: SCHOOLS   AND   BUSINESSES

For Lois
A.M.C.

For Eleanor and Michael
P.L.

Contents

We are stardust, million-year-old carbon.
We are golden, caught in the devil's bargain.
And we got to get ourselves back to the garden.
— Joni Mitchell
"Woodstock"

 *Introduction*

As the last line of the song "Woodstock" faded away twenty years ago, a new era began to dawn in America.

But the era did not take the form that the jubilant, stoned, dancing, muddy mass of humanity at that concert expected. In fact, it was not what anybody expected. Not Tony Casale, who spent much of the Woodstock weekend in a one-room trailer up on blocks along the banks of the Susquehanna River in Williamsport, Pennsylvania, trying unsuccessfully to lose his virginity. Not Philip Lerman, who spent Woodstock weekend in the basement of his parents' home in Far Rockaway, New York, listening to reports from Woodstock on WNEW-FM on the radio he had got for his bar mitzvah from his sister, and bemoaning the fact that he wasn't there.

Wherever you were on Woodstock weekend, you learned soon enough that something big was going down. The concert heralded the beginning of the Woodstock generation's roller-coaster ride, from protesting youth to mainstream adult.

The generation that was Woodstock expected its heartfelt idealism and vibrance to change the world, to carry on through the years.

It is fashionable today to say that the idealism of the Woodstock generation just faded away. But the values and ideals and beliefs and hopes of the generation do carry on, and are just now, as we move into the 1990s, beginning to be felt.

This is not a book about the Woodstock Festival, although the concert is its opening act. It is not just about ex-hippies, although many are encountered. It is not a whatever-happened-to book about famous people, although we will check in with some well-known old friends.

It is a book about the crazy-quilt Woodstock generation, about the idealism and strength that were born twenty years ago. About how that idealism was dashed in the 70s, submerged in the 80s, and is now surfacing as we greet the 90s. About the roller-coaster ride through the war and Watergate, disco and the Me Generation, to yuppiedom and the emergence of the generation's renewed soul.

Most of all, it is a book about everyday people doing everyday things, about a generation coming to grips with itself, and what this will mean to all of us.

Along the way we'll meet people you've heard of—Abbie Hoffman and Peter Max and Ken Kesey—and many you probably haven't, from an AIDS victim and pioneer to a cynical Vietnam veteran. Straights and freaks and cynics and idealists, Us and Them and people in between.

But from the kaleidoscope of images that make up their collected experience emerges the essential quality of a generation that has learned—to borrow a phrase from Edward Albee—that it is sometimes necessary to go a long way out of your way to come back a short way correctly.

CHAPTER ONE

 *Back to the Garden*

Richard Levine was hot. And thirsty. And he needed a cigarette.

For almost two hours he had been beating his drums to jazz, rock, and Latin melodies in a tiny nightclub in Swan Lake, New York, a quiet, rural town about a hundred miles north of New York City. Now Richard Levine needed a break.

He stepped outside in the warm August night breeze and stopped cold. In just the last few hours, the quiet country road that wound past the nightclub had turned into a good imitation of Manhattan at rush hour. Hundreds of cars were bumper to bumper. Levine, in his sweat-soaked tuxedo, watched silently as the column passed by. Long-haired kids in workshirts and jeans, or colorful paisley blouses with tie-dyed pants. One was wearing a white civil-defense helmet.

"Which way to Woodstock?" came a voice from the parade. Then Levine saw the speaker; he was standing straight in an old convertible.

Levine just shook his head. "I don't know."

Woodstock, Richard thought, I never heard of it. Then he turned and walked back to the bandstand.

In just a few hours Levine and just about everyone else in America and perhaps the entire English-speaking world would know all about Wood-stock.

In New York City Mark Hawthorne was just finishing his shift on the night rewrite desk of the *New York Times*. Hawthorne had heard of Woodstock. In fact, he and his wife were planning to leave for Woodstock in just a few hours. Then the massive news-gathering machinery of the *Times* shifted into gear, collecting information about sprawling traffic jams, food shortages, and abandoned cars.

Mark changed his mind. He would stay in New York. Besides, Woodstock probably wasn't such a big deal anyway, not for a young, ambitious reporter on the world's greatest newspaper.

Lois Kaufman was going to Woodstock; at least that's what she told her parents. She was really driving to Cape Cod to spend a few stolen days with her boyfriend. Lois was a sophomore at Brooklyn College, only a few miles from her home. She didn't have much time to be alone with her boyfriend; and besides, who would know.

Two days later Nat and Lillian Kaufman were frantically trying to reach their daughter, panicked by the scene they were watching on television.

As Lois Kaufman was motoring up the New England Turnpike and Richard Levine headed back to the bandstand and Mark Hawthorne was reading the Associated Press wire, thousands of young people were filtering into the seedy Port Authority Bus Terminal at Eighth Avenue and Forty-second Street in midtown Manhattan. They followed signs that said simply: Woodstock Festival . . . Load Here.

David Burak, a student activist at Cornell, had been to New York City delivering some books. Driving back to campus in Ithaca, New York, he stopped to pick up a hitchhiker at a tollbooth.

"Where are you going?" Burak asked.

"Oh, man, I'm going to Woodstock. Aren't you going?"

"No, man, it's going to be a drag."

"No," said the hitchhiker, "It's going to be the most amazing thing in the universe."

How, Burak thought, could anyone pass up the most amazing thing in the universe? So on a whim and with a smile, the man who in less than a year would lead one of the most bitter student protests of the 70s pulled off the highway a hundred miles short of home.

It's estimated that over a million people tried to get to Woodstock that weekend, August 15 to 17, 1969. Slightly less than four hundred thousand made it. Only fifty thousand had been expected.

What occurred became a focal point in American history; one of those few times that people will always remember where they were when they heard or saw or read about the concert in the rolling Catskill Mountains of upstate New York; just as they remember where they were when Neil Armstrong walked on the moon a month earlier, or when John F. Kennedy was cut down.

The Woodstock Music and Art Fair promised three days of peace and music. More acts were scheduled to play at Woodstock than had ever been slated for a single event before.

But it was more than music. It was a weekend that permanently stamped Woodstock in history and gave its name to an entire generation.

Many thought it was a beginning; the coming of age of the biggest, richest, most educated generation in the entire history of the whole damn country. For most of the 60s, young people had been consciously creating an identity separate from that of their parents; acting differently, dressing differently, even using expressions that left older Americans shaking their heads and wondering whatever happened to the English language. *Bad* was good and *far out* had nothing to do with distance.

And why not? Children of the 60s grew up thinking anything was possible; no achievement too great. If they wanted to change something—the language, say—who could stop them? Their vast numbers alone guaranteed they would be noticed and accommodated. One in five Americans was born in the baby boom, the inevitable result of so many virile young men returning home from World War II at about the same time.

When the children of the 60s flooded the schools, the nation built more schools. Housing developments erupted in places like Levittown, New York; Silver Spring, Maryland; and Orange County, California.

Their vision and dreams were no longer bounded by mere geography. Jet travel was available at affordable prices, and there was even a four-lane highway that stretched from New York to San Francisco with not one stoplight along the way.

More important, television allowed the babyboomers simultaneously to share feelings and events their parents couldn't possibly have imagined. The Vietnam War reached into their homes each night in living color—and it was for real.

For many, Woodstock was to be a beginning—the flexing of the generation's huge muscle; laying claim to its birthright; making things happen now . . . Why wait, man?

Today, twenty years later, we can see that Woodstock was not the beginning of a glorious revolution, but the last, great stand of a wide-eyed youthful idealism that would soon be shocked into reality by a sadder decade ahead.

The babyboomers kept the dreams but drifted apart, each with his own agenda of needs and wants. There were bills to pay, mortgages to meet, babies to raise.

They also learned there were things a generation, even the biggest generation in the whole damn country, couldn't control. And a lot of things just seemed to go wrong.

Vietnam would last five more years, and then another cold reality would set in. Watergate would create a numbing sense of disillusionment. Gas rationing would be a rude awakening for a generation that had never known bare shelves or empty pumps.

Gerald Ford would be an avuncular president who inspired little confidence. Jimmy Carter would offer fresh hope, but leave us feeling impotent.

But the spirit of Woodstock did not die. It would begin to resurface in subtle ways, blending with more traditional values in the 80s to form a more tolerant and energetic nation. It's as if you took the spirit of Woodstock, eliminated most of the naiveté, and sprinkled in some political savvy. Some may call it simply getting older and wiser.

People in the late 1980s began, subtly, again to reject authority. Protests surfaced, but mainly in a different form. People translated their need for independence into new lifestyles, job styles, new types of entrepreneurism. Minorities, women, gays, the elderly, and others expected to be heard. That was true whether you were a straight or a freak, a shorthair or a longhair. The young people of the 1960s had pretty well separated the country into Us and Them, but as they grew older they learned that Us and Them had more in common than they thought.

In some ways the 60s revival in the 80s would be superficial. The music of the 60s would return, often sung by Woodstock performers for new advertising jingles. Fashion would come full circle, from miniskirts to maxis to hotpants and back to minis.

But in other ways Woodstock's effects run deep. Twenty years later we can look back and trace the Woodstock generation, its music, fashions, and art, and the people like Abbie Hoffman, the activist, Mark Hawthorne, the *New York Times* reporter, and Lois Kaufman, the nice Jewish girl from Brooklyn who stole away for a weekend with her boyfriend. We can examine how politics and history have changed the way they live and how they will change the nation we'll share in the future.

The impact of the Woodstock generation is now being felt; it is only starting to exercise the muscle some thought it was flexing twenty years ago. To understand what will happen, it's important to understand what did happen—the fall and the rise of the Woodstock generation.

The Woodstock concert is just the beginning of the story.

The name was a misnomer. The Woodstock festival took place no closer to the village of Woodstock than, say, Philadelphia is to New York or Anaheim is to Los Angeles. The seed for the concert was not even sown in New York, as many still think, but sown several years earlier and more than a thousand miles away in a head shop in the Coconut Grove section of Miami.

The shop was owned by Michael Lang, a transplanted New Yorker who was looking for a business to start and a new place to live. Michael had visited Miami with his parents years earlier and liked it. So he packed his car in New York and headed south.

First, Lang visited a new artist who was making strange new color posters. They might sell well in Miami.

"I heard he was opening up a new business so I thought he would buy twenty, maybe even a hundred posters," recalls Peter Max. "Instead, he took three. It cost him six dollars."

Max didn't have to worry; in the next six months he would sell about four million more.

It was music that really turned Michael on. He wanted to get into the business but didn't have the talent to make it as a performer. He thought that promoting concerts and managing groups might be his ticket.

His first shot was copromoting a music festival in the middle of Gulf Stream Park, a local racetrack.

With only a few weeks' notice, Lang was able to sign the Mothers of Invention, John Lee Hooker, Chuck Berry, Arthur Brown, and Jimi Hendrix. Hendrix provided the highlight of the Gulf Stream show. Forgotten at the airport, he rented a helicopter and, stoned out of his mind on acid, descended a rope ladder from the chopper just as he was scheduled to go on. Lang was hooked.

Shortly afterward Mike moved to Woodstock, a rustic artists' community a couple hours north of New York City. He was in the music business, representing an obscure group, but Lang had bigger plans.

He wanted to arrange a series of concerts in the Woodstock area and dreamed of building a recording studio in the rolling hills. Woodstock seemed like an ideal place to set up shop; it was a town with a long history of the unusual.

A wealthy art patron, John Radcliffe Whitehead, founded an artists' colony there in 1902. In the next few decades it was the scene of scandalizing transvestite dances, served as the birthplace of the Communist Party in New York State (although the town voted steadfastly Republican), and drew sculptors, artists, and musicians from across the nation.

Pete Seeger lived there, as did Paul Butterfield, and Joan Baez was a frequent visitor.

Bob Dylan made Woodstock his home, moving into a large home in town but later switching to a secluded mountaintop home when young people, anxious to glimpse their idol, made life too difficult.

By the 60s, the Band and the Mothers of Invention and dozens of promoters and record company executives had homes there, and young people from as far away as Oregon and Washington began to straggle in, wearing fringed leather coats and granny glasses and sleeping on the village green or in the nearby woods.

The area had hosted other festivals. The Woodstock Soundouts, a series of small weekend folk rock concerts, were held only ten minutes from the center of Woodstock. The Blues Magoos and the Who had played there.

Unfortunately for Lang, the local citizens were tiring of the hippies that trooped into Woodstock. Two years earlier the town had turned down overtures from the Newport Jazz Festival to move its concert there. Peace and quiet were more important than money and fame.

The Woodstock town board also passed an "antihippie" ordinance, limiting the movements of the young people who wandered freely in the woods and slept anywhere they could find a spot. Still, Lang plowed ahead.

He mentioned the concert idea to another Woodstock resident, Artie Kornfeld, a songwriter and producer and vice president of Capitol Records. Kornfeld was excited, but they needed cash.

Through friends, Lang met John Roberts and Joel Rosenman, who had money and, like Mike, were in their early twenties, from New York, and interested in getting into the music business. Lang and Kornfeld met them in an apartment in Manhattan to lay out the Woodstock plan. They were sold.

Lang left to put together his first budget. It was done on two pages and totaled $500,000.

The concert was on, but publicity had to be arranged, artists hired, the stages designed, and a sound system hooked up (the entire show was taped on two eight-track systems).

What Lang had in mind was a music and art fair and his first job was to start signing acts, which wasn't as easy as it sounds. Copromoting a concert in a Florida racetrack didn't exactly put Michael into the big time. But he had a plan.

If he could sign just a few big groups, others would follow. They wouldn't want to be left out of such a big show. He was appealing, rightly, to their egos.

The first few acts charged double their normal rate, the princely fee of $10,000—modest by today's standards but much money for one show back in 1969. Lang signed Jefferson Airplane, Canned Heat, and Creedence Clearwater Revival, and then began working the rumor mill, letting word spread that a giant concert was planned for upstate New York. Other groups did sign on at their usual fees. Lang's gamble worked.

One star that didn't sign up was Roy Rogers. Lang wanted him to sing "Happy Trails" at the end of the concert, but Roy's agent, unfortunately, said no.

There was also another slight problem: finding a place to hold the concert. They looked at three or four sites before taking a $1,500 option on a piece of land in an industrial park in Wallkill, only a few miles from Woodstock. It wasn't perfect, but it would do.

The concert was officially announced in April. About the same time, another fortunate thing occurred: Michael met the Hog Farmers.

The Hog Farmers were a communal group living in New Mexico. They were true hippies, peaceful and sharing, not weekend flower children. Their leader, Hugh Romney, went by the name Wavy Gravy. Lang invited them to help work at the festival. Eighty of them would come by plane, at a cost of $17,000. They were worth every dime.

The Hog Farmers were vital for setting the right tone for the festival. They were the unofficial security force—the Please Force—and Wavy Gravy was the chief of please.

Wearing orange armbands showing a hog sitting on the neck of a guitar (the festival emblem was a dove sitting on a guitar neck), they ran the free-food kitchens, organized camping grounds, and finally oversaw the cleanup.

It was one of the few positive things that would happen for a while. Hard as he tried, Lang could not entirely escape politics.

Abbie Hoffman had heard about the Woodstock concert even before it was announced. He worried that the promoters were trying to rip off the public. He also felt that they should contribute something to his movement.

Hoffman, a leader of the yippies, was at the height of his fame. Only a year before he had been arrested protesting outside of the Democratic National Convention in Chicago. A year later he would make headlines again, this time as a defendant in the Chicago Seven trial, one of the most publicized trials in American history.

Hoffman would earn a reputation at the trial for volatile behavior, sometimes screaming at the judge and once even walking into the courtroom on his hands. But the Woodstock organizers already knew that Abbie was no one to take lightly. They worried that he could disrupt the festival so Lang met Hoffman at his place in Manhattan's East Village.

While the styles, the drugs, the music of the 60s helped create the right environment for his political movement, Hoffman also knew his message could get lost in that same atmosphere. He was determined not to let that happen.

Hoffman felt the organizers, the record companies, and the movie people were using the counterculture for their own commercial gain. Millions of dollars were going to be made and without someone watching out for the movement, the event wouldn't come off right, it wouldn't convey the right political message.

"You need us," Hoffman said. The doctors had no experience with people on bad acid trips. And the organizers, he felt, had no idea how many people might show up or even how to deal with them.

Besides, Hoffman and the Lower East Side street groups he represented felt they merited a place at the festival. They were the ones setting up shelters for people on bad trips and finding housing for runaways.

"Abbie started demanding—give us this, give us that," Lang said later.

"We're not ripping off the kids, we're not ripping off the culture, and we're not giving you anything," Michael answered.

The meeting threatened to break apart.

Finally, an agreement was reached. Lang donated $10,000. Half of that went to pay for a press to print political leaflets at the concert, keeping issues like civil rights, and the need for marijuana law reform an integral part of the concert. Much of the rest, Hoffman says, went to pay for food at the concert.

But Michael had no intention of letting the festival turn political. "There had been enough rhetoric about how we should live our lives; now it was time to start doing it."

Minor crises came one after another. Lang's partners were feuding, helicopters had to be arranged to fly performers into and out of the concert, there was trouble getting food services lined up. Then Lang heard that Bill Graham had already booked some of the same acts for the Fillmore East, his famous club in lower Manhattan, and was considering pulling those acts out of the festival. Lang met Graham, who agreed to close the Fillmore during the Woodstock weekend.

One by one, these problems were confronted, solved, or simply ignored until they went away.

But the most serious blow came in July, only a month before the concert. And this one did threaten to cancel the show. The Wallkill town board suddenly withdrew permission to hold the concert.

Michael knew he was in for trouble. A Concerned Citizens Committee had been formed to block the concert and gunshots had been fired at the little shed he used as headquarters.

After months of planning, preparing the grounds, designing the stage, selling thousands of tickets, and printing posters and news releases promoting the festival, suddenly there was no place to hold the concert.

Frantically they began searching for another location. Lang got a call about a piece of land, further west in White Lake in the town of Bethel. Lang drove up to check out the site. It turned out to be a swamp.

But on the way back Lang passed a large field; not perfect, but it would do. He started negotiating with the owner, who finally asked, "You mean you want something with a slope to it?"

Max Yasgur lead him a mile or so to a natural bowl created by gentle rolling hills with a lake in the background. It was a forty-acre meadow, big enough for the concert. There was even a little rise at the bottom of the bowl, perfect for a stage.

Yasgur agreed that day to lease his land for $50,000. But only a few weeks remained to move everything fifty miles from Wallkill to Bethel and start all over. The move cost $300,000, but the concert was saved.

Yasgur's meadow not only was perfect geographically, a natural amphitheater, but had spirit and history on its side. The area was settled in the mid-1700s by Moravian pioneers who believed in love of fellow man and peace, almost identical to the spirit of the hippie creed.

Bethel in Hebrew means a holy or consecrated spot. It seemed appropriate for the new Garden of Eden they sought to create.

Lang wanted to make a movie of the festival, from construction to cleanup. When no one seemed interested, he borrowed money and hired his own film crew. Finally, two days before the concert, Warner Brothers signed a deal to produce the movie paying Woodstock Ventures $100,000 for production costs and $500,000 for editing.

New roads were built, a water line constructed, electrical and telephone cables strung.

Lang had envisioned the festival as a concert and art fair with crafts and even a circus. But many of the artists never arrived and booths were never built for those who did. They had to be cancelled with the sudden move from Wallkill. The artists' booths lost out to necessities such as toilets and water lines.

Although the town board had agreed to the concert, it hadn't issued all the necessary permits and pretty soon someone came around posting Stop Work notices on poles around the site. Michael followed him around on his motorcycle, waiting until the man was out of sight and then tearing down the notices. Michael then dropped out of sight for a while, running the show with a walkie-talkie to avoid being served with a warrant for operating without a permit.

The blessed Hog Farmers arrived those final days and began setting up campsites and kitchens.

But on Thursday, only a day before the start of the festival, over three hundred New York City cops abandoned the concert after a warning by Police Commissioner Patrick Leary that their work as Woodstock security guards violated the department's regulations against moonlighting. Some of them came anyway.

In New York City there was a buzz on the street. Understand, it was very different from today. A little ad in the *Village Voice,* some word in alternative newspapers. But no TV spots saying "Coming Friday—Live

Coverage from Woodstock!" Even New York's WNEW-FM, one of the most progressive stations in America, didn't start talking about the concert until it was actually happening.

Today, Bob Geldorf would be interviewed by Jane Pauley before the concert; no such mechanism existed then. Nor was there a lead article in the *New York Times*'s Arts and Leisure Section the Sunday before. The grownups hadn't caught on. The word through underground channels was that something was happening on the East Coast in August 1969. Rumor had it that the Beatles would show up, and Dylan, and the Rolling Stones. None did.

Later the West Village would become trendy. Then the East Village was hot, very hot, with the Electric Circus, St. Mark's Place, the Village Theater, and of course the Fillmore. As the weekend approached, word spread all over the East Village that Woodstock was a Big Thing. Even the Fillmore planned to close, since so many of its acts were headed upstate.

David Colton, a student at Binghamton, New York, was working that summer running bumper cars in a local amusement park about twenty minutes north of New York City. He and his brother, hearing about the concert from the word around the East Village, figured there would be a mob scene and headed upstate Thursday night in their mother's Chevrolet Impala. David's girlfriend, Eilene, would go by bus and meet them, to throw her parents off the scent.

The scene would later remind David Colton of the *National Lampoon*'s "Lemmings"—everyone seemed to be going. The East Village was dead, St. Mark's Place was dead, and even the people who weren't going knew—in the parlance of the time—that Woodstock was where the energy was for the weekend.

Again, things were different then. Today people would go in vans, and bring backpacking equipment, tents and sleeping bags, and coolers with Pepsi and beer and ham sandwiches and hot dogs. Then, there were a lot of hippies that would live off the land. What they expected to find in the way of support equipment—bunkhouses, lean-tos, whatever—is unclear. At best, many brought a jacket and an extra T-shirt. Straights and freaks, longhairs and shorthairs—and there were plenty of both—left for Woodstock as if they were off to a local park and after the concert would go home.

There was no going home.

Before long, even the polyesters who showed up had opened their collars and, perhaps, taken their first toke.

The people at Woodstock, and those who weren't but felt they somehow belonged there, had by 1969 created a bonafide, tie-dyed-in-the-wool subculture. Its name, later, would be Woodstock Nation; its name then, for lack of a better term, was Us.

The generation had been written about, been talked of, and had created its own literature. It had its *Village Voice* and its *East Village Other;* its alternative newspapers and its alternative to its alternative newspapers.

As night fell on Thursday, it was still possible to get within two miles of the campsite. A long, long line of people wended its way through the hills in the sweet upstate evening. The local police seemed quite friendly, particularly to someone used to big-city cops. It wasn't unusual to see five or six persons sitting atop a police car that drove slowly toward the concert ground.

Those who arrived Thursday night found that the natural amphitheater in which the stage was set up was not all that crowded. Around this bowl was a line of trees. And beyond the trees, neighborhoods of hippies had blossomed.

These neighborhoods were established by the more experienced folk from the West Coast. California had its Summer of Love two years earlier, but that was a West Coast phenomenon.

The East Coasters might not have survived had it not been for the professional hippies—not just the Hog Farmers, but the people who lived in psychedelic buses and traveled around the country. Families, or tribes, they called themselves. They had long ponytails and grizzled faces tanned from months in the summer sun. They were the ones who set up tents and communal kitchens to feed the others. They became the festival elders, setting the rules—don't shit where the dogs are drinking, and such.

This area outside the festival ground was where the movie was shot. It was a crazy quilt of lean-tos and buses and Oldsmobiles and bikers and pools and mud, and was for many where the real festival was going on.

Across the nation, people of all walks of life considered themselves hippies. They were not all the same: some wore long hair, some didn't. Some smoked dope, some did acid, some didn't. But a connection between them was instantly recognizable and undeniable. It had to do with music, and drugs, and the war, and freedom, and love and sharing, and independence—a fuck-you attitude toward authority that infuriated the rest of the nation.

It was an outsider's attitude, except at Woodstock, where for one weekend in one place it was pervasive and triumphant. But as the years went by, and all those people who called themselves "One of Us" went off and got real jobs and stopped doing drugs and maybe even voted Republican, it appeared to vanish. Notwithstanding, that sense of connection did remain, a sleeping giant in yuppie America.

No one was straighter than Jimmy Holloran. He was the original all-American boy: an honors student, tall, muscular, athletic, and the product of a strict Irish-Catholic upbringing in Washington, D.C. He had captained the baseball team at Holy Cross University, graduated with honors, and gone on to Harvard Medical School.

Holloran and a friend traveled to Woodstock on a whim. Like many—at the concert and around the country—Jimmy would never be the same again.

A path led from this area back to the concert field. Signs posted on this trail dubbed it Groovy Way. Along Groovy Way were little booths with people selling tie-dyes and beads and pottery. These were the remnant of the "arts" part of the arts and music festival.

Back in the fields, away from the concert grounds, the Grateful Dead were setting up to play for the evening. Near the Hog Farm setup was a sort of Grateful Dead communal area, where the Deadheads from the West Coast had settled down for the weekend.

It was basically background music; the Dead were not yet an East Coast phenomenon. People wandered around, shared the brown rice handed out by the Hog Farmers, and then bedded down, drifting off easily while in the distance Jerry Garcia's nine fingers strummed a long version of "Uncle John's Band."

And as they slept, people kept coming.

Bethel citizens awoke Friday to find people as far as they could see. One homeowner leaving home in the morning even stumbled over a couple making love on his front porch.

Friday morning, before one song had yet been sung on the festival stage, promoters issued an announcement to radio stations: anyone who was still thinking of attending the concert, please stay home.

Traffic was backed up for ten miles in every direction. Cars by the hundreds were being abandoned on the sides of roads. People were walking five, eight, ten miles down the center of highways to reach Max Yasgur's farm.

A crew of reporters and photographers from *Rolling Stone* magazine, then one year old, never heard the radio report. They had decided to beat traffic and left early in the morning for the hundred-mile trip.

They made it to within eight miles of Bethel before encountering a solid wall of cars along the two-lane road.

"Automotive casualties looked like the skeletons of horses that died on the Oregon trail," wrote Greil Marcus in *Rolling Stone*. Others compared the scene to Napoleon's retreat from Moscow or the Bataan death march.

Townspeople and vacationers (this was the Catskills, after all) gathered in small groups to watch the parade. Surprisingly, there was little jeering or snickering from either side. Some residents smiled and offered water from their wells and faucets.

Almost two hundred thousand tickets had been sold, but authorities estimated that seven hundred fifty thousand to one million people were on the road to Bethel. The townspeople watching the parade were like millions of other Americans that weekend: curious. What could bring so many people so far? And why did they look and act so differently from their older brothers and sisters?

American youths were asserting their separate identity. Almost twenty years later, in a survey done for this book, 70 percent of all babyboomers said they wish they had gone to the Woodstock festival.

That morning, refreshed from a good night's sleep in the fields, some fed by a wonderful sweet oatmeal prepared in big vats by the Hog Farmers, others returning from bathing nude in a far-off pond, campers walked down Groovy Way to the concert ground, through the trees, and stopped dead at a scene filled with so many people that it looked as though it had been staged by Cecil B. DeMille, not Michael Lang.

And still the people came.

By the time the music started Friday afternoon, cars were no longer allowed to enter the area and the New York State Police had transferred 150 officers to help deal with traffic. They had already given up trying to make drug arrests.

Drugs were not nearly as plentiful as legend has made them. Still, the wafting musky scent of marijuana was pervasive enough that, some visitors would say, you could get high just by walking through the crowd.

Already food was scarce. The hot-dog stands left were running low—later, they would burn down—and even in nearby towns like Ellenville, stores were running out of food.

Tickets to the concert became meaningless. The six-foot chain-link fences had been broken down, partly by gate crashers, partly as a symbolic gesture of hippie openness ("Fences, man? That's what this concert is about. No fences"), and partly from the crush of humanity. The concert was declared free, costing Lang and his partners about $9 million.

Richie Havens was the first to play. He walked on stage wearing a rust-colored, striped, ankle-length tunic, strummed a few chords on his guitar, and called the festival to order.

Even as he sang, a five-person helicopter flew back and forth, shuttling performers over the wriggling mass below.

Years later Havens would be stopped by a man on a New York City street. The stranger had seen Havens' performance in the movie *Woodstock*. It had been projected on a big rock in Ghana. Such would become the magnitude and reach of this concert. Again, the music was wonderful but it was not just the music.

Woodstock, like Vietnam, Watergate, disco, and Reagan, would define and challenge the American psyche in the coming years.

It was on Friday night when Michael knew, really knew, that the festival would work. That's when the Hell's Angels rolled in. There were rumors the Angels would start trouble.

Michael stood on the stage and watched as they motored up the road and were absorbed into the crowd. There was no trouble.

Rock day was to be Saturday. Even though the order on the program would become totally confused (neither the movie nor the audiotape presented performers in the correct order), Friday remained mostly folk day. Joan Baez played on Friday but had to wait awhile, but that was all right by her.

"Maybe there will be a few more people here by then. . . . I don't like a puny gathering like this," Baez joked a few hours before she went on in the pitch black.

She was pregnant with David Harris's child. Harris was in a federal prison for draft evasion and she dedicated a song to him and to the hunger strike he had just started.

Baez was followed by John Sebastian, Arlo Guthrie, Tim Hardin, Melanie, the Incredible String Band, Sweetwater, and Ravi Shankar. Most of the groups played for over an hour, some longer.

The sound system was decent, but not nearly strong enough to reach the whole crowd. The people on the stage were tiny dots, and never was there a moment—not even when Country Joe gave the Fish chant—when the entire crowd was focused on the stage.

What was happening in the crowd was another matter. New arrivals were bringing copies of the *New York Daily News,* with banner headlines proclaiming that a hippie festival had closed the New York State Thruway. It began to dawn on people just how big this thing had become. They were part of a News Event.

Now, there was a three-hour wait to use the few pay phones. On the other end of the lines were the frantic parents: My god! Where are you? I see on the news that there's no food! No electricity! No shelter! No toilets!

But it was all right. In a way the parents couldn't understand, it was all right.

In its own way, the mass of humanity was the perfect organism, the perfect distribution system. If the blanket next to you had a soda, you didn't say, "Excuse me, may I have a sip, please?" Rather, the soda would be passed to your blanket, and the brown rice from your blanket would pass to theirs. No one had any food, and there were virtually no vendors, but everyone ate. Everyone had something to share. Someone was cooking hamburgers. Someone was cooking chicken. Someone had a candy bar. Someone held up a half-eaten hot dog and called out, "anybody want a hot dog?" And, like Wimpy in a Popeye cartoon, someone came by and took it, and handed someone else his joint.

This impressed Gary Stoces. Stoces, five hundred miles away in Washington, D.C., was about a year (or a lifetime) out of Vietnam but still working for the Marine Corps, writing a book about something euphemistically called pacification.

Stoces and his marine buddies heard that hordes of hippies were going to Bethel for a weekend of craziness. Like many Vietnam veterans, he was personally touched by the antiwar sentiment.

Vietnam was the first American war in which returning soldiers were not lined up for parades but for drug tests. Stoces found it hard to understand the hatred he sensed from hippies. He felt no hatred for them. In fact, he was impressed at how peacefully the Woodstock weekend was going.

Stoces sat in a bar with Sergeant Smith, who had returned from Vietnam with him.

"Geez," Smith said as the bartender brought him another beer. "Imagine putting three hundred thousand marines in one place for a weekend. Within forty-eight hours they'd be beating the shit out of each other."

Stoces smiled at the thought. He had spent the day writing about how to "win the hearts and minds of the Vietnamese people" by having marines live and work with them. The term for it, in the alphabet-soup tradition of the government, was CAC—Civilian Activities Companies. It was, Stoces realized with some irony, the perfect term.

CAC, pronounced "kack," was the Vietnamese word for penis; and in Vietnam it was the year of the cock. In some way, he realized, everyone was getting fucked.

Stoces thought of this and started to laugh.

Back in Woodstock Abbie Hoffman was laughing too, enjoying the scene and his part in it. Within seventy-two hours his laughter would end with a bitter ring. Abbie felt that one of his missions was "keeping the concert political," making sure the message of social injustice, of the war, of the government, would be a part of the scene.

He would soon be hooted and howled at by the very people he was trying to reach.

By Friday afternoon, the weekend hippies were arriving. Again, it was different from the West Coast. In Berkeley it wasn't unusual to see a worker emerge from a manhole with long hair flowing from under a hard hat with a big peace symbol pasted on its side. But in New York you carried your beads and peace buttons in your pocket, and put them on when you left the office. These were the people arriving now, in what had become a blisteringly hot afternoon.

A weekend hippie named Paul arrived with his girlfriend. She was one of Them, a straight. She was well dressed and upset at the mud and the dust and the heat, and would be remembered for years afterward for her own silent protest: throughout the Who's set she faced away from the stage, her arms folded.

She didn't want to be there.

Midway into Friday evening an announcement was made from the stage.

"We've had thousands and thousands of people come here today; many, many more than we knew or even dreamed or thought," the speaker said.

"The one major thing you have to remember tonight when you go back up in the woods to go to sleep or if you stay here is that the man next to you is your brother. And you damn well better treat each other that way because if you don't we blow the whole thing and we've got it right there."

The world was watching and for three days peace prevailed. It was a good thing. Even as a gentle rain began falling that Friday, a detachment of national guard troops equipped with tear gas was mobilizing a hundred miles away in Albany, waiting for trouble.

Abbie Hoffman watched it rain and looked out on the thousands of people. It's crucial that this event survive, he thought to himself, and it ain't headed for survival.

"I might not be the brightest organizer in America," Hoffman said, "but I'm the fastest."

He began dividing up the responsibilities. Wavy Gravy and the Hog Farmers could handle the bad-acid trips. God knows they'd had enough practice. But the instant city was enormously understaffed for dealing with general injuries and illnesses.

Near dawn on Saturday Hoffman took his first action: he commandeered the pink and white press tent to the right of the stage. Kicking out the journalists, none of whom was too pleased by this, he declared it a hospital—actually more of a makeshift M*A*S*H unit. Hoffman had no real authority to do any of this, but Abbie was Abbie, so who was to question?

By 7 A.M. the hospital administration was set up, with Hoffman, of course, in charge. He was on a bullhorn, directing his staff. Everyone was addressed by his first name and function—there was Anne Quartermaster, Jerry Admissions, Doctor Mack Surgery, and, of course, Abbie Director.

The omission of this scene, and of Hoffman, from the Woodstock movie and the general Woodstock lore would rankle him even twenty years later.

"You'll see Wavy Gravy in the movies because he's not a threat to them," Hoffman said. "But the people in charge of the hospital—some of them were political, up-against-the-wall-motherfucker people—they're not going to put these people on TV. These are people who are going to be underground with the Weathermen in two years. None of them are on cozy terms with the rock establishment, and none of them are gonna be featured in the ads."

This split, between the rock establishment and the political people, would flare up not only at the concert (involving Hoffman, naturally) but also again and again in the decades to follow.

Rock music was, plainly and simply, the voice of the people. But very quickly the performers became as rich, as powerful, and as distant as the leaders their songs opposed. This growing split between the rockers and rock audience would become a part of the growing disillusionment that led to the breakup of the Woodstock generation.

By Saturday the New York Port Authority had stopped selling tickets to anywhere near Bethel. The huge, seventy-foot by eighty-foot revolving stage had also stopped moving.

Still, the music went on and continued till Monday dawn—Creedence Clearwater Revival; Sly and the Family Stone; Canned Heat; the Grateful Dead; Jefferson Airplane; Janis Joplin; Santana; Mountain; Country Joe and the Fish; the Band; the Paul Butterfield Blues Band; Blood, Sweat, and Tears; Crosby, Stills, Nash, and Young; the Jeff Beck Group; Joe Cocker; the Moody Blues; the Who; Johnny Winter; and Jimi Hendrix.

Meanwhile, the citizenry of this instant city walked around and looked at itself, wondering who was tripping and who wasn't, who were the real hippies and who were play-acting for the weekend.

Word was spreading that the concert had been declared a disaster area. A few people decided to leave, unwilling any longer to cope with the shortages of water, food, toilets, cool air, and space.

Further east, in Woodstock itself, citizens read the *New York Times,* saw the pictures on television, and talked about seeking a court injunction to prevent festival promoters from using the name Woodstock. In the end, they did nothing.

Music was scheduled to begin at 1 P.M. Saturday and run for four hours. It began midafternoon and went far, far into the night. The size of the crowd was overwhelming to some of the performers.

Crosby, Stills, Nash, and Young were one of the big winners at Woodstock. A relatively unknown group, it played a great set. "This is only the second time we've played together in front of people and we're scared shitless," Stephen Stills told the crowd.

Country Joe McDonald was also nervous. "I had performed solo in coffeehouses but this was terrifying," Joe said later. "What's worse, I walked on the stage and nobody seemed to notice."

Joe hesitated for a moment and wondered if he could get away with doing his Fish cheer. Finally, he screamed into the microphone, "Gimme an F . . . gimme a U . . . gimme a C . . . gimme a K." The crowd echoed each letter with a lusty roar.

It's easy to overstate the sense of communion going through the crowd because there was also a sense of paranoia. There were rumors that the military was sealing off the area and would keep people in detention. Many nervously joked that if they wanted to get rid of Us all, which they did, this would be the time to do it.

Army helicopters did in fact appear, but dropped food and supplies and ferried doctors and medical aids into Yasgur's farm.

Saturday afternoon gave way to Saturday night. Creedence Clearwater Revival followed the Grateful Dead at about 3:30 A.M. Sunday.

Creedence, riding a wave of popularity at the time, waited and waited. Finally, its turn came to go on. About a third of the way through the set the performers noticed everyone was sleeping.

"I looked out past the floodlights and I see about five rows of bodies just intertwined, They're all asleep," John Fogerty later told *Rolling Stone.* "Stoned and asleep."

"Well, we're up here having a great time," Fogerty said. "I hope some of you are too."

Then across the meadow in the darkness Fogerty saw someone flicking a lighter. Then a yell came from the same direction. "Don't worry about it, John. We're with you."

Fogerty played the rest of the set for that one person.

On Sunday, the Who's manager demanded his money before his group went on stage. Lang offered to give him a check and guaranteed it would be good the next morning when he went to the bank. That wasn't good enough and the argument became heated.

"Wait here," Lang said. "I'm going to go out and make an announcement that the Who will not play until they get the cash and we'll see how that goes over with the crowd."

The Who performed.

The political people at the concert were becoming a little concerned. They liked what was going on: this was their music, the music they carried into battle in marches on Washington and Chicago and New York. But a feel-good weekend without a message was an opportunity lost; and time was slipping away.

Somehow, they thought, this energy had to be focused on issues so that a week later four hundred thousand people would not only remember a great party, but also see themselves as part of a great movement.

This split came to a head while the Who was about to go on stage.

Abbie Hoffman had been working round the clock in the hospital or in the booths since the concert began. Saturday night came and there was a break, to tear down one group's equipment and put up another's.

The Who was due on stage in about thirty minutes. Community announcements were now being made—about water, people who had lost other people, bad drugs—as well as cheery poetry readings.

Hoffman was sitting on the side of the stage with Lang and other organizers, who felt things were going well. They weren't going to make money; it had become a free concert—although in the back of their minds there was still movie and album revenue. But they were feeling copacetic, knowing that Rockefeller was wrong for readying the National Guard and that the *New York Times* was wrong for calling this the "nightmare in the Catskills."

"I can see things aren't going too well financially," Hoffman said to them, "but obviously this is going to be an incredible movie."

He proposed using a percentage of the movie revenue to set up a fund for people who had been arrested.

The organizers, Hoffman recalls, thought it was a great idea and promised to announce it near the end of the concert.

Hoffman, being Hoffman, decided that sooner is better than later, walked up to the mike and started delivering a political rap. For all the political issues the concert would become associated with, this was perhaps the first and last political speech of the weekend.

Hoffman talked awhile about politics, the war in Vietnam, and the war back home. Finally, someone turned his microphone off, and Abbie kicked it over and walked off stage.

"Bummer, Abbie, that was horrible."

"You brought us all down."

"Bummer, we were on cloud nine, we're having a good time."

What happened next was unclear. In hippie lore, Peter Townshend of the Who, pissed at Hoffman, hit him with his guitar.

Is that what happened?

"We bumped," Hoffman recalled later.

Was it intentional?

"Well, we both read about it so much over the years, I think we tended to believe it."

Townsend was a little more direct. He told *Rolling Stone*, "I kicked him off the stage.

"I deeply regret that. If I was given that opportunity again, I would stop the show. Because I don't think Rock & Roll is that important. Then I did. The show had to go on."

Lang and other organizers remember it a little differently. They don't recall agreeing to set up an arrest fund. They do remember that Abbie, stoned and exhausted from working at the hospital, was yelling that he saw someone with a knife who Hoffman believed was trying to kill him. Michael looked under the stage for the would-be assassin but found no one. In the meantime, Hoffman had jumped onto the stage and started talking about someone having been arrested for having a single joint of marijuana. It was then that Townsend conked him with his guitar and Abbie leaped from the stage never to be heard from again the rest of the weekend.

Michael and the other organizers were still worried that the radicals would disrupt the festival. Movement City was located next to the Hog Farm. Here resided the representatives of the Weathermen, SDS, and other groups. There was a lot of activity in Movement City, but mostly because it had the only public telephones.

The booths manned by the various political groups were rarely used. The printing press ordered to print newsletters was soon ruined by the mud.

Joe Cocker would begin the festival's third day; it would end sometime toward dawn Monday with Jimi Hendrix.

As Cocker was finishing what might be the greatest live performance of a song ever—"A Little Help from My Friends"—the skies opened. It had rained off and on throughout the festival; but now came roiling clouds, like something Steven Spielberg would create fifteen years later.

"Hold on to your neighbor, man," the stage implored.

Stagehands hurried to disconnect electrical equipment and instruments.

"Hey if you think really hard, maybe we can stop this rain," the stage pleaded.

"No rain . . . no rain . . . no rain," thousands chanted.

"Fuck the rain . . . fuck the rain," answered thousands more.

But the rain came down in sheets and the wind blew the tarps and shook the towers holding lights and speakers. The mountains of garbage became soaked and mud, a problem throughout the weekend, became thoroughly pervasive.

By the time the rain had ended, the area was a thick glop of chocolate pudding. The only way to survive was to get into the mud. People began sliding around in the mud, laughing through chattering teeth.

It had gone from incredibly hot to incredibly wet. Some took off their clothes and threw Frisbees. Others danced in the nude or bathed naked in the lake.

Sitting on his farm almost three thousand miles away in Oregon, America's most famous hippie wasn't happy with the news coming from Woodstock.

Ken Kesey had become famous a year earlier as the subject of Tom Wolfe's bestseller *The Electric Kool-Aid Acid Test,* even more famous than from his own books, *One Flew over the Cuckoo's Nest* and *Sometimes a Great Notion.*

Ken had planned on going to Woodstock. In fact, he helped organize a contingent of nine busloads of his tribe, the Merry Pranksters. Then, at the last minute, Kesey changed his mind.

"I went out to get on one of these buses and the women had moved in with their kids and I didn't want to be part of a moving commune."

Hearing the reports from Woodstock, Ken knew he made the right decision. He had no use for what was described as "acres and acres of bare titty," heavy drugs, and far-out vibes reverberating from the East.

No, Kesey wasn't happy with the news from Woodstock; but the truth was, he wasn't happy with his own life either. And when the Pranksters returned home, they found a different Ken Kesey.

Late Sunday afternoon Max Yasgur climbed the stage to speak. It was only appropriate since without Max Yasgur there might not have been a Woodstock; he did much more than provide the land.

Shortly after the move to Bethel some prominent local officials suggested that a payment of $10,000 would probably prevent some problems and hassles Lang might run into. Michael told Max and Max "went crazy." Yasgur, one of the most prominent people in the community, from then on accompanied Lang to almost every meeting to make sure things went smoothly.

Max had a heart condition and sometimes when Michael visited Max would take him to his bedroom and get into his oxygen tent as he heard about the next problem facing the festival.

"The important thing you've proven is that a half a million kids . . . can get together and have three days of fun and music and have nothing but three days of fun and music, and God bless you for it," Max told the audience. They cheered, not really knowing how much Max had done to make the festival a reality.

The weekend was remarkably peaceful. There were no injuries as a result of violence. A seventeen-year-old was killed in an accident and one died from an overdose. There were hundreds of drug-related illnesses, as well as stomach infections and flu caused by exposure. About a thousand people a day were treated for some type of illness.

The promoters issued a call for doctors. The army ferried some in; others came from nearby communities. A few came from the crowd, including Jimmy Holloran.

Holloran was twenty-seven, older than most of the Woodstock crowd. Although he came to hear a concert, he ended up treating drug-overdose and flu victims in the Red Cross shelter.

The people who knew Holloran were struck by his upbeat, optimistic approach to life. Few knew he was hiding an agonizing secret.

Waves of people streamed away from the concert after the Sunday afternoon thunderstorms. Many were tired and hungry and still in shock from the experience of the weekend.

Some farmers complained that the young people were trying to milk their cows and others grumbled about the drugs, drinking, and nudity.

But the Monticello police chief called them "the most courteous, considerate" group of people he ever met. Neighbors provided free food and water, and the Jewish Community Center in Monticello made sandwiches.

By Sunday night enough people had left that it was possible to get near the stage, and the music became more of a focal point—as did the bonfires that sprang up. It was cold. The sense of magic was hidden somewhere behind the need for coping.

By the time Jimi Hendrix finished the show at 8:30 Monday morning, only a few thousand people remained around the stage. His electric-guitar version of the "Star-Spangled Banner" marked more than the end of a concert. It signaled the passage from one age to another.

Never again would the hippie creed be so exalted. There would be other attempts at other Woodstocks but none generated the same enthusiasm, the same sense of brotherhood experienced on the road to Bethel.

As the cars left, posters were given away. Imagine! After all that—"And now, here's your free commemorative poster." After three days of little food or shelter, a tiny semblance of the original organization appeared.

The four hundred thousand scattered across the nation.

Mark Hawthorne, the *New York Times* rewrite man, would learn he had more in common with the Woodstock Nation than he ever dreamed.

Jimmy Holloran would cast aside the honors and dreams of a million other American men to start a new life.

David Colton, who ran the bumper cars that summer, got back into his mother's Impala with his girlfriend and his brother. When they reached Sam Goody's record store in New York they stopped, three longhairs, caked in mud, saying, "Hey, we're just back from Woodstock." The people in the record store looked at them as if they were survivors of the *Titanic.*

Abbie Hoffman would go back to being Abbie Hoffman, for a while.

He would be asked at the Chicago conspiracy trial where he resided.

"I reside in Woodstock Nation."

"And in what state is Woodstock?"

"It is in the state of the mind."

That's what stuck with people of the Woodstock generation once they washed off the mud. Not the drugs or the politics, but a state of mind.

The real influence of the Woodstock generation would not be felt for years. It would be a long, tough, fascinating road ahead.

Anthony Greenlee of Nyack, New York, was fifteen years old when he went to the concert. Ten years after, he said, "Woodstock Nation lasted exactly as long as the concert. We went from a generation that cared about others to a generation that only cares about I, me, mine. It's too bad. We came so close."

In many ways Anthony Greenlee was right. And in many ways he was dead wrong.

CHAPTER TWO

The Last Hurrah

By the time the Merry Pranksters had arrived home from Woodstock, turned off Interstate 5 into Pleasant Hill, Oregon, and driven up to the Kesey homestead, Ken had planted a big sign to greet them at the front gate. It read simply: NO.

Some took the hint, and turned and left. Others were more persistent, and Kesey took them out to the interstate and pointed them in the direction from which they came. A few had to be thrown out.

If the Merry Pranksters were surprised, expecting to be welcomed home with open arms, it was because they didn't understand that Kesey, like the country, was reaching a turning point.

After Tom Wolfe turned the spotlight on Kesey in *The Electric Kool-Aid Acid Test*—a massive bestseller, required reading in hundreds of schools— many looked to Kesey as a spiritual leader. In reality, the spotlight "burned like a big ultraviolet eye," Kesey wrote later. The voltage generated by it scared him and excited him at the same time, and he needed an escape before it swallowed him up.

Everything had got too big, too uncontrollable. Too many people, too much rock and roll—too trendy. Kesey, like the nation, would soon go in search of himself.

America after World War II was a homogeneous nation. Americans believed they were in the best, the richest, the most morally righteous country in the world. They felt secure in their technology and knew that tomorrow would always be better than today.

But a series of 1960s shocks made Americans question if they were really as good and as blessed as they had thought: the assassination of John F. Kennedy, then those of Martin Luther King and Robert Kennedy; the riots in the cities and on the campuses; and, of course, Vietnam—all of which were brought into our living rooms by the unblinking electronic eye of television, interrupted only by a message from our sponsor.

The images evoked such strong feelings that Americans began to take sides: for or against the war, for or against the civil rights movement, for or against Nixon; Us against Them. America—Love It or Leave It.

But more than anyone else, the Woodstock generation began choosing sides, making changes. The trappings of the 60s remained. People still wore their hair long, still wore jeans with American flags sewn across the ass, and still painted peace signs on the sides of their Volkswagen bugs. But inwardly, it was as if a time clock were going off and a hidden voice saying, "It's time to move on."

The generation that reached puberty during John Kennedy's presidency was hitting adulthood with Richard Nixon.

By all outward appearances, the Woodstock generation remained thoroughly infused with the festival spirit. It seemed ready to explode like a seed pod and spread its energies across the nation.

But just the opposite would happen.

It would start with a series of deaths, betrayals, outrages.

The deaths—of Martin Luther King, Robert Kennedy, Janis Joplin, Jimi Hendrix, Jim Morrison—would impart a sense of mortality to those who felt immortal. They were people who helped shape the generation, in its moods, its feelings, it beliefs, its very consciousness.

Each new outrage—the chaining of Bobby Seale at the Chicago trial, the revelations about My Lai and the bombing of Cambodia, and more than anything else Kent State—would bring a sense of impotence to those who felt omnipotent.

Each new betrayal—the failure of Richard Nixon to end the war, the stagnating economy, Ted Kennedy's Chappaquiddick, the breakup of the Beatles—would bring a sense of disillusionment to those who tried to keep the faith.

At the time each event seemed like a sad, isolated moment. Collectively, they began to chip away at the generation's spirit and cause it to wither and atrophy. Bit by bit, death by death, outrage by outrage, the glue that bound the generation together would crack and disappear.

If Woodstock was about believing that the generation could change the world, then each of the events of those next few years was proof that the world could change this generation. For all Woodstock's braggadocio, the odds for changing the system became slimmer and slimmer.

After years of walking in step—talking the same, dressing the same—the Woodstock generation looked around, reexamined itself, and moved off in different directions, politically, culturally, and individually.

It was as though the great electromagnet in the middle of the generation, the magnet that pulled all those people to Woodstock, had begun to lose its power, short-circuited slowly by a dozen different events. And without that magnet, the generation could not hold together as one. It would not explode like a seed pod, spreading its energies across the nation. It would merely fizzle.

Americans would grow more concerned with their personal agendas: finding a job, paying the rent, and having children. Even their causes would become more personal: gay rights, women's rights, the rights of singles, the rights of the elderly.

Certainly, many things still kept the Woodstock generation together; the war and the protest against it were most obvious. But something larger, a sense of belonging made up of dozens of little pieces, united the generation. For some, those pieces were drugs and sex and rock and roll, and jeans and bell-bottoms. For others, those pieces were political—hippie and yippie, Panther and NAACP.

Soon, only the war would remain a unifying agent. All those other pieces would fragment, and the unity of the generation would dissolve, and with it the sense of belonging. Moving through Altamont and Vietnam and the campus protests, a generation that had chanted "Yes I can and yes I will," began to feel, maybe I can't.

Ken Kesey, the symbol of the Woodstock generation for many, was one of those who would feel a distance, move away, and begin to doubt. It would be a difficult period for one of America's best, most interesting writers. He would begin living his own myths and walking dangerously close to the abyss.

Kesey's troubles actually began a year before Woodstock when he was convicted, a second time, for marijuana possession. He fled to Mexico but returned, and was arrested. Kesey was sentenced to three years in prison but served only five months and eleven days in the San Mateo jail. But to someone who couldn't tolerate institutions, jail was hateful. Sitting in his cell, he wondered how anyone could look down the dark tunnel of real jail time, ten years or so, and not go stark-raving mad.

Jail seemed an unlikely place for the person voted most likely to succeed by his classmates back in high school.

Ken Elton Kesey was born in Colorado but his family, like the characters in his book *Sometimes a Great Notion,* leapfrogged the continent until almost bumping into the Pacific in Springfield, Oregon.

Kesey's family started poor, but prospered when his father, Fred, began a successful dairy cooperative. Ken swam in the local rivers, fished, and wrestled. He enjoyed magic and science fiction, was a star athlete and student, and even married his high school sweetheart, Faye Haxby, in 1956, a year before graduating from the University of Oregon.

Ken spent a year knocking around Hollywood hoping to make it as an actor. When that didn't work, he enrolled in a graduate writing program at Stanford University.

It was here, in 1959, that Kesey was introduced to serious drugs even before many future hippies were out of diapers. Kesey became one of the first people in the country to use LSD—ironically, at the invitation of the United States government.

LSD was new then; it was even legal. For $75 a day Kesey let doctors at the Veterans Hospital in Menlo Park use his body to test the effects of acid and other hallucinogens. It was like giving sight to a blind man. Suddenly everything was bigger, larger than life; his mind thought more precisely—the undetected became obvious. It was like opening a door that had been shut.

Kesey stayed on when the experiments ended, working as a night attendant in the mental ward, sometimes going to work high on drugs himself. Out of the experience of the mental ward grew his first and most famous book, *One Flew over the Cuckoo's Nest*. The hero is Randle P. McMurphy, a prisoner who fakes insanity to escape from the drudgery of a work farm and into the comfort of a nice, cushy mental hospital.

McMurphy tries to liberate his fellow inmates by injecting a sense of humor into the gloom of the ward. He is loved by them but hated by uptight bitch Nurse Ratched. He defies her authority and they struggle for the hearts and minds of the ward. She has McMurphy lobotomized and he is mercifully killed by a fellow inmate who then escapes.

The novel formed the perfect metaphor for the early-70s world of America; it was a microcosm of a land in which power was being misused and creativity struggled against stifling influences.

The failed "revolution" in the mental ward would be prophetic of the Woodstock generation. A few would be liberated; the masses would gain small bits of freedom but would remain confined within the institution. In the end, the institution would go on—softened, but intact. The revolution, in the end, would result in only small changes.

And the leadership would die.

The book was an instant winner. *Cuckoo's Nest* became a Broadway play and a hit film, winning five Oscars in 1976. But Kesey was mentioned only once, by director Milos Forman.

"I felt pride and hurt at the same time," Kesey told Bob Green of the *Chicago Sun-Times* after the awards ceremony.

Ken was paid only $28,000 for the movie rights. The film grossed over $40 million. Hurt and angry about the money and how the screenplay was written, Kesey refused to see the film.

Even before *Cuckoo's Nest* was a hit, Kesey moved back to Oregon, where he worked as a logger to research his second novel, *Sometimes a Great Notion*.

Kesey took the title from the song "Good Night, Irene."

Sometimes I live in the country,
Sometimes I live in the town;
Sometimes I get a great notion
To jump into the river ... an' drown.

Notion is a sprawling story of a family-owned logging dynasty. Again, the reviews were wild: "A blockbuster of a book, a huge turbulent tale ... this book establishes beyond doubt that Ken Kesey is a novelist of unusual talent and imagination."

Notion also became a movie and marked Kesey as one of the young writers with a chance of having a real impact, a genius before thirty.

Kesey had moved to La Honda, fifty miles south of San Francisco, to a big log house equipped with all types of stereo equipment, tape recorders, movie cameras, and projectors. At La Honda Kesey finished *Sometimes a Great Notion* and there he entertained a continuous parade of visitors; some of them just stayed on—and became the Merry Pranksters.

The acid-rock and psychedelic movement were just getting started in the early 60s; San Francisco was the center, La Honda the leading edge. Kesey served LSD-spiked Kool-Aid to groups like the Jefferson Airplane and the Grateful Dead and they returned to San Francisco and spread the word. They experimented with light and color, wore spectacular clothes, and painted posters with psychedelic visions of their LSD trips.

Ken Kesey was the high priest of psychedelia and the Pranksters were his acolytes. He discovered LSD before Timothy Leary did and advocated its use as a way for people to understand themselves better and solve their problems.

Then it was 1964, the year of the Trip. Kesey and thirteen Pranksters traveled cross-country in a Day-Glo-colored 1939 International Harvester bus, from San Francisco to New York. It was The Trip made famous in *The Electric Kool-Aid Acid Test*.

The Trip was compared with Jack Kerouac's journey a decade earlier, a trip glorified in his book *On the Road*. Kesey did for the hippies what Kerouac did for the beatniks.

Kesey and Kerouac met during the Trip, at a party in a New York Park Avenue apartment where the Pranksters were staying. Kerouac was sullen, uninviting. He liked *One Flew over the Cuckoo's Nest*, but considered Kesey a symbol "for a new generation—a generation he considered 'disrespectful' and 'illiterate,' " according to Gerald Nicosia's biography of Kerouac, *Memory Babe*.

"Jack was further bewildered when one of the Pranksters tied an

American flag around his neck. The couch was also covered with flags," Nicosia wrote.

Kerouac, despite living far outside the mainstream, treated the flag with great respect.

The symbol of the 50s and the symbol of the 60s had met and each turned away, equally bewildered. Kerouac resented the intrusion. Kesey would soon know the feeling.

Kesey returned west. Over the next few years he was arrested twice for possession of marijuana. The second time, in 1968, he fled to Mexico. He returned, was arrested in San Francisco, and sent to prison. Although the jail time was short, Kesey and the Merry Pranksters were never the same.

Jail put a serious crimp in the activities of Kesey and his band. It made him more than a little paranoid. "It makes you jumpy, makes you flinch every time you see a cop. It's like being an Olympic diver. You're going off the board and somebody fills your butt with buckshot."

It was time, Kesey decided, to make a serious attempt at getting his life back together. He was drawn back to his roots, to Oregon, to the land, the animals, the hard, sweaty work.

He bought a seventy-acre farm in Pleasant Hill and moved Faye and their four children into a converted barn, working the fields and trying to become a solid citizen.

The children went to local public schools and Kesey, once an alternate on the U.S. Olympic wrestling team, helped coach local teams. Still, he suffered from a powerful writer's wanderlust and craving for dark adventure.

Kesey embarked on several world-girdling trips, for *Rolling Stone, Esquire,* and other magazines. He went in search of a secret pyramid in Egypt, a Chinese philosopher in Beijing, and the Beatles in London. All too often, all he found were drugs and disappointment.

Kesey grew frightened by the drug culture he had helped create. And rather than be spurred into action by political movements, he was disgusted by them. The 1968 Democratic Convention in Chicago was seized upon by "Johnny-come-latelies" like Abbie Hoffman and Jerry Rubin, who, Kesey thought, felt they understood and he didn't.

He and Hoffman traveled in different orbits and seldom met. The radicals wanted to take the movement down a road Ken believed it should not take. They wanted confrontation—"We hoped to step over that hurdle instead of tripping on it." Kesey's kind of hippies were flower children, not bottle throwers.

If Ken Kesey was the guru of the counterculture, he was a disenchanted guru at best. Increasingly, he found its music, its violence, its dirty, unkempt refugees distasteful and joyless.

Kesey's farm had become a kind of commune. There was a constant stream of lost, doped-up visitors and motorcycle crazies to contend with, each more distasteful than the last; looking for shelter, sympathy, and good times. "The legion of the dangerous disappointed," he called them.

Disenchantment turned to disgust. Woodstock was Kesey's turning point and the NO sign went into the front yard just before the Pranksters returned home from Bethel.

If Kesey was trying to find himself, so was the rest of the country. It was a time when everything just seemed to go wrong. Older people, those who fought and won World War II, wondered why America couldn't do anything right anymore. Younger people lost confidence in their leaders and questioned the rightness of what they were doing.

The relentless optimism of the 50s and 60s began to fade just before Woodstock as the three-pointed knife of death, betrayal, and outrage began to cut at the generation's core.

In April 1968 Martin Luther King was standing on a terrace of the Lorraine Motel in Memphis when one shot from a 30.06 rifle shattered his spine. King's murder touched off rioting in hundreds of cities and towns across the nation.

One of the marchers in King's funeral procession was Robert F. Kennedy. Less than two months later he was shot dead by a Jordanian immigrant, Sirhan Sirhan.

Their deaths would create a sense of loss—more specifically, a sense that something had been stolen—throughout the Woodstock generation. The feeling of superhuman strength—the we-can-change-the-world attitude—was shattered forever.

Twenty years later, the Woodstock generation would overwhelmingly vote Martin Luther King and Robert Kennedy as the two most influential people of its lifetime.

The sense of betrayal was symbolized best by the breakup of the Beatles and the way the generation reacted to Bob Dylan. Earlier, Dylan, perhaps the most listened-to voice in recent years, had infuriated fans with his experiments in electric music. Now, after a motorcycle accident, he would become first reclusive, then eclectic, putting out country-style albums that made it seem he was thumbing his nose at those looking to him for songs of political importance. Two decades later these albums—"John Wesley Harding" and "New Morning" among them—would be counted among his best works. But in the late 60s the generation was looking for leaders and it appeared that Dylan was taking a hike.

The outrage came over Vietnam; by this time even Walter Cronkite was questioning American involvement.

The North Vietnamese launched their biggest offensive of the war, striking during Tet, their lunar New Year. Almost sixty thousand troops simultaneously attacked almost every southern city of Vietnam, virtually cutting the country in half. Vietcong commandos even got onto the grounds of the U.S. embassy in Saigon.

This happened only weeks after U.S. officials assured the nation that peace was at hand, further widening the credibility gap between the American people and their leaders. Over a half million U.S. troops were stationed in Vietnam; and thanks to television, Americans for the first time could see their sons falling and bleeding in jungles thousands of miles from home.

On hundreds of campuses across the nation, students struck or marched or sat in to protest the war.

The year was a succession of disasters, one shock after another that shattered the emotional stability of the nation.

The shocks continued in 1968. In Chicago more than eighty peace groups came to Chicago for the Democratic National Convention. They were met by twelve thousand police, with another twelve thousand army troops and National Guardsmen standing by.

Throughout the week bloody battles were fought between demonstrators and nightstick-swinging police. Hundreds of people were hurt and arrested. Dozens of journalists were injured and delegates to the convention were maced by the cops.

On Wednesday, the night of Hubert Humphrey's presidential nomination, demonstrators planned a nonviolent march. They taunted police with shouts of "Pig" and "Oink." The response from the policemen was out of proportion. Swinging nightsticks, they charged the crowd. Hundreds were beaten and arrested—all in the plain view of television, all amid chants of "The whole world is watching."

The clash was later officially termed a "police riot"; yet a grand jury indicted eight antiwar protesters for conspiring to incite trouble at the convention. The trial of the Chicago Seven, a year and a half later, would be one of the most incredible court proceedings in American history.

The original defendants were Abbie Hoffman, Jerry Rubin, Tom Hayden, Bobby Seale, Rennie Davis, David Dellinger, Lee Weiner, and John R. Froines. The mood of the trial was set on the first day when Defense Attorney William Kunstler requested a mistrial—he didn't like the dramatic way Judge Julius J. Hoffman read the charges to the jury.

In what would become one of the most powerful symbols of the decade, Seale, a Black Panther, refused to be silent and was gagged and tied to his chair. He was tried separately.

Hoffman wore love beads and at one session showed up in judicial robes. Another time he called Judge Hoffman "a disgrace to the Jews."

One afternoon he confronted Mayor Richard Daley of Chicago. It happened just after a lunch break.

This was the scene. Daley and his cronies were attended by about sixty members of the press. The galleries were full, but the prosecutor, the judge, and a couple of the defendants were late. Hoffman was early.

"I come bouncing in over the ropes, and I have this fringe jacket on, my boots, which were standard apparel, and Daley is standing right there," Hoffman remembers.

"And I walk up about ten feet from him, and I put up my dukes, and I say, 'What do we need all these lawyers for? Let's settle it, me and you! Right here!'

"And there's this hush over the room. My God, he's got bodyguards, they've got blackjacks out, they're ready!"

"And he starts laughing. And all his cronies start laughing. And I said, 'See! I'm here, I'm ready. You're not ready. And I walked out of the room.'"

The eight were acquitted of most of the charges. Only Davis, Dellinger, Hayden, Hoffman, and Rubin were convicted, and only on charges of crossing state lines to incite a riot. Judge Hoffman sentenced each to five years in prison, a $5,000 fine, and $50,000 in court costs.

The convictions made some believe that the system was unbeatable and they gave up. Others decided that more violent tactics were necessary; the protests did become meaner and more dangerous. It was one of the first forks in the road, where the generation would begin to divide.

By the time the convictions were reversed, it was too late—the dissolution and breakup of the movement had already started, and would continue through the 1970s.

There would be many reasons.

The end of the draft in 1973 would eliminate those who were involved for selfish ends; without the threat of the draft, there were no personal reasons to be involved.

Worsening economic conditions, high inflation and unemployment, made living on the fringe that much tougher. And within the movement police intervention was growing; more FBI undercover agents were posing as hippies.

The movement had its own troubles anyway—it became hard to have regular rallies and demonstrations, since the leaders had accumulated enough bad will and done enough on-the-edge deeds that they knew they could be arrested at any moment.

The movement was also becoming more polarized, with a small but vocal faction pushing to use violence, to increase the stakes.

Hubert Humphrey won the Democratic nomination for president in 1968, but lost the election to Richard Nixon when Chicago's streets erupted in view of the TV cameras.

One of the most poignant moments of the campaign was a young schoolgirl holding up the sign Bring Us Together during a Nixon Campaign stop. Even Nixon was touched.

Of course, Nixon would do anything but bring the country together. He promised to withdraw the troops from Vietnam; instead, he escalated the war, ordering the secret bombing of Vietcong bases in Cambodia.

By 1969 the number killed in Vietnam had surpassed the losses from the Korean War. Finally, public opposition started to mount.

Jimmy Holloran, who tended the sick at Woodstock, opposed the war. He thought it a waste, the killing senseless.

But a guy like Jimmy didn't take to the streets; not a good Irish-Catholic boy from northwest Washington, D.C., who was taught to say his prayers at night, stand up straight, and be a model for his four younger brothers and sisters. It was a heavy burden being the oldest, setting the benchmark, being the first.

Besides, Jimmy Holloran was fighting his own war. Like the war in Southeast Asia, it would separate him from his family and friends, and cause him terrible loneliness.

It would ultimately take his life.

Even though the Vietnam War was not over, it was already starting to wane in importance. For many Americans, it was replaced by concerns more personal, if no less socially important: a drive for acceptance by some who had been shunted off into the back alleys of American life. It was women winning equal wages for comparable work, gays expressing their preference, jobs for the handicapped, and respect for the elderly.

People like Jimmy Holloran would stand up and make Americans face issues other generations had hidden away.

Jimmy was everything that a family could want in a home where family meant everything. He was a gifted student, a loving son, a star football player, and center fielder who could hit the long ball. He was one of those rare people to whom everything came easy. Even rarer: he was so honest, so decent that no one seemed to mind much.

Jim and Betty Holloran used to discuss this with their son. Betty remembered that when she was in high school many of the top athletes had learned to drink too much, studied too little—had wasted their lives. She didn't want this to happen to Jimmy.

They didn't have sitdown talks, but it would just come up in conversation, and Betty Holloran would make her point, the way mothers do. Jimmy, as always, would do the right thing.

The Holloran household was one in which you said grace before meals, went to parochial schools, and never, ever missed mass on Sunday morning. Jimmy grew up embracing God; he became an altar boy and even talked of going into the priesthood.

He was a football and baseball star at D.C.'s Gonzaga High School, but his interests went way beyond sports. He won poetry contests and became president of the student council. He went to dances, often chaperoned by his parents, and had dates with the prettiest girls in school.

By his senior year, schools like Harvard and Holy Cross were asking him to attend, not only for his athletic ability but for his brains. They sent alumni to meet with Jimmy and woo his parents.

Jimmy chose Holy Cross, in Worcester, Massachusetts. Some of his friends from Gonzaga were going there, many of them from the football team. It was an all-boys school; and, of course, it was Catholic. This was important to his parents, who favored Holy Cross; they were afraid he would go to Harvard and lose his religion.

One afternoon in April, near the end of his senior year in high school, Jimmy walked into the house and told his mother that he was talking with a priest about something important, something very personal. The priest had suggested that Jimmy see a psychiatrist. He made the appointment. Would his mother go with him?

"Certainly, I'll go," she said.

Jimmy was quiet as they drove to the Georgetown University Hospital. He went in to see the doctor and Betty waited outside. About an hour later, the doctor told her to come in.

"I think Jim should still accept his scholarship to college," the doctor said. "I can recommend a doctor for him in Boston."

Betty said okay.

The doctor never mentioned to her why Jimmy had come to see him; neither did Jimmy, not on the way home, not the next day, not for almost two decades.

Betty Holloran didn't ask. She and Jim had discussed it. Jimmy would tell them when he was ready.

"If he doesn't want to tell me, I shouldn't question him," Betty said.

Jimmy knew his parents were curious. Why would their eighteen-year-old all-American son want psychiatric help? But he just couldn't tell them the truth and he wouldn't tell them a lie. Instead he went to church and prayed to God to help him and went to Holy Cross, where once a week, on Wednesday, Jimmy would put on a coat and tie before dinner and disappear to downtown Boston to see his psychiatrist.

Stuart Long, Jimmy's classmate from Holy Cross and Gonzaga, asked him once, "Jim, where do you go on Wednesday nights?"

He responded, "You don't want to know."

Jimmy disliked the rigid authoritarianism and the religiousness of Holy Cross. But much about the school he did like. In the fall he had football and as soon as that was over he would start swinging a weighted bat, doing it for hours, grooving his swing for spring baseball. He acted in school plays and wrote and went on dates.

Jimmy loved to act and write. He devoured books and would have been happy as a writer, or a journalist, or doing something in film. He took advanced English courses but majored in premed. Becoming a doctor seemed like the right thing to do for the first person in his family to go to college.

Jimmy would have also loved to play professional baseball. He made All–New England and played in the college world series; there were those who felt he could have made it to the Show, the big leagues. But Jimmy had what they call a short arm—couldn't get the ball into the infield fast enough. He had practiced for hours to become as good as he was, and he knew he didn't have the talent to make it to the major leagues.

Jimmy also had long talks with the priests at Holy Cross, particularly the younger ones: on religion, on ethics, on right and wrong and decency and fairness—particularly in the Catholic church. This was something he enjoyed. Growing up in the church, law was the church law and you accepted it along with meatless Fridays and the infallibility of the pope, no questions asked.

"If someone was committed to life in a mental hospital or a prison," Jimmy asked the priest, "why couldn't the husband or wife remarry? Why was that a sin?"

Jimmy had seen his mother drag herself to church on Sundays no matter how sick or how tired. Why, he asked, was it a sin to miss mass on Sundays? Why was the church so stubborn?

Why were women treated differently?

Why was the church so inflexible about homosexuals, making it a sin for a man to share his life with another man?

Jimmy was really asking about Jimmy. Why did God make him the way he was? Why was he so tormented? Why did he have to keep this terrible secret? How could others accept him if he couldn't accept himself?

In 1964 Jimmy Holloran scored the highest mark in the entire history of the Harvard Medical School's entrance exam. This time, when Harvard offered a full scholarship, Jimmy took it.

He graduated and for his internship moved to the West Coast, to Harbor General Hospital in Los Angeles. He loved California. It was sunny and bright, particularly enticing after seven years in Boston. And the people were less uptight, more tolerant. Still, when his internship ended, Jimmy returned east. He took a job in New York and a house in Connecticut and each day became one of the crowd, one of tens of thousands who rode the train to Manhattan to work.

Jimmy surprised his friends in 1969 by announcing that he was getting married. It wasn't as though there weren't women; in fact, they flocked to him. After all, he was tall, handsome, brilliant, certainly destined for greatness. But he had never been seriously involved.

This woman, Diane, was different. She was beautiful and spunky and clearly confident about her sexual prowess.

An August wedding was planned, invitations sent. But a few weeks later the couple sent postcards to all their guests. The wedding was off; no explanation was offered.

Jim and Betty Holloran couldn't understand it then, but after a while they came to understand that Jimmy knew the relationship was wrong for him, and they admired him for his honesty.

Instead of getting married that month, Jimmy went to Woodstock with his old friend Stuart Long. They took two women with them, and Long and the women camped on the edge of the huge amphitheater while Jimmy worked in the Red Cross tent comforting bad trips, and treating people for diarrhea and exposure.

For the first time he saw hundreds of thousands of people doing what they wanted to do; they were round pegs in round holes, not forced into square molds. They had a freedom he craved but never experienced: the freedom to be themselves.

After Woodstock, Jimmy withdrew, became more distant from his family. He wasn't angry or worried or bitter; he just seemed preoccupied. He decided to move, to return to the sunshine of California.

"I'm not going to stay on the East Coast any longer," he said. "It's too conservative."

Jimmy moved to San Francisco, to the area around Castro Street, and took a job as an emergency-room doctor at a local hospital. His ties to home became even more fragile.

When writing to his parents, Jimmy would list only his office address, never his home, so they wouldn't know the neighborhood where he lived.

When speaking with them on the phone, he would sometimes grow quiet, as though he no longer wanted to talk, as though wanting to forget the East.

Washington and Boston meant pain and hiding. Jimmy Holloran was determined to start a new life, a freer life; to be like the people he saw at Woodstock in 1969.

Because the shocks changing the generation were coming in dribs and drabs rather than in one tumultuous upheaval, it still seemed as if anything, even a freer world, were still possible.

One major shock, a major betrayal—the death of the Beatles—was eerily foreshadowed by the strangest story of 1969, the "death" of Paul McCartney.

A Detroit disc jockey claimed Paul McCartney had been dead for several years. It set off a nationwide deathwatch, with "signs" of Paul's death discovered in everything from lyrics to album covers. John always insisted that at the end of "Strawberry Fields" he was saying "cranberry sauce"—not "I bury Paul"—but people believed this as much as they believed that "Lucy in the Sky with Diamonds" didn't stand for LSD.

The death myth escalated with the release of "Abbey Road"; on the album cover, Paul is walking barefoot (like a corpse) while the others are dressed in what could be described as the garb of a pallbearer, a gravedigger, and a priest. He's stepping with his right foot, and the others aren't (the three others, this was believed to signify, were "left"). And a license plate visible on a white Volkswagen on the cover read "28 IF"—Paul would have been twenty-eight *if* he had lived.

Supposed signals were found everywhere. Entire magazines sprang up just to examine them. A TV show presented a mock courtroom in which evidence was presented for and against the argument that Paul was dead.

Paul was very much alive but the Beatles were on their deathbed. McCartney married Linda Eastman on March 12, 1969 and went into seclusion. Eight days later John Lennon and Yoko Ono wed at a private ceremony on the Rock of Gibraltar. They went to a hotel room where they told reporters they were going to bed for a week to protest violence in the world.

Later they released "Give Peace a Chance" by John Lennon and the Plastic Ono Band; it was, for all practical purposes, the end of the Beatles. One year later Lennon and McCartney each released albums containing only their own songs and Paul announced he was leaving the Beatles.

Other groups would surpass the Beatles musically; other songwriters would create more thoughtful lyrics. But the Beatles were the first. They were the Adam and Eve of the Woodstock generation's move into and away from the garden. They were the assault troops of the British music invasion of the 60s. They were the reason that thousands of kids who never wore anything but a crew cut stopped going to barbers.

For years afterward, whenever one of the Beatles would perform at a concert, thousands would attend simply on the odd chance that the Beatles would get back together. They never would. But the search for a Beatles reunion mirrored the larger search: they wanted the 60s back. Again, they were betrayed.

The breakup marked an incredible low for the Woodstock generation, in a year of incredible highs and unbelievable lows for the nation.

The highest high began at 9:32 A.M. on July 19, 1969 when Apollo 11 lifted off from Cape Kennedy for the moon. The command vessel was called the *Columbia* and the lunar module, the section that would sit down on the moon, was the *Eagle*.

The *Eagle* landed at 4:17 P.M. Sunday, July 20. A few hours later almost a billion people across the world watched as a television camera mounted on the *Eagle* followed Commander Neil Armstrong backing down a narrow ladder and stepping into the thin lunar dust.

"It's one small step for man, one giant leap for mankind," Armstrong said.

Back on earth, summer 1969 was being called by some the summer of festivals. Not all were as peaceful as Woodstock.

First, there were skirmishes between policemen and concertgoers in Palm Springs, California, when the officers tried to cool off a crowd outside a baseball stadium by turning on the underground sprinkler system. The cops used tear gas, the crowd panicked, and two people were shot by the terrified owner of a nearby gas station. Hundreds were arrested and hundreds more hurt.

A few weeks later 115 young people were arrested during a concert in Los Angeles. Fans also clashed with police at the Newport Jazz Festival in June. The same thing happened a week later in Denver.

This is what made Woodstock so special. Almost everything that could go wrong did—but it still worked. Even the *New York Times* relented, calling it "a phenomenon of innocence."

This was also the summer of the Rolling Stones's first American appearance in several years. The group's nationwide tour culminated in a free concert at the Altamont Speedway in California. The Hell's Angels were hired for $500 worth of beer to provide security. It was a fatal mistake.

The British promoters didn't understand the Angels. Hell's Angels in England rode little Hondas, not big Harley Hogs, and they were more of a motorcycle club than a way of life.

At Altamont the Angels meant business. Many carried pool cues and clubs, and they pounced on anyone who approached the low-slung stage. Several people were badly beaten and one man was stabbed to death while Stones' singer Mick Jagger sang on.

Michael Lang, the man who made Woodstock come off so flawlessly, was standing in the crowd in Altamont. Lang just shook his head. It was a good example of bad planning, he thought.

But it was more than that. If Woodstock was one of the high points of the year, and the decade, Altamont was one of the lowest. The violence seemed like a self-fulfilling prophecy to those who shook their heads at the sight of hippies. It seemed like one more step away from the garden.

It didn't help that the most bizarre crime of the year, perhaps the decade, was committed by a would-be hippie living in a commune.

Movie star Sharon Tate was blonde, bosomy, and carrying the child of producer-husband Roman Polanski. She was murdered and mutilated along with four friends in her Los Angeles home. Four months later Charles Manson and several members of his commune near Death Valley were arrested.

Manson was a long-haired ex-convict who held a mystical sway over his followers. The longest trial in California history ended more than a year later when Manson and three of his female followers were convicted of killing Tate and six others.

There would be other shocking deaths that year. The Woodstock generation sank its roots in the Kennedy years, and reaped its pain in Robert Kennedy's death. Senator Edward M. Kennedy inherited much of his brother's psychic energy and warmth. This is why the Woodstock generation felt yet another sense of betrayal when the Chappaquiddick story broke.

After a party, a car driven by Kennedy plunged off a bridge and passenger Mary Jo Kopechne drowned. Rumors were rife of an affair; other rumors had it that Kennedy left Mary Jo to die, that her family was paid off.

Kennedy survived, but his presidential ambitions were another fatality. The Woodstock generation had lost one more potential hero.

Years later, when people began to wonder why the generation had lost its ability to believe in heroes, these deaths would loom large and dark and deep.

The first draft lottery since 1942 was imposed in 1969. In thousands of homes, dormatories, and student unions across the nation, men and women listened to numbers being called on the radio. Each birthday was assigned a number from 1 to 365. They listened, knowing their fates, and the fates of their brothers and friends, were being determined far away. A high number meant they could get on with their lives; a low number and the question was not if, but when they would receive a letter from the Selective Service.

June 17 landed number seventy-three in the lottery and a letter came ordering Tony Casale to report to the post office in Chambersburg, Pennsylvania. There he was herded onto a bus with fifty other scared-but-afraid-to-show-it young men and driven to the U.S. Army Depot in New Cumberland, Pennsylvania.

Once inside the sprawling complex of one-story buildings they stripped to their underwear and each was given a jar and a bag. Wallets, money, jewelry went into the bag; they peed in the jar, and that's how they spent the next several hours, holding their valuables in one hand and their urine in the other.

They marched from station to station, an eye test here, a hearing test there, and finally into a large room where they were divided into two lines facing each other. Then they were ordered to drop their underpants and bend over while a doctor walked up and down behind each line getting a unique view of America's finest.

Finally they were allowed to dress, were given a box lunch of a stale ham sandwich and an apple, and waited to be called into a doctor's office for the Conference.

The conference was where they received the verdict: 1A, qualified for service; 4F, go home and relax; 1Y, physically unfit, but could be called if the war got worse.

The draft brought out American ingenuity at its best. A Pennsylvania man, hearing that eggs could raise your blood pressure, ate four dozen the day before his physical. He got sick but was classified 1A.

In Brooklyn a man ate turkey for weeks hoping to raise his uric-acid level. This was only after trying to figure out how to stretch his shoe size, which was already thirteen and a half. Thousands professed to be homosexual, a ticket out of the military.

Casale, waiting in line for the conference, heard the man ahead of him confess to being a practicing homosexual, an immediate ticket home.

"When was the last time you got laid?" the doctor asked. The kid got so flustered by the bluntness of the question that he stammered. The doctor marked him 1A.

Antiwar protests were everywhere. San Francisco State University was closed for three weeks. At the City College of New York, the auditorium was burned. Harvard rioted on April 9. Massachusetts State Police were called and fought their way into University Hall.

Two-hundred fifty students took over Willard Straight Hall at Cornell.

At the University of Wisconsin, black students called a strike and exchanged blows with conservative white students. May 15 was Moratorium Day, hundreds of thousands of protesters marched against the Vietnam War.

Over four hundred universities had strikes or were forced to close. Worried lawmakers in New York, New Jersey, Massachusetts, West Virginia, South Carolina, and Texas hurried to pass laws prohibiting handguns on campuses.

Nixon responded to the demonstrations with his own plan for ending the war; he called it Vietnamization. U.S. troops would be replaced by Vietnamese troops. By year's end sixty thousand Americans had returned home. His vice president, Spiro Agnew, called the protesters an "effete corps of impudent snobs."

Agnew didn't limit his criticism to students, however. He and Nixon both felt that the news media were fostering an antiwar mood in the country. Agnew attacked the "group of men, numbering perhaps no more than a dozen," who control the news media, calling them the "unelected elite."

Agnew struck a spark. Hundreds of letters agreeing with the vice president poured into the TV networks and newspapers like the *New York Times* and the *Washington Post*.

But attitudes toward the war soured even more as fall began. Charges began surfacing that Americans had committed war crimes in South Vietnam. The place was a village named My Lai. The platoon leader was Lt. William L. Calley, Jr.

Soldiers in the American division had helicoptered into My Lai. Several were killed by Vietcong snipers and booby traps.

Angry GIs rounded up the civilians into the center of the village where, according to witnesses, many were shot at point-blank range and dumped into an L-shaped ditch.

Calley was convicted of murder two years later. A federal court eventually overturned the conviction and Calley was released from the army in 1974.

The reaction to Calley and My Lai came from two very different directions, but the result was the same.

Some felt betrayed—Americans were doing what they could not believe Americans would do, kill women and children.

Others felt outrage. Many so sincerely believed in the immorality of the American presence in Vietnam that they simply assumed that such atrocities were commonplace, and they were infuriated at the hypocrisy of setting up one man as a scapegoat.

From both sides sentiment against the war continued to grow. In spring 1970 a national poll showed over half of all adults in sympathy with antiwar demonstrators.

Opposition to the war started appearing in more subtle ways. The popular film *M*A*S*H,* starring Donald Sutherland and Elliott Gould, poked fun at the pettiness and bureaucracy of the military. Two years later it would become a top-rated television program, using the Korean War to make a point about Vietnam. "M*A*S*H" retired from service in 1983, eight years after the Vietnam War.

On May 1, 1970 Nixon ordered U.S. troops into Cambodia to destroy Vietcong basecamps and storage depots. In return, Communist troops attacked the Cambodian government supported by the United States, creating a two-front war in Southeast Asia.

The third front was back in the United States. There the antiwar movement was becoming more confrontational. Feelings were running so high that tragedy was certain to occur.

It struck first at the University of Wisconsin. One person was killed when the Army Mathematics Research Center was bombed. Not long after, two people were killed and nine wounded when police officers opened fire on a student protest at Jackson State, a predominantly black school in Jackson, Mississippi.

But the event that most gripped the nation occurred on a quiet Ohio campus with little history of protest or student activism. Ironically, the war had little to do with starting the trouble at Kent State. A motorist threatened to drive into a group of young people dancing outside a bar. The car's windows were broken and the kids set fire to some trash barrels. Police used tear gas to force the kids back to campus.

Angry students held a demonstration the next night. A few shouted antiwar slogans:

One two three four,
We don't want your fuckin' war...

Some flares were thrown through a window into the ROTC building and it burned to the ground.

Mayor LeRoy Satrom requested and got National Guard troops to help keep order. Five hundred arrived the next day equipped with tear gas and M1 rifles.

A few students held a quiet demonstration Monday afternoon but most simply went about their business, scurrying back and forth to class. The guardsmen appeared and ordered the campus commons cleared. Students responded with their middle fingers and a few hurled stones at the guardsmen.

Guardsmen fired tear gas into the crowd and a small detachment pursued one group of students. What caused the next episode is the subject of debate. What happened, however, is fact. The guardsmen knelt, aimed, and fired.

Thirteen students were shot; four were dead. None had been a campus militant and one of the dead was even an ROTC cadet. An official inquiry determined later that the guardsmen were never in any physical danger.

Ralph Fogel heard about the Kent State killings over Armed Forces Radio while lying on his bunk in a barracks in Quang Tri Province of Vietnam, not far from the DMZ.

Ralph had joined the U.S. Naval Reserve when he was about to be drafted. He expected to be on a ship somewhere, anywhere, far from Vietnam. Instead, he ended up in the Seabees—combat construction battalion—in the northern province of South Vietnam. He was under frequent rocket and mortar attack. Once he fell on a chaplain during a barrage and the brass, thinking he was trying to protect the clergyman, gave him a decoration.

Ralph talked occasionally with his fiancée back home and she told him about the antiwar protests and riots. He wanted to be home, protesting too. It is a bad war, he thought; we have no right being the policeman of the world.

But here he was, in Vietnam—unable to stop the war; unable to do much to win it. Then the news came on the radio about the deaths in Kent State.

"Those bastards were protesting," one of the other men said. "They deserve it."

Ralph just rolled over on his bunk and cried.

These kids were my age, he thought. This isn't my America.

By the time the spring semester had ended, more than four hundred college campuses had been disrupted by protests against the war. Some colleges simply closed early for the year but that didn't stop the protests. Washington was the next target.

More than a hundred thousand marched on Washington during the week of May 9, 1970. Nixon tried to make a gesture of conciliation by visiting them as they slept on the grounds of the Lincoln Memorial. They wanted to talk about issues; he talked about football and surfing.

Interior Secretary Walter J. Hickel warned Nixon that a vast segment of young people feel there is "no opportunity to communicate with government." His letter was published in several newspapers. Hickel was unceremoniously fired.

Nixon had other problems. Wages and salaries were rising but the gains were being stolen away by inflation. Inflation hadn't been a really serious problem since before World War II. But credit-card use, which had expanded by almost 400 percent in the past five years, fueled inflation; so did spending on the war. When the government cut the money supply to slow inflation, unemployment soared.

The next year Nixon announced his New Economic Policy, wage-and-price controls to get the economy back on track.

Babyboomers were learning, firsthand, some hard facts of economic life. Inflation or unemployment or both would grow with them over the next ten years. The widespread wealth with which they grew up allowed them the freedom to indulge in the luxury of questioning society, of protesting, of trying alternative lifestyles. Now, the faltering economy made it more difficult. People who may have remained, or become, involved in the antiwar movement, or the environment, or helping the poor, had to turn their attention to paying the rent and feeding their young families.

Another story, another key betrayal, was developing in Washington but the headlines would come later. The White House put together a group of secret operatives to find and plug leaks in the administration. They were called the plumbers.

The plumbers also developed a list of Nixon political enemies, including columnist Jack Anderson and actors Jane Fonda and Paul Newman. Some were harassed by FBI checks and the administration tried, unsuccessfully, to get the IRS to audit its enemies. The plumbers even broke into the office of a Beverly Hills psychiatrist looking for the files of a patient, Daniel Ellsberg.

Ellsberg, a Harvard graduate and worker at the Rand Corporation, angry about the invasion of Cambodia, had leaked secret documents detailing U.S. involvement in Vietnam. The Pentagon Papers were published in newspapers across the country.

Americans became more and more frustrated with the war, both at home and in the battlefield. Deaths reached forty-five thousand and more than half of all adults felt it was time to end the war.

Troops in the field wore peace symbols on their steel helmets and it was estimated that two of three soldiers were on drugs. Nixon's popularity waned badly. By the winter of 1970 less than half of all Americans approved of his job performance.

If Americans were split over the war, there wasn't much doubt that the Woodstock generation was changing the way America lived. The Census Bureau reported that the number of people living with unmarried partners of the opposite sex had risen 70 percent since 1960. Living together was not only more acceptable than ever, but safer. This was the first generation of women who, thanks to the pill, didn't have to worry about getting pregnant.

One of the big debates of the year was over sex education in schools. A Gallup poll found that almost three of four adults approved of sex education, and over half favored courses explaining birth control. Each town and community seemed torn by the argument.

Eighteen-year-olds got the right to vote in 1970, the fiftieth anniversary of women's suffrage. There were dozens of women's marches across the nation, and newsrooms everywhere debated the question whether to use Ms. or Miss or Mrs. They got a partial answer a year or so later when *Ms.* magazine was formed; it was a publication edited by women for women.

Forty percent of all married women were now employed. One reason was inflation, which was silently stealing the spending power of the dollar. It simply became harder to survive on one paycheck. Another reason was the change in women themselves and in their expectations about life.

Fewer and fewer women were willing to settle for the role of household helpmate. Thousands entered male-dominated professions such as law, medicine, architecture. So many women entered journalism that fifteen years later activists complained that newsrooms were becoming "pink-collar ghettos." To the tune of Helen Reddy singing "I Am Woman" women marched into the workplace becoming one of the greatest forces shaping American life.

Still, the average woman made only about 60 percent of what a man made for the same job, a gap that would close very slowly during the next two decades.

On television the "Mary Tyler Moore Show" depicted for the first time the real-life problems facing single working women. "All in the Family" was another TV breakthrough, using humor to confront issues like racism and homosexuality.

"All in the Family" was followed by "M*A*S*H," but these were only a few bright spots in an otherwise dim picture. The entertainment industry was in crisis.

Entertainment was becoming more innocuous, less offensive. Movies like *Easy Rider* a year earlier and *Alice's Restaurant* challenged viewers to reassess their values.

But the early 70s brought us *Love Story,* an overly sentimentalized bittersweet romance with almost no point. Yet, millions lined up to see Ali McGraw tell Ryan O'Neal that "love means never having to say you're sorry."

The movie *Airport* came out, to be followed by *Airport 1975* (which came out in 1974), *Airport 1977,* and *Airport 1979: The Concorde. Airport* was the harbinger of a long line of disaster films, such as *The Posiedon Adventure*, *The Towering Inferno*, and *Earthquake*, designed not to expand the mind but to babysit it. They were pure action, pure suspense, and little plot. The few intelligent movies that continued to be made would have an increasingly hard time competing for audience attention with escapist fare; by decade's end they would lose the fight altogether.

Escapism in films entered a new phase: The movie *Deep Throat* introduced the early 70s film movement of porno chic. The plot evolved around star Linda Lovelace, who leads a sexually frustrated existence before learning that her clitoris, through some anatomical accident, was located a few feet too high—in her throat. Suddenly porno became fashionable and skin flicks were in. *Deep Throat* parties were organized and the guests driven to the movie houses in limousines; entire offices attended.

Deep Throat was followed by such films as *The Devil in Miss Jones* and *Behind the Green Door* (which caused considerable embarrassment for Procter and Gamble when it was revealed that the movie's star, Marilyn Chambers, was also the angel-faced blonde on the Ivory Snow box).

While film drifted away from the message movies of the 60s, music was entering a deeper crisis.

The summer of festivals would not be repeated. As soon as a promoter announced a concert, city councils and citizens groups mobilized to pass ordinances blocking the show.

More important, some stars lost touch with their audiences or simply self-destructed. It became common for groups to arrive hours late for concerts; sometimes they were too drunk or too stoned to perform well, and sometimes they would not show up at all.

One hit record would earn more than an average worker in his lifetime. The money and the adulation made some performers feel bigger than life.

Two of Woodstock's biggest stars, Jimi Hendrix and Janis Joplin, died within three weeks of each other in 1970. Jimi was twenty-four; Janis twenty-five.

Hendrix, one of the greatest guitar players ever, died in his sleep in London after talking an overdose of pills.

Joplin, whose excesses in sex, drugs, and booze became legendary, injected a massive overdose of heroin into her body. Six months later "Me and Bobby McGee" hit the top of the charts. It was her only number one single.

The deaths of Hendrix, Joplin, and later Jim Morrison, and others, coupled with the breakup of the Beatles, took the soul out of the music industry, and weakened the glue that held together the Woodstock generation.

Music was becoming more generic, more trivial again. Peter, Paul and Mary scored with an inoffensive song, "Leaving on a Jet Plane," and B. J. Thomas had a hit with "Raindrops Keep Falling on My Head" from the movie *Butch Cassidy and the Sundance Kid*.

A wave of nostalgia hit the generation. When people become disenchanted with the present, they often look back to simpler times of the past. Howdy Doody was hot on college campuses. Sha Na Na cashed in on the 50s rock-and-roll revival, and back by popular demand were Elvis Presley, Chuck Berry, the Everly Brothers, Fats Domino, and Little Richard. Woodstock was only a song, sung by Crosby, Stills, Nash, and Young, a group which, appropriately enough, got its big break at Bethel.

The Woodstock generation was becoming so disillusioned that entertainers went to drastic lengths to get its attention. It was called glitter rock. Alice Cooper performed on stage with his eyes blackened and a boa constrictor wriggling around his neck and between his legs. David Bowie appeared with orange hair and lipstick. Elton John did a concert dressed like Donald Duck, right down to the tail. There were even a few performances in which live chickens were killed on stage and the blood splattered into the audience.

The unity that music provided only a few years before was shattering as rock itself splintered.

Rock and roll was moving in many directions. The Osmonds, David Cassidy, and the Ohio Express introduced bubble-gum music, which was more style than substance with such lyrics as "Yummy, Yummy, Yummy, I've Got Love in My Tummy."

A reaction to the acid rock of the 60s and the glitter rock of the early 70s was religious rock. *Jesus Christ Superstar* came out as an album and opened on Broadway as a hit play a year later. It was followed by *Godspell* and George Harrison's "My Sweet Lord."

The religious movement really exploded with EXPLO 72. Billy Graham called it a Christian Woodstock as thousands of freshly scrubbed young people from across the nation jammed a Texas football stadium to sing and shout the praises of the Lord in front of a huge backdrop with the word *Jesus* in psychedelic colors.

The religious movement was one reaction to the disillusionment of those who thought they could do so much but who were accomplishing so little.

This disillusionment took hold in other ways. Mark Hawthorne, the *New York Times* rewrite man who never made it to Woodstock, did make it to California in the early 70s; it was a poor-tourists trip to see plays and sightsee around Los Angeles.

A friend offered him a visit to a commune near Mendocino. It was the perfect end of the vacation, and the perfect tourist-guide-to-hippiedom. After a day of skinny-dipping in the warm sun, he was offered a hit of psylocybin.

Mark had smoked his share of marijuana, but this would be his first acid trip. It was amazing—everything an acid trip was supposed to be but only occasionally was. After a time—how long? it's hard to say, since time was a concept becoming harder to believe in—he started understanding that sense of oneness he'd heard friends talk about.

As the acid rush lighted his eyes and the river tickled his knees, the feeling grew within him. He tossed a Frisbee and felt connected to it as it sailed away. He laughed, and felt the laugh still inside him and apart from him as he heard it echo off the distant hills.

Mark felt connected to something, something larger than himself. This was where he wanted to be all the time.

He returned to New York, to the *Times,* but events moved quickly: he split with his wife, quit his job, and returned to California—to Berkeley. Behind him were college, the air force, the Peace Corps, the marriage, a child, the *Times*. He took the name California and worked odd jobs and hung out with the street people. He tripped a few more times but that feeling of oneness, the loving connection, never returned; something was missing.

"Woodstock, and the hippie period, were about positivity, of l-o-v-e," he said, spelling it as if it were a dirty word. "We tried it and burned out. It didn't work. In San Francisco, the summer of l-o-v-e was centered on Haight Street. I think it was telling us: don't forget hate."

He began going with a woman named Sarah, and instead of saying "I love you" to each other, "I hate you" became their term of affection. When the relationship ended after two years, there was none of the bitterness and resentment he had felt after the breakup of his marriage.

Clearly, he was on to something. Then it came to him: love, sweet love, isn't enough; the world also needs hate.

He had taken to hanging out at the Posts, the place where the Berkeley campus meets Telegraph Avenue, watching the straight people on their way to work, watching what appeared to be fake smiles stapled to their faces. He walked away from the Posts to a nearby building surrounded by steps on which workers drank their morning coffee and hippies sipped their morning tea. To his friend named Sky he said, "You know, people are really fucked up." And Sky said, "I know. Don't you just hate them?"

And, in the parlance of the times, it just . . . clicked.

He began standing near the Posts, saying to passersby, "Fuck you . . . I hate you . . . Have a lousy day." And people laughed, and a crowd gathered to see Hateman.

"It was like popping a cork in a champagne bottle. I didn't know what I was doing but I was on to something."

The crowd remained around him, this hippie freak espousing hate with love in his eyes, and the performer in him took over. He moved a hundred yards north, to a fountain that remained dry because of a drought, and stood inside the circle of the fountain and perfected his act.

It took awhile. He tried the idea that maybe violence was caring. He gave that one up when a thirteen-year-old boy began showing up every day to beat him with a stick.

Hecklers would appear, but like any good standup comic he learned to deal with them. He had the comic's sense that the heckler is the person paying the best attention. And after a while, after giving them his "I hate you" rap with those steely blue eyes boring into them, he made them laugh, and smile, and listen.

"After a while, I wouldn't trust you unless you said, 'I hate you.' It gets people to acknowledge negativity. Once I hate you, I accept you—I stop trying to reform you. Christians are always trying to reform you."

As time went by, Hateman began refining his art: pushing people's hands rather than shaking them, saying "I hate you" and "Have a lousy day." People cared for him as if he were touching something deep inside their souls. Hateman was going beyond the failed-love-generation idea and, in his own way, preserving a piece of it.

Gradually, he became enamored of breaking rules, rules like look both ways before crossing (which landed him in the hospital) and men should wear pants. Hateman took to standing at the Posts wearing a dress open to reveal his trademark brassiere, outlandish earrings, and a bright red straw hat trailing streamers that mixed with his graying hair.

His ever-present shopping cart contained the cans and bottles he collected all day to make money to buy cigarettes. Dragging behind on a string was an empty Tide container, there for a purpose, like the dress and the crazy hat: to get people to notice him. Tourists took his picture and moved along, but the braver ones would come up to chat. "I hate you," he told them, and made them push hands, which kept his caring feeling flowing.

"We're in a crisis. Old alliances have been based on rapport—clans, families, communities. We're now in a period of intense individualism. What this means is, we're coming into conflict with each other.

"My way of operating—push-pull and I hate you and acknowledging negativity verbally and physically—is a way to restructure relationships, of saying, 'Okay, you're different from me.'"

Eventually, Mark Hawthorne dropped the name California and took the name Datura. But he saved his warmest smile and push of the hand to those who came by and said, "Hey! Hateman!"

There were hints in 1971 that the world, just maybe, was getting a little less hateful. President Nixon shocked the nation by announcing that he would visit mainland China. The Soviets were irate so Nixon said he would visit Russia too.

One constant remained, however, and that was the war. In the spring of 1971, Nixon ordered a new offensive to break open the stalled peace talks. South Vietnamese troops attacked Vietcong strongholds in Laos but they were caught in a trap, losing ten thousand men in six weeks. Clearly, Nixon's policy of Vietnamization was not working. An overwhelming majority of Americans now felt the United States should not be in the war.

Gary Stoces, who had watched Woodstock with a mixture of admiration and bewilderment, was one of them.

Gary Stoces had earned his freedom from the Marine Corps two years earlier, walking up to a guard at a marine barracks gate with a joker in his hand.

He spent a lot of time just tooling around Washington, D.C., in a 1963 Corvette. Driving was comforting; it gave him a feeling of control over something. He also drove very fast, giving him a thrill that he hadn't experienced since Vietnam. But the thrill was undercut by a feeling of purposelessness, a sense of going nowhere fast. Still, on through the muggy Washington nights he drove, propelled by the strange notion that if one moves forward fast enough, the past can never catch up.

Of course, the past was close behind. It followed him around. Parts of the past, anyway. Cleveland, on the other hand, was a distant memory. Gary left Cleveland just as the 60s were dawning, and he never looked back. He was bored to death in high school. He passed the time with mindless activities, like stealing hubcaps from 1956 Oldsmobiles, the ones that looked like silver roulette wheels. He had no desire to vandalize. He only wanted to cut through the boredom, the boredom that sent him to the marines and to Vietnam.

Among the things he learned there was the fine art of pacification—the winning of hearts and minds. A squad of marines would be brought to a village. They lived there, and brought medical teams to inoculate the children against smallpox and polio. Little by little the villagers came to trust them, to give them information.

Then these squads would be yanked out of the villages. The Vietcong would come. Because the now defenseless villagers had helped the Americans, the Vietcong would blow the villagers away.

Besides writing a book on pacification, Gary held other jobs in the marines over the last few years. Among them was duty on the parade team. One of the great paradoxes of the time was that amid all the antiwar protests, twice a week an old-fashioned military drill was held at sunset: on Friday at the marine barracks, on Tuesday at the Iwo Jima Memorial, in Arlington, Virginia.

They would stand on the bus on the way to the memorial, so as not to crease their trousers. The word *Vietnam* was never mentioned at these parade drills. The marines marched around looking pretty. Gary was one of the guys carrying a sword.

There was no ammo in their rifles, there was no police protection—and none was needed. There were never protests at these drills. "We'd get applauded," Gary remembers. "They were really incredible drills. People with hair down to their ass were applauding these marines, and meantime they hated the war. It was a very strange time."

The gallows humor that all marines know was along for the ride too. At the Iwo Jima Memorial parade drills a firing squad marched around the base of the memorial. In tribute to a fallen comrade, the squad would fire its guns. In the silence that followed the loud crack, you could hear the retort echo off the buildings and nearby hills.

The morning after one such tribute, Gary came into the barracks to see written on the blackboard: Marine Barracks 1, Civilians 0. A major was crowing, "Hey, the firing squad got one yesterday! Guy heard the guns, got a heart attack, and died."

It was the gallows humor, and the Us against Them attitude, that made this all right. And it made Gary laugh.

But always the past was close behind. By 1970 it had come to be too much. "George Bernard Shaw had the great line, 'If you have to refer to what you're doing as your duty you're ashamed of what you are doing,'" Gary said. "You know what I had to look forward to? I had outgrown the Marine Corps. Another tour in Vietnam? Hell, after two hours I'm a refugee from the law of averages. I'm going to go back in the infantry for something I didn't believe in, nobody else really believed in? I just knew there was more out of life than another tour in Vietnam."

He got out of the marines on a Monday morning. He was running a 103-degree temperature. "I don't care if I had spinal meningitis; I would have crawled out of that gate and died a free man out in the streets of Washington."

The previous weekend, three days from freedom—two-and-a-wakeup—a sergeant major had tried to talk him out of leaving the Marine Corps. When Gary left his office, the sergeant major noticed a playing card on the desk.

It's an old marine tradition: when you have fifty-two days left, you buy a deck of playing cards. Every day you leave one somewhere. The joker goes to the gate sentry.

So Gary strode through the barracks on that chilly morning and handed his joker to the gate sentry, who put it in a pile with a dozen others. Many were leaving the marines these days, Gary thought.

He marched across the street, at Eighth and I streets, to have a drink with the winos near Quick Cash Kelley's Pawn Shop. Then he took his 103-degree temperature home to bed.

Before he lay down, he threw out everything he owned that had anything to do with the marines. Except the socks. He kept those.

Then he worked at, of all places, the Pentagon, installing telephones for the phone company. Much as he hated the hippies who had berated him on his return, he sort of enjoyed the fact that because his hair was long they called him the "hippie phone man" around the Pentagon. In Vietnam, as he came to think the war was stupid, he had been chided as the Leftist Sergeant, which couldn't have been further from the truth. Now at the Pentagon they cackled, "Hide the pencils, the hippie phone man is here." While he despised the war for its stupidity, its meaninglessness, he despised being identified with hippies. So he shaved his head, and it remains shaved today.

He had a fantasy, which is fairly normal: he wanted to kill former defense secretary Robert Strange McNamara.

"When I came back from Vietnam, I swore—and thank God I didn't, living here in Washington, but I swore—if I was ever in a restaurant and I saw Robert McNamara, I would have killed the guy with my bare fucking hands, and I'll tell you I think I would have been stupid enough to do it.

"There is one man I could never forgive. I hope every misfortune that could happen to a human being happens to him. I hope he dies of some incurable painful cancer. No, better than that. He gets hit with some kind of kerosene heat explosion and he gets burns over 95 percent of his body and he slowly fucking dies in a burn ward. That's how much I despised that man.

"Now I could see the guy and I wouldn't piss on him if he were on fire. I couldn't care less now, but I found that was a normal veteran's reaction. A lot of veterans fantasized about killing McNamara."

But of course he never did. He just worked, and drank, and partied. On breaks he noticed that the Vietnam veterans and the World War II veterans at the Pentagon avoided each other—sitting on opposite sides of the room—and he came to feel that the World War II veterans were treating him worse than the hippies did.

It didn't bother him much. Nothing bothered him much. Until one afternoon in April 1971. He was working in a wire closet next to room 5D565 on the fifth floor of the Pentagon, installing a new phone system for an antisubmarine warfare group. It was boring work, and he had a transistor radio on.

That week Vietnam veterans were marching on Washington to protest the war, a protest called Dewey Canyon Three. Gary wasn't going to join, but he liked the idea. He figured that everyone else had had his say about the war. Why not the veterans?

Then he heard the report: the Supreme Court had ruled that the veterans could not sleep on the mall.

"I said to myself, this is bullshit. They let the fucking KKK sleep on the mall; they've had the Boy Scouts on the mall."

Gary blew up. He locked up his tools and stormed into his boss's office. "I'm outta here," he said, fuming. "I just heard this thing on the radio. I want the rest of the week off. You can do it with or without pay, but I'm not coming back until Monday."

He went home, changed clothes, asked a friend to feed his cats for a few days, and—having been too broke to replace the expired tags on his car— walked to the mall.

A group of the veterans were marching on the Supreme Court that Wednesday afternoon, and about a hundred twenty-five of them were arrested. Everyone was too broke to make the $25 bail. But someone in the big holding cell had a great idea.

"We all get one phone call," he said. "Let's call ABC, NBC, CBS, and the Red Cross. The Red Cross will give you $25 for a pint of blood. We'll get the Red Cross down here. We'll have the networks down here televising all these Vietnam veterans in Washington, D.C., selling our blood and giving it to the city so we can get out of jail."

They never got a chance to find out if it would work. The police got wind of the plan, and—not having their hearts in this anyway, since many of the policemen were veterans themselves—let everybody go.

Back on the mall Gary was standing next to a veteran who had come back from the 101st Airborne with a bad leg. A fifty-ish lady walked by, seeing the two men huddling against the cool evening air, one's shaved head and the other's long cane forming a sort of inverted exclamation point.

"You're a disgrace to your country!" she told them. "You shouldn't be protesting. What are the troops going to think?"

"Lady," said the man with the cane, "we are the troops."

It was a tense moment, but things would get much tenser. As night fell, park policemen gathered. Everyone expected them to sweep through on horseback and chase the veterans off the mall.

Gary was sitting next to a friend, RJ, who turned to Gary and said, "If the cops come, they may get me"—he pulled two hand grenades from his coat—"but I'm taking some of these motherfuckers with me."

Holy shit, Gary thought. This is getting serious!

Just then the head of the park police approached the tired, nervous, angry horde of veterans. Through a bullhorn he read a proclamation, telling him that that they were in violation of that day's ruling. A long, long silence followed. The next move would be crucial.

The shadow of flags played across the faces of the Washington Monument. The park police chief raised his bullhorn again. The electronic voice again crackled across the mall: "If Nixon wants you arrested, let him do it."

A stunned silence was broken by hoots and cheers and applause. People ran off and came back with blankets and sandwiches and beer and settled in for the night.

The protest ended on Friday with a moving ceremony. Vietnam veterans, one by one, walked up to a statue and discarded their medals. This touched Gary deeply; he knew what a medal meant to a veteran. He knew that for some of them, medals were all they had left. Finally, a symbolic tree was planted in the name of peace.

Gary couldn't believe what happened next.

"These guys threw away their medals, which is symbolically their guts, their hearts and soul. Fucking tourists started scavenging through there. 'I got a silver star!' 'Hey, I'll trade you for a bronze!'

"I threw up. I got so sick. It was the most disgusting thing I'd ever seen. That's when I figured, this country ain't worth a fuck."

The past had finally caught up. The stupidity over there had finally met the stupidity over here, in Gary's mind. He had no use for either anymore.

He slept that night in the old Tom Jones bar. Meanwhile, the Woodstock Nation was heading into town for its own protest.

The next morning Gary said to a friend, "Let's go down and see what the revolution looks like." So they went back to the mall, and saw "these kids, getting out of cars, Cadillacs, big Buicks—their mommies and daddies are driving these kids to the revolution!"

There wasn't much left for Gary to do now, so he bummed around the next few years. The events of that week in 1971 had brought his cynicism about the war back home to him, finally. Now he would have to live with it.

The "revolution" began on May 1, May Day. Tens of thousands of protesters marched on Washington, vowing to stop the government. They stood in intersections, abandoned cars in roads, and lay down in front of buses.

Police skirmished with protesters for three days. More than twelve thousand were arrested.

The protests, however, were wearing thin for some. One poll showed that almost two-thirds of all college students were tired of disorderly protests, and the campuses became quieter.

September hosted another battle, at a state prison in rural western New York. In the years that followed, Attica would become synonymous with repression and violence.

Over twelve hundred rioting prisoners took thirty-nine hostages. After four days of stalled negotiations, state troopers burst through the doors while police sharpshooters picked off targets on the ground.

More than a hundred twenty men were killed or wounded. Eleven guards were slain. Prison officials reported that some of the slain guards' throats had been slashed by inmates. Autopsies revealed, however, that all the dead guards had been shot, and the prisoners had no guns.

It was just one more blow to the credibility of government officials, one more reason why cynicism was beginning to outweigh hopefulness.

The year 1972 ended the 60s—not the decade itself, but its spirit.

The big story of the year was a burglary. It would take two years for it to unfold, but by the time it did the Woodstock generation would be more jaded, less trusting, and more cynical than ever.

It began late on the night of June 17 when security guard Frank Wills discovered a break-in at the Democratic National Committee headquarters in the Watergate office complex in Washington. The White House plumbers had run amuck.

Nixon fundraisers received millions of dollars in illegal contributions for the president's reelection campaign. How to spend the money?

Suggestions included kidnaping antiwar leaders, hiring prostitutes to lure prominent Democrats into compromising positions, even hiring people to break into the office of the Democratic National Committee to tap their phones.

That was the burglary Frank Wills discovered. He called the police. Four men were arrested and a massive coverup began.

The *Washington Post* linked the burglars to the White House and the CIA. A short time later it reported that Attorney General John Mitchell controlled a slush fund that was used to play dirty tricks on Democratic candidates.

Even though the case against the president grew, a Gallup poll less than a month before the election revealed that only half of all registered voters had even heard of the Watergate break-in.

The campaign itself was a joke, starting with the political conventions.

The Republican campaign was choreographed to the minute. The only disruption was from a group of former soldiers, Vietnam Veterans Against the War. They had traveled across the country to Miami on what they called the Last Patrol. Just as Nixon stood at the podium to begin his acceptance speech, they started chanting: "Stop the bombing, stop the war."

If Nixon heard, or if he cared, no one seemed to know. The convention went on as scheduled, never missing a beat. The opposite was true of the Democratic Convention. It started off in a mess and got worse.

George McGovern's forces, led by future presidential candidate Gary Hart, the senator's campaign manager, made up their own rules. They ran roughshod over the old Democratic guard, alienating the very people they would need to make a respectable run at the presidency.

McGovern even had problems finding a running mate. He was turned down by six candidates before Sen. Thomas Eagleton, of Missouri, accepted the vice presidential nomination. The convention was so far behind schedule that McGovern's acceptance speech came after most of the nation had gone to bed.

If McGovern had any chance to defeat Nixon, it was dashed within weeks when headlines reported that years earlier Eagleton had received electroshock treatment for an emotional disorder.

McGovern supported Eagleton. "I'm fully satisfied. I am behind him 1,000 percent," he said.

But within a week Eagleton stepped aside at McGovern's request, to be replaced by Sargent Shriver, John Kennedy's brother-in-law.

The Kennedy magic didn't rub off. Nixon carried forty-nine of fifty states; only Massachusetts went for George McGovern (spawning "Don't Blame Me, I'm from Massachusetts" bumper stickers a year later when the notoriety of Watergate finally began to catch up with Nixon). It was the most lopsided election since 1936.

Two events foreshadowed the future: the U.S. began work on a reusable space vehicle to be known as the Shuttle and, in a strange story (out of California, naturally), astrologer Linda Goodman claimed Gov. Ronald Reagan was a secret astrology freak. Hardly anyone believed her.

Vietnam, the one great force still uniting the Woodstock generation, was about to end. One final desperate battle remained. South Vietnamese troops were routed as the North launched its strongest attack since Tet. Quang Tri was lost and An Loc, sixty miles from Saigon, was surrounded.

The North Vietnamese attack was broken by wave after wave of B52s. Hanoi and Haiphong were pounded, along with the rail lines leading into and out of the north. The navy mined harbors and shelled coastal areas. It was a virtual blockade.

The North Vietnamese thrust withered under the pressure and Hanoi decided to negotiate. In October, just weeks before the U.S. election, Secretary of State Henry Kissinger promised that peace was at hand.

Negotiations broke down again, after the election, and Nixon ordered the bombing renewed on an even larger scale. There were over a thousand raids a week. Hospitals and civilian neighborhoods were destroyed along with military targets.

On December 30 the White House announced an end to the bombings. About a month later the United States officially withdrew from Vietnam.

Altogether, 2.5 million Americans had served in Vietnam. Just over fifty-six thousand died and a third of a million were wounded.

America itself was a casualty. The nation was more polarized than at any time since before World War II—America-firsters versus those who said we had to spend more and fight harder to stem the spread of communism; those who felt the nation was almost always wrong versus those who said, "My country right or wrong."

But within the Woodstock generation itself, there were cracks and fissures tearing at its heart and soul, threatening to fragment it forever.

CHAPTER THREE

Expletive Deleted

President Nixon was inaugurated on January 20, 1973 in a multi-million-dollar bash planned, orchestrated, and celebrated by future felons riding a wave of popularity to a second term in the White House.

The war in Vietnam was over—or at least the killing of Americans had just about stopped—and the draft was winding down. Nine days before his inauguration the president announced he was ending wage-and-price controls and three weeks later the first American prisoners of war finally came home.

The president had taken his oath of office earlier in the day and his popularity was at an all-time high.

Some protested the inauguration. A special protest mass took place at the Washington Cathedral, some petitions were delivered to the White House, and the Vietnam Veterans Against the War held a march. These drew little attention outside Washington.

The nation had just come through five tough years of self-examination. It needed a break. And it seemed like a good time for one. Now, at last, the Woodstock generation could move forward. For much of the last decade, part of the generation had been at war and part had been protesting the fighting. Now, it seemed, all of it could simply go about the business of life.

Unfortunately, it didn't work out that way. Instead, Americans were heading into an even more difficult and confusing time. For the Woodstock generation, it would continue its great slide down to the 80s.

The end of the war relieved the generation of its need to protest, but also took away its rallying force. Never again would there be an issue so clearly righteous and unifying. There would be causes; but the end of the war, combined with the deaths, the outrages, the betrayals, caused the Woodstock generation to splinter into many groups.

The defeats came in a steady drip-drip-drip of events. This allowed the generation slowly, irrevocably to drift apart, and before anyone realized what was happening its sense of unity had been torn, the Us shattered.

It became a hollow shell, ripe for the invasion of disease and the symptoms were cynicism and active disinvolvement.

The effect was the loss of the great potential of the generation to change the world. As a unified, loud, ubiquitous voice, it undeniably carried enormous weight and strength. Splintered, it lost that potential, that weight, that force. Now the generation's self-proclaimed mandate to change the world no longer seemed an inevitability; it no longer even seemed likely.

Mindlessly entertaining movies would seduce the generation away from social conscience; the hoopla around Patty Hearst would embarrass it away from involvement. The Us was gone; its core, its leaders, fractured into hippies and yippies and Panthers and Weathermen; its central philosophy was splintered into violence versus nonviolence, drugs versus no drugs, this versus that.

Each event of this next period—from the seemingly innocuous advent of video games to the grownup change in *Rolling Stone* magazine—emitted a tiny signal that the generation was moving in different directions.

But the dominant event of the period—the rise of Watergate and the fall of Richard Nixon—would seal the generation's fate.

Watergate left the nation feeling dirty, defiled, disgusted. It was a sobering, disillusioning experience. Had there been a way to channel that disgust—to reunite the generation in this time of crisis—things would have been different.

Perhaps, like the great movements before—the civil rights movement and the antiwar movement—this disgust could have been channeled into action, involvement, and ultimately change.

But this time, there was no clear direction to channel all the energy and, most important, no great leaders left to show the way.

For a generation raised on trust and abundance these would be shattering years. From the corruption in the White House to the energy crisis, to the worsening economy, our problems demanded aggressive leadership and unified action.

But there was no one. Nixon was simply trying to survive Watergate and the nation's problems were allowed to grow and fester. Within the Woodstock generation the leaders had died or given up or were about to go into hiding. And so the generation, disappointed and disgusted, turned its back on the world.

For most of the inaugural partygoers still celebrating Nixon's reelection, Watergate still seemed more of a nuisance than a problem. They love us out there, the Nixon people thought. Watergate is more of a public relations issue than anything else. Just keep the cap on the bottle and things will blow over.

They were wrong.

Weekly, sometimes daily, revelations were surfacing in the *Washington*

Post, the *New York Times,* the *Los Angeles Times,* and other newspapers. Stories linked the Watergate break-in to the White House, and raised issues about payoffs and coverups and dirty tricks committed against the Democrats to ensure not just a Nixon win, but a Nixon landslide.

In February the Senate formed a committee to conduct its own investigation into the growing scandal. It was headed by Sam Ervin, a good-old-boy from North Carolina whose backwoods humor and no-bullshit approach would make him a genuine American folk hero by the end of the year.

A month later the original Watergate burglars were sentenced by John J. Sirica, a federal district court judge in Washington, D.C., nicknamed "Maximum John" for his tough sentences. Maximum John gave the burglars thirty-five to forty years in prison. They had one out, Sirica hinted: cooperate with the government's investigation. Some took the hint and one of them told the Watergate Committee that former Attorney General John N. Mitchell knew about the break-in before it took place.

Mitchell headed Nixon's reelection committee and was one of the president's closest friends. The cap was off the bottle.

One month later the investigation led into the White House itself. Nixon's closest aides, H. R. Haldeman, John D. Ehrlichman, John Dean, and Attorney General Richard G. Kleindienst, the nation's highest law-enforcement officer, were implicated in the coverup.

Watergate was no longer merely a public relations problem.

Nixon went on television and promised the nation he had taken no part in Watergate or the coverup. In a desperate attempt to regain credibility, he appointed Elliot Richardson, one of the most respected men in government, to be his new attorney general.

Richardson named Archibald Cox, an old professor of his at Harvard Law School, as a special prosecutor to get to the bottom of the Watergate mess.

Nixon's predecessor, Lyndon Baines Johnson, died January 22, 1973 of a heart attack on his Texas ranch. Johnson was a long-time target of the hippie movement, particularly during the Vietnam War. But even as he died, the hippie movement was doing the same.

The fun was simply going out of it. To be sure, hippies and a few communes survived into the 80s, but, by and large, the movement died during the middle years of the 70s.

"I knew the peace and love movement was over when you couldn't leave your marijuana plants out on the window sills anymore," recalls Bradley Pattison. "Someone would take them."

Bradley had just trimmed his waist-length hair, taken off his earring and love beads, and started wearing shoes. Now that he was getting older— Bradley was twenty-six at the time—"it was time to get more serious about my career."

He had come to New York in 1966 from an upper-middle-class Illinois family to be an actor and quickly got into the New York street scene— hanging out a hell of a lot more than he worked. He spent most Sundays at the Bethesda fountain near the lagoon in Central Park.

"It was like a festival every Sunday; packed with people; making music, smoking dope. Children. No one was ever hassled by police. It was easy to meet people; you just had to go there twice."

During the week the scene was Washington Square in the Village, where things were a bit more intellectual if not quite as much fun; the few beatniks still around mixed with the hippies who were moving in. Still, you could smoke and talk and get a feel about what was really going on in the world.

Pattison lived in the old Ansonia Hotel on Broadway where he shared three rooms in what used to be Enrico Caruso's suite.

He had small parts in a few dinner theaters, a few road shows but lived mostly on the $75 his family sent every week. "New York wasn't too expensive yet; pizza was twenty-five cents a slice and a lot of nights pizza was dinner."

One of his most thrilling moments was watching the *Eagle* land on the moon in July 1969, watching it with thousands of others on a huge screen set up in Central Park.

Then, of course, there was Woodstock. Pattison went on the spur of the moment in a Volkswagen van with some people he had just met at Bethesda fountain. He didn't even bother to pack clothes. People did a lot of that in those days.

Want to go on a trip? Sure, why not. Somehow you just knew that you would find food and a place to sleep and a way back home.

"I didn't have much to do and I didn't have any money so I went along. The people I was with were so stoned I was lucky we got there at all."

When he got there he couldn't wait to leave. Some people didn't enjoy being at Woodstock and Bradley Pattison was one of them.

"It was a hassle; everyone was stoned, people were getting sick on bad drugs, I was so far from the stage—it was pretty much of a pain in the ass."

Bradley had used drugs, not heavy drugs, but grass and hash and a little acid. Sometimes he awoke at three in the morning to drop acid and then went back to sleep so he could wake up stoned.

He stopped dropping acid in the early 70s. The last time was in Cape

Cod, where he was appearing in a play: "We were down by the ocean watching the sun and having a spectacular time. Then I realized that everything was wonderful but there was a chemical in my body making it wonderful. I wanted to feel that way naturally."

And then the whole thing began to die for him. The drug scene got scarier and he no longer felt the sharing feeling of the 60s. "Having possessions became important again and people even started complaining, 'How come you don't bring out your dope when I'm at your house?' More and more people were taking their earrings out during the week and putting them back during the weekends."

Then some of his theater friends became more successful and Bradley Pattison was struck by the disease of ambition. "I was surrounded by people who were achieving success, and I wanted some for myself. That's when capitalism first came into my heart."

Three times he auditioned for *Hair;* it was his dream to be in the show. Three times he wasn't chosen.

Not getting any younger and his career not getting any hotter, Pattison moved to Arizona, where he began supporting himself by painting.

"The 60s gave me the opportunity to explore myself and know myself and not have other people tell me what I should be or what's expected of me," Bradley said. "But you get to a point where it's time to move on."

Years later Pattison's father died and left him enough money to become financially independent. "I was once so crazy that I told my father, 'When you die, leave your fortune to my sister.' Fortunately, he didn't pay any attention to me."

Ambition changed the way Bradley Pattison lived. And ambition was one of the things tearing the generation apart. Many in the generation were already ambitious, but just didn't know it yet. It's a lot easier to hide your ambition when you're seventeen and free than when you're twenty-three and caring for a family.

Moreover, for the first time in their lives the generation was facing deprivation, from the growing recession to waiting in line for gasoline.

And ambition—*Blind Ambition,* as John Dean's book later called it—was at the heart of Watergate and other scandals now erupting in Washington.

On March 20, a Senate subcommittee heard shocking testimony that the International Telephone and Telegraph Company and the CIA plotted to disrupt free elections in Chile, to prevent Salvador Allende, a Marxist, from being elected president. Some members of the Woodstock generation rose in protest. But many, for the first time, felt too tired or too spent to get involved. Perhaps they just didn't care. Though it was the first time, it would not be the last.

Then the Watergate hearings started on May 17. It was a drama played live on television and on the front pages of newspapers across the nation. Millions watched as Washington's pompous and powerful swore to tell the truth and then settled in a leather chair to face the inquiry. The witnesses ranged from minor bureaucrats to those closest to the president—the very men who shaped the nation's policies over the past four and a half years. This time it was their turn to answer questions, not ask them. Their names became household words: McCord, Haldeman, Ehrlichman, Dean, Magruder. Their testimony was replayed nightly at dinner tables across America.

It was former White House aide Jeb Stuart Magruder who confirmed that former Attorney General Mitchell had approved the Watergate burglary.

In late June, Dean told the committee that President Nixon took part in the Watergate coverup. Nixon and his aides had discussed using the CIA to block the FBI's investigation into the scandal.

But it was lesser-known Alexander Butterfield, a Haldeman aide in charge of ushering people into and out of the Oval Office, who dropped the biggest bomb and pitched the nation into the most serious constitutional crisis since the Civil War—Nixon had bugged himself.

An elaborate, voice-activated taping system had been installed in the Oval Office. It went on whenever anyone spoke. Nixon had meant to preserve his words—to bequeath them to the library he was already planning—for historians and posterity.

Instead, the tapes would be the instrument of his disaster. For months the question had been asked: What did the president know and when did he know it? Now there was an answer.

Special prosecutor Cox and the Ervin committee each moved swiftly. Both wanted the tapes. Nixon refused. The courts would decide the matter. But what if they ordered him to give up the tapes and the president still refused? What if he told both the Supreme Court and the Congress to go to hell?

No one was quite sure what would happen

The year 1973 was becoming strange indeed, marked by all sorts of weird goings-on.

Jimmy Carter, the governor of Georgia, set out to become president of the United States. Many laughed and the press labeled him "Jimmy Who?"

Airline passengers were required to pass through metal detectors on the way to flights and it became a crime even to joke about hijacking at the airport.

The draft officially ended June 30.

A survey of high school seniors showed they shared most of their parents' values and ideals. The exceptions: sex and marijuana. Oregon became the first state to decriminalize marijuana. A leader of that campaign was the original Merry Prankster, Ken Kesey.

Atari sales hit $1 million a month for Pong, a video ping-pong game popular in bars. It was a harbinger of the video-game craze to come. No other symbol better indicated the generation's growing active disinvolvement. People were not only shying from involvement, but also seeking something to occupy their senses, to numb their minds. Pong was the perfect answer.

As escapist movies saw their heyday begin in the Watergate years, so did video games. Bars were now no longer a place in which to sit and have long, impassioned political arguments into the night. A quarter and a video machine let you turn your back on the bar and on the political argument.

Which is just what the generation was doing.

It found many other ways to escape. "Star Trek" had been in reruns for years, but groupies—"trekkies"—made it more popular than ever. Thousands attended "Star Trek" conferences where they bought scale models of the Starship *Enterprise,* authentic Federation uniforms, and even Vulcan ears like those worn by Mr. Spock. Members of the original cast showed up to sign autographs, and there was even talk of a new *Star Trek* movie.

The Woodstock generation was turning to a television show of its youth—rerunning its past in syndication.

There were symbolic hints of the emergence of the women's movement. Women applauded as Billy Jean King defeated male chauvinist Bobby Riggs in straight sets in tennis. In music, women vocalists became successful as solo acts; the last wave in women's music were the "girl groups" of the 60s. But now Diana Ross emerged from the Supremes with the immensely successful "Touch Me in the Morning." Others included Roberta Flack, "Killing Me Softly with His Song"; Olivia Newton-John, "Let Me Be There"; and Cher, with "Half Breed." But the emergence of the genuine women's movement was still a few years away.

Rolling Stone became more of a general-interest magazine, adding politics to music as its readers aged and began to settle down. And a lot of settling down was going on in the Woodstock generation, aided by much mindless entertainment to ease the way. On television, variety shows emerged: Sonny and Cher, Carol Burnett, Donny and Marie, and Flip Wilson.

Movies focused mostly on pure entertainment, or on fond looks at the past.

One of the big hits of the year was *American Graffiti,* which harkened back to happier days in the early 60s—drag racing, lover's lane, and cruising in the street. Introduced in it were Richard Dreyfuss, Harrison Ford, Suzanne Somers, an adult Ronny Howard, Cindy Williams, and Candy Clark. All became stars in the years ahead. It spawned the TV series "Happy Days," which gave us the Fonz and a succession of imitators.

But unlike the series that followed, *American Graffiti* carried a bittersweet message for the Woodstock generation. It didn't merely glorify the innocence of youth; it bade that youth a sad, puzzled farewell. Throughout the movie, Richard Dreyfuss floats through the last night of high school, searching in vain for a mystical blonde-in-a-Thunderbird. At the end of the movie he flies away to start a new life, and from the plane sees the Thunderbird rolling smoothly along the highway below, the highway he leaves behind forever.

Superman returned, starring Christopher Reeve—who had to work out to build up his body to fit the man-of-steel role. It made $100 million.

Dirty Harry returned in *Magnum Force,* James Bond returned in *Live and Let Die,* and Robert Redford and Barbra Streisand returned in *The Way We Were*—another movie that took a bittersweet look at a magical past gone forever and that captured the Woodstock generation's sense of moving on.

The biggest moneymaker of the year was not a movie that recalled the generation's struggle, but an escapist thriller, *The Exorcist.* Movies would never be the same; mindless slash-and-gash films—from the *Halloween* series to the *Friday the 13th* series to the *Nightmare on Elm Street* movies—would come out every year like clockwork.

In August Judge Sirica ordered Nixon to hand over the Oval Office tapes. Nixon refused.

One week later a Los Angeles grand jury indicted Ehrlichman and three others, including G. Gordon Liddy, for the 1971 break-in at the office of Daniel Ellsberg's psychiatrist.

Explosive as Watergate was, it was just the central core of a series of events that would launch a critical and decisive few months for Nixon and for the nation. The ramifications would be felt for years.

On October 6, Egyptian and Syrian forces launched a surprise attack on Israel. It was Yom Kippur, for Jews the holiest day of the year. The Arabs had the early advantage, pressing their attacks into Sinai and on the Golan Heights, pushing back the Israelis who were running dangerously short of supplies. The White House ordered a massive airlift.

It was Nixon at his best, ordering "everything that will fly" into the air carrying millions of tons of supplies and spare parts to Israel. It easily eclipsed the peak of the Berlin airlift. Israel counterattacked, and pushed the Egyptians and Syrians back deep into their own territory.

Many non-Jewish Americans watched the war with little more than passing interest. The stories were interesting. Each side bused newsmen to the front to get its side of the story so it could be graphically portrayed on television. Public relations, learned from Vietnam, was becoming an important part of making war.

Americans took a deeper interest in the Middle East a few days later when Arab oil-producing countries banned exports to the U.S. in retaliation for helping Israel.

On October 10, the country was shocked again. Vice President Spiro Agnew pleaded no contest to income-tax evasion and resigned from office. Agnew began taking payoffs from contractors as a public official in Baltimore. The payoffs continued and even in the White House Agnew had taken envelopes stuffed with cash.

A leader who had taunted the generation was being discredited. The generation, however, would feel more disillusioned than victorious.

Two days later Nixon called Republican congressional leaders together to announce his new vice president. The president was smiling and happy, and never mentioned Agnew's name as he stepped to the podium. He started the announcement and then stopped to let the drama build. He smiled again. All that was missing was a drum roll.

And the winner was: Congressman Gerald Ford, of Michigan.

Two months later Ford gave a speech in which he said, "I am a Ford, not a Lincoln." This proved accurate.

Nixon actually didn't want to choose Ford. He had several other candidates in mind. Speculation, it is now eerie to note, centered on a key figure from the past and one from the future: former Texas Governor John Connally, who had been shot during the Kennedy assassination, and California governor Ronald Reagan.

But Nixon needed to pick someone "safe"; someone Congress would accept without a battle. Nixon was in too much danger over Watergate to pick a fight with anyone.

Two days later, Nixon's smile turned to a frown. The court of appeals ruled that he must turn over the tapes to Judge Sirica.

Special prosecutor Cox asked for even more tapes. They were essential, he said, to getting at the bottom of the scandal, to finding out who knew what, and when.

Nixon was enraged and on Saturday, October 20, in what came to be known as the Saturday Night Massacre, ordered that Cox be fired. Attorney General Richardson, who had hired Cox, refused to carry out the order and quit in protest. Nixon then fired Deputy Attorney General William Ruckelshaus when he also refused. Cox was fired by Solicitor General

Robert Bork, but Nixon had done himself more harm than he could possibly have imagined.

The Saturday Night Massacre created a firestorm of protest, uniting all the anger and bitterness people felt toward the deepening scandal. The White House switchboard lit up and for the first time came widespread calls for Nixon's resignation. Even conservative *Time* magazine editorialized that "the president should resign."

Three days later a White House attorney announced that Nixon would turn over the tapes. There was a problem, however: two of the nine subpoenaed tapes did not exist. Nixon offered later to supply his own written notes.

In November the nation was told of an eighteen-and-a-half-minute gap on another tape—the result of an error made when transcribing the tape, the White House said. The break occurred in the middle of a conversation between Nixon and Haldeman just three days after the Watergate burglary. Experts would later conclude the gap had to be the result of several deliberate erasures.

It was also reported during the fall that Nixon paid less than $1,000 in income taxes in 1970 and 1971.

Not only had he lost the confidence of Congress and other national leaders, but now Nixon had also lost the confidence of the public. Only a small minority felt he was telling the entire truth about Watergate. Nixon had passed the point of no return.

So had Abbie Hoffman.

The events that would overtake Hoffman in the next few months reflect two key dynamics that kept the Woodstock generation from fulfilling its mandate: the loss of its leadership, and the splintering of the movement.

Abbie's sense that things were closing in—that one of these days he would end up in jail or dead—grew and grew.

They missed us in Chicago, Abbie thought. We got out, we found loopholes. But he was being arrested regularly around the country, now; and tempers were heating up.

So after Kent State and Jackson State, and with police getting tougher and meaner with protesters, and with the leaders of the movement under constant watch and harassment, going underground became a more likely option.

Yet, going underground was also a difficult, painful step. For one thing, it meant getting involved with the people who created the underground in the United States—the Weathermen.

The Weather Underground was one of the most violent factions that had split from the movement. With a legacy of bombings and a motto of If You Don't Believe in Guns and Violence, Then You Aren't a Revolutionary, the Weathermen represented the deepest division in the counterculture.

The split was also one of the most important. For the first time there was a segment of the movement with which many average, everyday hippies—those only partly or peripherally involved—truly disagreed.

"The majority of everyone I knew above ground couldn't stand the Weather Underground," Hoffman says. "We couldn't stand their politics, we couldn't stand certain acts of indiscriminate violence, we hated their ideological rigidity. But we recognized that the development of an underground in the United States and its ability to survive were extremely important."

It was indeed extremely important to Hoffman. After thirty-eight arrests and fifteen trials he was now facing the most serious charges of his life.

It would be wrong to cite that night at the Diplomat Hotel in New York City as the only turning point. But cocaine did change hands in the hotel that night, and Hoffman found himself facing charges that could lead to a life sentence.

That's a helluva incentive to think seriously about your options.

Hoffman admits involvement, but says he had only arranged a meeting with two groups because both sides trusted him. He was not dealing cocaine, he says, but was in the wrong place at the wrong time.

"To this day, to tell the story, I can't because there are other people involved and I've never snitched on anyone in my life," Hoffman says.

"I will say this to you. Both the police and I were guilty. I was there, but the police acted on both the selling and buying end. So I was guilty in the sense that I shouldn't have been there—in the room, with the cocaine—I should have known better. But, of course, I was on cocaine at the time, and it gives you that 'Superman of the Moment' feeling, as Malcolm X said about it, and I was a little out of my head and out of my element.

"So what can I say? The police have testified that I was not a dealer, but it was under strange circumstances."

Hoffman had been through the court system before, but he was getting a little tired of it, and the charges were more serious this time.

Other matters were weighing on him too. There was pressure from inside the movement. The movement in this country has always been anti-elitist, suspicious of people who become famous. Abbie was getting famous.

It was not unusual for Hoffman to get a 3 A.M. call from some kid from Texas who said he was going to crash Hoffman's pad that night. Or to get a plea to attend a rally in Philadelphia two days later. When Hoffman told the caller he couldn't crash, or declined the plea to attend the rally because he had to be elsewhere, he was called an elitist asshole who cared only about himself.

Finally, Hoffman felt a growing need for privacy—not in small part the result of having a one-year-old child and wanting a more sane family life.

"So going underground was partly because on both sides I didn't know how to perform in the role of Abbie Hoffman. There are no leaders who survived that period."

He was living in New York City, on the fringe of what is now Soho. Ahead of him were new identities on new passports, plastic surgery in Los Angeles, and a trip to Mexico to lose his Boston accent "because all the movies told me that's where you're supposed to go."

For his new identities he would pick what he called "wallpaper names." "I went back to the kids on my block that nobody paid any attention to. There was a Mark, there was a Barry, there was a Howie."

Much has been made of the name Barry Freed, under which he lived in upstate New York; it's been seen as a Hoffman joke, living as a fugitive under the name Freed. "The last names were assimilated Jewish names," he explains. "Fried with an *i*, Freed with two *e*'s. There was no idea of that 'freed' thing. That was a quirk."

So, with the external pressures of the trial and the internal pressures of being Abbie Hoffman, he made the decision most painful to anyone, and especially to anyone with a one-year-old child: he would go underground.

"If you're asking me emotionally what it felt like," he says, "it was horrendous."

As Hoffman was preparing to go into hiding, the Watergate Committee was asking Nixon for more revelations. It wanted five hundred more tapes and documents. Nixon, vacationing in California, replied in writing: no. Several congressmen called for Nixon's impeachment. Dozens of newspapers and even some Republicans asked the president to resign.

On January 30, 1974 Nixon delivered his State of the Union Address to the Congress and the nation. Supreme Court justices and cabinet members sat only a few feet away. "One year of Watergate is enough," he implored. "Let's move on to more important matters."

In a sense, he got his wish. Watergate would not continue another full year. On February 4, the House of Representatives voted 410—4 to conduct an impeachment inquiry, the first step toward removing Richard Nixon from office.

Just a few weeks later, Americans felt the impact of the Arab oil embargo. Babyboomers were raised believing that a big car and a full tank were their birthright. Many still had the big car, but for the first time in their lives had to wait in line to get gas, and then probably couldn't fill up.

By February half the gas stations in the East were closed, and those that were open had lines up to six miles long. In many states you could buy gas only on alternate days, odd or even, depending on the last number of your license plate. Others limited purchases to two or three dollars.

New-car sales fell through the floor and thousands of auto workers lost their jobs as the sale of small, fuel-efficient imports soared. To conserve fuel, the speed limit was cut to fifty-five miles per hour and Daylight Savings Time was adopted. As a result, worried mothers found their children going to school in the dark.

The oil embargo ended and gas shortages in most places lasted only a month or so. But dollar-a-gallon gas was not only a reality, but in some places a bargain.

The most bizarre story of 1974 was the kidnaping on February 4 of newspaper heiress Patricia Hearst by the Symbionese Liberation Army (SLA). The SLA demanded that Patty's father provide $2 million in food to feed the needy people of California. He did, but a month later got another message: Patty had joined her captors. Enclosed was a photo of her posed before a cobra-emblazoned flag of the SLA.

In April she was captured on film with other SLA members robbing a San Francisco bank. She was holding an automatic rifle and appeared to be a willing participant.

The nation became obsessed with the Patty Hearst story. She was reported in Pennsylvania, in Ohio, back in California. "Where's Patty Hearst?" T-shirts sold by the thousands.

She was finally arrested in San Francisco more than a year after her kidnaping. At first defiant, she began to tell the story of her kidnaping, and how she was brainwashed by the SLA, locked in a dark closet for days at a time, and raped repeatedly.

Still, she was found guilty of armed robbery and sentenced to seven years in prison.

A Free Patty Hearst movement started. Petitions were signed by tens of thousands. She served twenty-two months in prison before being pardoned by President Jimmy Carter.

Whereas some members of the Woodstock generation saw her as a victim, others saw her as the poor little rich girl playing revolutionary for a while, then crying for her rich daddy to save her when the game got rough. She didn't mean it; she had been brainwashed, she said. Just what parents always wanted to believe about their own good-kids-turned-hippies.

Her lawyer wasn't even the liberals' William Kunstler, but the establishment's F. Lee Bailey.

The Patty Hearst story read like the movie that it did become. Ken Kesey was already in Hollywood working on his own movie and it made him feel like a captive too.

Kesey was playing the role of Hollywood writer, doing the screenplay for *One Flew over the Cuckoo's Nest*. It was not going well; in fact, the 70s weren't going much better for Ken Kesey than they were for Richard Nixon.

While maintaining a semblance of normal life on the farm, shoveling compost, helping a cow give birth, retreating to his study to write, he describes bouts of trembling and shaking, staying up night after night, "grassing and speeding."

Meanwhile, his agent was calling about fresh material he promised his publisher and his wife was reminding him that the loan office hadn't been paid. At one point he referred to himself as a "fat, old bald, retired writer."

On one of his *Rolling Stone* assignments, he wrote of flying to Cairo in search of a secret pyramid and the first thing he did was buy five pounds of hash. He was either drunk or stoned most of the time, smoking dope in a tomb, throwing up on the face of a pyramid.

"I'm high like a motherfucker," he boasted.

Tripping on acid made him feel superhuman; he could swim, fly, throw a steer, he could leep over the walls of vicious conformity.

He could also relax, writing little more than occasional pieces for underground publications, living the life of the not-too-badly-heeled farmer, bestowing his wisdom upon visitors, storing up observations about life—all the while waiting for a block of time and energy to come along.

"It's very hard when you're doing a novel like *Great Notion*," he said. "It requires real solitude for long periods of time."

Somehow, through all the turbulence of his life, Kesey was able to keep his marriage to Faye intact for more than thirty years.

"I don't know many successful writers who can keep a big heavy novel together and a family together," he said. "They require so much of the same energy. And you get mean and you get irascible and your brains begin to run out your nose. Finally you say, 'It's too hard, I'll wait until I'm a little older and I'm alone.'"

But not too alone.

Most writers, Kesey contends, "die of loneliness." His friend Richard Brautigan, author of books like *Trout Fishing in America*—once a bible to the Woodstock generation—shot himself in a remote cabin and his body wasn't discovered for several weeks. "What a sad statement of your life.

You get off so far from your friends and family nobody knows you're dead for a month."

Kesey loathed, too, the part of writing that has nothing to do with writing. "To take it to New York and go into those offices and go to the talk shows, it's a bitch. When I go to Hollywood or New York, especially Hollywood, I always come out of it feeling that something has been clipped off and I'm a little bit less than when I went in."

Kesey turned his land into a dairy farm, causing his beef cattle to "heave a sigh of relief." He, brother Chuck, and their sister Sue started the Springfield Creamery, a dairy that boasts some of the best yogurt in Oregon. "It's the only legitimate work I've ever done," he says, half serious.

Kesey marveled to a *Rolling Stone* interviewer about a simple equation: he's watering the field, the grass is coming up, the cows are shitting on the field. It was good karma. For Kesey, "stuff started falling into place."

He was looking for, as he once put it, "toe-to-toe truth and love."

His farm, fifteen miles outside Springfield, Oregon, had cows, ducks, chickens, a peacock, three dogs, two buses, a tractor, a hay wagon, and a used and rusting bus. He and his family lived in a converted barn beside the milk barn. Nearby are the chicken house, an unfinished geodesic dome, and a cottage.

The Day-Glo bus, the bus that he and the Pranksters took across America, was parked—and still is—in a field near his house, biodegrading nicely. "Some want me to restore it," Kesey said. "I plan to let it go back to the ground whence it came."

He was getting nothing accomplished, he said, except life. It was straight farming: cut the hay, fix the machinery, feed the cows, fix the fences. "The whole show," as Kesey put it.

"They say, 'Why don't you hire somebody?' What for? That's like having Marilyn Monroe living in your yard and hiring somebody to screw her. If you're going to have a big beautiful piece of stuff like that, you might as well get into it yourself."

This was a hell of a lot better, it seemed, than pressing keys on a typewriter.

His friend and fellow Prankster, Neal Cassidy, had a lot to do with his losing interest, at least temporarily, in writing. "I saw that Cassidy did everything that a novel does, except better 'cause he was livin' it and not writing about it."

And yet Cassidy, who had seemed to Kesey the man that nothing could kill, wandered off into the desert one night counting railroad ties, and died of exposure.

Kesey didn't stop writing, but what he wrote was, like his article for *The*

Last Whole Earth Catalog in 1971, obscure and laced with drugs. The "tool" he recommended for shedding light was the Bible, best taken in a quiet place "with a bit of hash and some chamomile tea with honey and lemon in it."

Take your time, he suggested. Ease your way through the Bible with the help of a purple satin bookmark, a chapter or two at a time before bed. It will "wipe the slate of your mind clean."

And if that doesn't help, try the philosophy of I Ching, "the tool of the way." As he puts it, "give the Ching a ring."

Kesey found other worldly diversions that kept his typewriter quiet but his global consciousness happy. He discovered the environment and joined crusades to save it. Oregon's first-in-the-nation returnable bottle and can law, passed in 1971, is a piece of work he is happy with and helped accomplish. It was one of a series of issues he got involved in.

He produced a distinctly minor book in 1973, *Ken Kesey's Garage Sale*, which Arthur Miller called "a transparent attempt to capitalize on twice-published material lying at the bottom of the drawer."

He wasn't having much more luck a year later writing the screenplay for *One Flew over the Cuckoo's Nest*. In fact, Kesey became terrified because of what he was doing with his life.

The movie's producers felt that the way to get him thinking about mental institutions again was to send him to a psychiatric conference at Disney World. Kesey went, got shitfaced, and stayed that way.

He found himself haunted by guilt. "The air is thick with broken promises coming to roost," Kesey says. His father was dying and he failed to call home. Kesey wanted to bring something home for his son, but all he had to show for the trip was a broken cocktail glass.

Kesey was preoccupied with "the bleak and bottomless rock of failure" to which he, like Prometheus, was chained.

His biggest fear was entropy, the loss of energy. The superego increasingly fails in its job of letting the good thoughts in and shutting the bad ones out, leaving the world a little bit crazier. He dreaded a return visit to the Portland mental hospital where the movie was being filmed, but finally, a half-blind, half-crazy inmate snapped him out of his despair. As in the book, the insane had more sense than those whom society judges sane.

Kesey wrote a version of *Cuckoo's Nest* for the screen, but Hollywood didn't like it and didn't think much of his ability to meet deadlines. The script was surreal and, like the book, written from the point of view of Chief Broom, the giant Indian mental patient who fakes muteness, mercifully kills McMurphy, and escapes. Instead, said Kesey, "they wanted 'Hogan's Heroes.'" The final script was written by someone else, from McMurphy's point of view.

Writers lose the right to do their own screenplays all the time in Hollywood, so that wasn't what angered Kesey. "I didn't mind it so much as them saying I didn't do the work."

Kesey stayed on the farm and, except for occasional magazine articles, did little writing in the mid-70s. He continued to be known for his first two novels, though he tried to downplay their importance.

For many, Kesey and his friend Brautigan were the key writers of the Woodstock generation. Now, one was clearly losing it and the other was headed toward suicide. The generation wasn't doing too well either.

It was, however, finding a strange new mindless way to blow off a little steam. It was called streaking, and it began—where else—on college campuses. A door would open, a nude body would dart across a street or down a sidewalk and disappear.

It might be a solitary naked body racing across a busy intersection. It might be many streakers, dozens, in some cases hundreds, of students. Contests were held for the longest streak, the most streakers, and streaking in the worst weather conditions. Most streakers were men, though a number of women stripped and joined in.

A few older members of the Woodstock generation saw what the college campuses had come to, and shook their heads. Is this what we fought for? they asked. Is this our legacy?

The failure of the college campuses to carry on the protest and political traditions born in the Woodstock years was disheartening. It made so much of what had gone before seem meaningless. It was one more step away from the garden.

The most prominent streak took place during the Academy Awards presentation on nationwide television. David Niven was speaking when the streaker, an unemployed press agent, raced across the stage behind him. Niven delivered the line of the night: "The only laugh that man will probably ever get is for stripping and showing off his shortcomings."

On March 1, seven former Nixon administration figures were indicted for plotting to block the Watergate investigation. Nixon was named as an "unindicted co-conspirator"; the grand jury concluded the president aided in the coverup.

Nixon's popularity plunged to an all-time low. When it appeared things couldn't get any worse for the president, they did. The Internal Revenue Service ruled that he owed $465,000 in back taxes. Nixon agreed to pay, but by now fewer than three in ten adults approved of his job performance.

Meanwhile, the Watergate investigation continued to uncover facts of its own on a trail that seemed to lead directly to the Oval Office. Investigators sought even more tapes and the public was asking, "What's Nixon got to hide?"

On April 29, the president answered on national television. Huge piles of bound transcripts were stacked behind him. Nixon surrendered over twelve hundred pages of transcribed conversations, but he refused to yield the tapes themselves.

The transcripts revealed that Nixon's Oval Office conversations were often punctuated by profanity and vulgarity. The phrase "expletive deleted" was coined by editors to cover the worst of the gutter language. Even fellow Republicans called conversations disgusting and immoral—not just for the language, but for their revelations about the coverup. A majority of Americans thought Nixon should resign.

Vice President Ford admitted he was "a little disappointed" by the tapes. Yet he continued to travel the nation proclaiming the president's innocence. Despite Ford's loyalty, a group of the vice president's friends began to meet secretly each week in Washington to put together a transition plan for the next president.

On May 9, the House Judiciary Committee formally started impeachment hearings. Nixon tried to duck the heat, first by visiting Egypt, where he met with Anwar el-Sadat at the foot of the great pyramids. He returned to the U.S. and within a week set off for Moscow for his third and last summit with Leonid Brezhnev.

Billy Hayes followed the Watergate developments, at least as best he could from Sagmalcilar Prison, twelve hundred miles away in Istanbul. He was in a section of the prison reserved for Turists, the name the Turks gave foreign prisoners. The Turists kept track of events back home by listening to Armed Forces Radio and reading newspapers and magazines that arrived weeks, even months, late. Billy sometimes got stacks of them at once. He put them in order and read them as if they were current news.

"Watergate was like reading about Elmer Fudd and Daffy Duck," Billy said.

Prisoners sometimes asked him what in the hell was going on in America. "How the fuck do I know," Billy answered. "I've been in here for three years."

Billy was arrested on October 7, 1970 in Istanbul, as he tried to board a flight that would take him from Istanbul to Frankfurt to London and finally home to New York, where he would sell part of the two kilos of hashish he had taped under his arms and around his stomach. The rest Billy would use himself.

He had the rotten luck to get caught in a spot search for hijackers. A guard patted him down, and the next thing Billy knew, a pistol was pointing at his chest. Billy was in trouble, just as his father had predicted when he dropped out of Marquette University.

College was the first time he was really away from home and from his good Catholic upbringing and he wanted to experience life. Billy spent the first semester of his sophomore year bumming on the West Coast, surfing in California, visiting Mexico—all of which made his father less than happy. He returned to school to keep from losing his student draft deferment, but his grades went downhill. He joined a few protests—Billy did oppose the war—but he went mostly because he liked the energy and the girls.

Then he dropped out of Marquette University during his senior year and his father warned him it would be a mistake. His father worked for a large insurance company, had never gone to college, and wanted his kids to do better. Their relationship was strained even more when Billy was ordered to report for his draft physical.

Billy fasted for three days before his physical and then ate a bunch of hash. Then he told the military psychiatrist about his dream: to move into the deep woods of British Columbia where he would play his saxophone and through the music make contact with Sasquatch, the Big Foot.

"The army said 'Don't call us, we'll call you,'" Billy said. He was ruled psychologically unfit for duty.

Not long afterward he decided to visit Europe with a stop in Turkey. Now, in the heat of a Turkish August, Billy Hayes was in prison far from home. He wrote a letter to his parents.

"I cry to think how I'm hurting you," he wrote. "Forgive me."

Billy learned quickly that Turkish prisons do not have the same rules as American jails. The first week there he was beaten across the legs and the soles of his feet until he couldn't walk. There wasn't much he could do but sit back and wait for court; for that, he'd have to stay in jail until December.

He developed a routine. He awoke early so he could enjoy the stillness of daybreak, before the other prisoners began turning on their radios; then yoga twice a day, while waiting for his cell to be opened so he could walk into the prison courtyard. Then he talked with his fellow prisoners, drank some tea, and maybe smoked a little hash.

Sometimes in the courtyard Billy peered into the sky and remembered stories about aliens kidnaping earthlings to examine their bodies and then returning them to earth. They can take me, he thought, perform any test they want on my body, and drop me anyplace on earth, anyplace but Turkey.

The December court date came and Billy hoped for bail so he could try to escape. Or maybe he would get a short sentence. It shook him to learn what the prosecutor was asking for: life in prison.

His next stop was a mental hospital—a seventeen-day checkup to see if he was sane enough to stand trail. It was such a hellhole that he longed for his old cell. Prisoners were fighting over beds and urine-soaked sheets. He tried to convince the doctors he was crazy, hoping they would send him home. It didn't work. Two and a half weeks later he was back at Sagmalcilar.

Billy had been in prison for seven months by the time he stood before the judge at his trial, unable to speak or understand the language. The judge sentenced him to fifty months in prison. With time off for good behavior, he would be free in July 1973.

He thought about escaping. He could drug the guards with LSD or he could get transferred back to the "bug ward," where escape would be easier. Was he serious? "As serious as you can get without stepping over the line . . . which means not serious at all."

Finally, he settled on one plan. He would have help from the outside, from his old friend Patrick, who would come to Turkey from Germany where he was working to save enough money for the escape. Then, a few days before Patrick was scheduled to come, he was killed in Germany, stabbed with a bayonet.

"After Patrick died, I just thought, well, I'm supposed to be spending my time here."

Billy settled back and decided to do his time. In 1973 he made himself a calendar to count down his remaining time in jail. With only fifty-four days left, less than two months, the roof caved in on Billy Hayes. The Turkish high court reviewed his sentence. The prosecutor again wanted something harsher.

In September 1973, three years after he was arrested, two months after he was originally due to be released, Billy Hayes was sentenced to a lifetime in prison; with good behavior he could be released in the year 2000.

For three years Billy's parents had told people he was sick in Europe. Now they revealed the truth and started a letter-writing campaign. They wrote Sen. James Buckley, newspapers, government officials, anyone who could help. A campaign started at home to convince the Turks to allow Billy to do his time in an American prison. But that could take months, years, forever. Billy talked to the American consul, but little happened. Then he read about Watergate and wondered how the American government could help him if it couldn't help itself. The U.S. government, he realized, couldn't do anything. What happens to Billy Hayes was up to Billy Hayes.

At home, the growing recession produced the worst inflation the country had known since the 1940s. By July the rising cost of living had replaced the energy crisis as the chief concern among Americans, according to the latest Gallup poll. People couldn't understand why prices were rising so much faster than their wages.

Also high on Americans' list of worries were distrust of public officials and corruption in government. Crime was also on the upswing; some blamed it on the baby boom—more kids, more crime—but others cited the poor example of government leaders.

There was a shift toward law and order. More than a dozen states revamped their criminal codes to provide for tougher sentences. Some reinstated the death penalty. For a generation raised on calling policemen pigs, the trend toward law and order could have raised its hackles. Again, it didn't. The riotous protesters of only a few years ago were quiet.

On July 27, the House Judiciary Committee voted 27–11 to send to Congress its first article of impeachment against the president, on the grounds that he obstructed justice in the investigation of the Watergate burglary.

On August 5, the White House released one more transcript, this one of a tape made June 23, 1972, six days after the break-in. In it Nixon ordered his aides to block the FBI from investigating the burglary. Ford was warned to prepare himself to take over the presidency.

Three nights later Nixon went on television. "I've never been a quitter," he said. "To leave office before my term is completed is opposed to every instinct in my body."

But Nixon did quit, less than two years after his landslide reelection victory. The combative language was gone. Nixon acknowledged that some of his judgments might have been wrong and expressed the hope that his departure would evoke a "process of healing that is so desperately needed in America."

On August 9, 1974 Richard Nixon, the nation's thirty-ninth president, signed a single-sentence statement of resignation. At exactly noon the power of the office shifted to Gerald Ford. At 12:05 Ford put his hand on a family Bible and took the oath of office.

It was a symbolic end to a bitter, divided period of American life.

Thousands of miles away in Istanbul, Billy Hayes heard about Nixon's resignation and the thought came to him that Nixon was now no better off than he was. So he sat down and wrote a letter to the former president of the United States. He began: "Dear Fellow Prisoner."

Many hoped Nixon's resignation would be the beginning of a new era. The U.S. was out of Vietnam and now, finally, Watergate was over. Student protests were a thing of the past.

But the innate trust Americans had in their leaders had been shattered a piece at a time. It would not be restored for decades, perhaps never for some of the Woodstock generation, born in an America that could do no wrong, and now living in an America in which nothing seemed to go right.

The splintering and active disinvolvement of the generation in this period would give way to an even deeper disfranchisement. The lack of focus would lead to an ennui bordering on mindlessness.

CHAPTER FOUR

The Boring Years

It was the bicentennial year, 1976; 200 years of government of the people, by the people, and for the people, with just a few interruptions like the Civil War, Spiro Agnew, and Watergate.

Can you imagine? Richard Nixon would have been president of the United States during the biggest national party of the century if only he had played by the rules. But he didn't and so he wasn't. Gerry Ford was the first appointed president in those 200 years, and he was running against a Georgia peanut farmer named Jimmy Carter to determine who would lead the nation into its next decade.

This should have been a big election, a critical moment in American history. It was the bicentennial, the first election since Watergate, and the first since the end of the Vietnam War.

When in the 80s people traced the evolution of the yuppie movement—why people became selfish and alienated—they looked back on this period as a lost opportunity. With Nixon gone, this could have been the time to recapture the generation's heart and mind, to restore it to its proper role as leaders and idealists. Instead, the generation moved further away.

The Woodstock generation should have felt proud, proud for helping to end the war and proud of the nation for vanquishing an evil administration. Instead, it was a time for feeling not much of anything.

This was the period between the resignation of Richard Nixon and the election of Jimmy Carter—summer 1974 through fall 1976. The remnants of the hippie movement were becoming scarcer and scarcer. Fewer hitchhikers lingered at highway tollbooths. It was harder to find an ounce of halfway decent pot for twenty bucks. And seldom did one greet another with the peace sign anymore.

Most important, there was no movement to easily become a part of anymore. While many dedicated activists continued to fight for social change, it took much more determination and dedication for those on the fringe to get involved. It was easy to become part of the movement when there were mass rallies to protest and festivals to listen to music en masse. But suddenly the hippies had no easy venues for feeling like "one of us."

What they had around them, instead, was the soporific Gerry Ford, to be followed by the quietly seductive Jimmy Carter.

What they heard was the sound of the most soulless music of their lifetime: disco, a commercially viable Musak with no discernible backbeat or message.

Disco was the Valium of music and Gerry Ford was the Valium of presidents. With no leaders to inspire rage or passion—and no Us to shake Them out of their stupor—the generation slip-slided into the soft, thick, unthinking mist.

It's not that people didn't know what was going on around them. They did. But they felt detached from the world, as though they were loaded on Valium. The Woodstock generation saw what was going on but its senses were far too deadened to care.

Newspapers and television news were filled with stories about voter apathy and predictions of a record low turnout. At least one comic asked, "What if we gave an election and nobody came?"

Artist Peter Max was thinking about this the Tuesday before the election. He had been watching Ford and Carter debate on television as he painted late into the night, accompanied only by his girlfriend at the time, model Rosie Vela.

By 2 A.M. Peter had finished the piece but still had some paint left. As was his custom, he decided not to waste it. Rosie was sitting on the floor against a wall with a light shining across her face. She was a beautiful woman—"One of the most beautiful women in the world," Max called her. Although her name might not be familiar, her face was. She had been featured on the cover of *Vogue* and many a television commercial.

Using his last bit of paint (Max hates to waste paint) Peter painted Rosie as Miss Liberty against the wind. It was a glorious painting, inspiring enough, suggested Rosie, to use as an election poster to counteract some of the apathy.

"That's a lot of work," Peter said, "and besides the election is only a few days off."

They went to bed, but like Scrooge in "A Christmas Carol," Peter was awakened in a dream. He was sleeping on a single cot and two men were kneeling facing him on either side. Peter recognized them—one was George Washington and the other Thomas Jefferson.

"I'm lying there on this cot and these two great men are talking to me in this old English speech, 'Peter, you've got to do this poster. You've got to get people to vote again.'"

Suddenly, the dream switched and Peter was standing on Sixth Avenue in Manhattan, the street also called Avenue of the Americas. His back was to a huge poster, his poster. He looked left, then right. Peter saw his posters up and down the street.

A TV reporter from ABC approached. She asked, "Peter, this is a beautiful poster but who paid for it?"

"Lady, I'll tell you who paid for it," said another person, a man dressed in a gray printer's uniform. "He (Max) had us print this poster and told us, 'Bill it to my country.'"

And with that Peter Max, perhaps the Woodstock generation's favorite artist and certainly its most patriotic, awoke and decided to do something for his country. He didn't sleep the rest of the night. At 7:30 A.M. he called for a car and he and Rosie carried the still wet painting to a printer who told him, "You gotta be crazy."

This was Wednesday morning, and the election was less than a week off. There was no way the poster could be ready in time.

By 9 A.M. they were at a second printer.

"I'll make a drawing. I'll sign posters for everybody in your family, anything," Peter pleaded, "but, please, print this poster."

The printer agreed but bad luck struck. The presses broke down and it wasn't until 6 P.M. Friday, four days before the election, that Max got his posters, 5,000 of them. Peter pulled $500 out of his pocket—all the cash he had with him—to pay for carting the posters through Manhattan rush hour to a gallery five blocks away.

Max drew a map of New York, divided the city into regions, and then hired people to put up the posters. Three thousand went up on Saturday, most of the rest on Sunday.

He also rolled about two hundred posters into tubes and shipped them overnight to station managers, news directors, and TV anchormen across the country. Many were signed and all included pleas to use these to urge people to vote.

And so on election day 1976 Rosie Vela's portrait as windblown Miss Liberty appeared on television stations in forty cities across America. Underneath her image were the words: "My Love Is America . . . Vote."

But hard as he tried, not even Peter Max could save this election.

It wasn't merely that Ford and Carter were an unimpressive pair, although that certainly was the case. And it wasn't that most of the nation didn't really care, although that too was the case.

The truth was, the Carter-Ford election came at the end of a period when the nation was just plain tired. By Nixon's resignation—after the trauma of the 60s and early 70s—the nation needed to decompress, to take a break. And we got it. The Ford Years.

"This sounds terrible, but I don't recall much about them," said Robert Baron, who had camped on a hillside at Woodstock and woke the next morning to find himself at the bottom of the slope.

"What years were they?" asked Lois Kaufman, who had lied to her parents about Woodstock and spent the weekend with her boyfriend in New England.

Do you remember pet rocks?

"Yeah, I remember pet rocks," she said.

Do you remember the bicentennial?

"Sure, I remember the bicentennial and the tall ships."

Do you remember disco?

"Of course, I remember disco."

And that's the way it was with these years, the ones between Watergate and Jimmy Carter. People remember a few specific occurrences and fads, but not for the sum of their parts.

These years did nothing to slow the slide of the Woodstock generation into the depths it would reach by the end of the decade. Nor would they speed its descent. They were simply a rest stop, a breathing spell on the long, strange trip.

The new president, Gerry Ford, seemed to be what we needed at the time—a caretaker, someone to maintain the engine of America until it was back on the road again. The most common description of Gerald R. Ford was: "He's a really nice guy, someone you would love as a neighbor."

For more than two decades Ford had represented Grand Rapids, Michigan, in the House of Representatives. He had advanced to the House Republican leadership thanks to his single most endearing characteristic: his ability to offend as few people as possible.

That's one reason, maybe the main reason, Richard Nixon chose him to replace Spiro Agnew—nobody hated Gerry Ford. Besides, good ol' Gerry was a team player, someone who had done Nixon's bidding in the House with little argument.

He was a center on the University of Michigan football team. And the joke attributed to Lyndon Johnson and told thousands of times since was that Ford had played too many games without a helmet.

Gerry had been right in 1973 when he said he was a Ford, not a Lincoln. He wasn't a star but a plodder. He was perceived as a nice guy, an amusing bumbler who slipped on stairways and drove golf balls into crowds. Press secretary Ron Nessen more than once angrily jumped to the defense of the president's coordination.

But Ford was also perceived to be straight and honest, and right now, after Watergate, and the War and Spiro and Dick, straight and honest were enough.

The nation was curious about its new president. Reporters did stories about his good-looking kids and his wife, Betty, the former dancer. They even got up early and filmed Ford making breakfast for himself, recording for posterity how he made the perfect English muffin. Some secretly felt a sense of relief: humanity had returned to the White House after the imperial presidency of Richard Nixon.

A Gallup poll in late summer of 1974, shortly after Ford took office, showed that more than 70 percent of all Americans approved his performance, but that's as good as it got. A series of miscalculations and errors would erode his support. For those who had not yet succumbed to the growing indifference, his performance would make them easy targets.

Only a few weeks into his presidency Ford let it be known that he would run for election in 1976, prompting more than a few snickers, since he had promised during his vice presidential confirmation not to run.

Then on September 8, exactly one month after President Nixon announced his resignation, President Ford announced that he was pardoning Nixon for any crimes he may have committed. The White House switchboard was alight with protest and Ford's public support plummeted.

The next week Ford announced his amnesty plan for Vietnam War draft evaders. Many compared the plan with Ford's treatment of Nixon, noting the disproportion between the rigid conditions of the amnesty plan and the leniency bestowed upon Ford's disgraced predecessor.

In one fell swoop Ford had managed to alienate the Woodstock generation in two ways: pardoning the man it hated most, while being not nearly as understanding with those who refused to fight in Vietnam.

Hoping to rally the public behind him on some issue, Ford declared inflation Public Enemy Number One. In the fall of 1974 inflation was rising at an annual rate of over 17 percent, the gross national product was dropping, and unemployment was over 5 percent—it would hit 6.5 percent by the end of the year, the highest since 1961.

The Ford people came up with a slogan: Whip Inflation Now. WIN buttons were handed out and a song was even composed to give the campaign an identity. It fared no better than Herbert Hoover's similar attempt when he asked for a song that would make people forget the Depression; the song was instead a melancholy testament to hard times:

Once I built a railroad, made it run,

Made it race against time.
Once I built a railroad, now it's done;
Brother, can you spare a dime?

Finally, the White House admitted what it had refused to acknowledge but everyone else already knew: the nation was in a recession.

If women didn't already have enough reason to enter the work force, the recession gave them one.

The workplace was only one of the many areas in which women were making their presence felt. Indeed, if any group in the nation was moving forward, it was women. In fact, the growing energy of the women's movement contrasted starkly with the inertia of the majority of the Woodstock generation.

Ella Grasso, of Connecticut, became the first woman to be elected governor outright without being preceded by her husband.

The number of women in medical schools increased by two-thirds (although it still totaled only 15 percent).

By 1975 over half of all women were working and the average household size had shrunk from above four to just under three members. Woodstock generation women were bearing fewer children and having them later. The next year Congress passed a bill admitting women to Annapolis, West Point, and the Air Force Academy for the first time.

Barbara Walters debuted as the first anchorwoman on a network news program, NASA announced it would accept female astronaut applicants, and for the first time Rhodes Scholarships were available to women.

Despite these gains, American women, particularly those of Woodstock age, found a new set of social values emerging. The birth-control pill allowed women greater control over their bodies. The year before, 1973, the U.S. Supreme Court legalized abortion during the first six months of pregnancy. The changing mores now made it acceptable for women to make sexual demands on men.

All of this marked the beginning of a confusing time in the war between the sexes, confusion that would continue well into the 80s. Men and women were trying to adjust to enormous social changes. More women were working and becoming more independent. Married women wanted more say in how much to spend on a car or a home or how much to invest.

Sexual roles became gradually blurred, and both sexes—men and women—had trouble handling the fallout.

One woman meeting the challenge was Lois Kaufman. By this time, she had left Brooklyn College, went on to New York University to get a master's degree and then a doctorate in communications. She taught at Brooklyn College, New York University, Keane College, and finally Rutgers University.

She helped start a technical communications program, turning jargon into English. On the side, she did consulting for corporate executives, teaching them how to speak, how to make presentations, how to develop marketing plans, how to deal with the media. Gradually, she decided this was more exciting than teaching "and it paid a hell of a lot better."

Unlike most other professors, Lois started asking for 8 A.M. classes, evening classes, anything to keep open a chunk of the day for her growing business. The more she succeeded, the more she wanted to succeed.

The company she had started, INFOCUS, grew, so she left Rutgers. She worked first out of her bedroom and then a two-room office in Princeton. Later, she rented two floors of a commercial building.

Lois Kaufman, like tens of thousands of women moving into business, were challenging old rules and changing and growing. Many would pay a price.

For Lois it was a failed marriage—although she doesn't like to call her divorce a failure; she calls it "growing and changing." She and her husband had dated through high school and college, but gradually they grew apart as she took on more and more challenging roles, more and more challenging assignments. Like tens of thousands of young women she was growing more independent, more excited about a life outside the home.

"I used to come home and tell Richie about the things that happened to me during the day and he would tell me to calm down. The last thing I wanted to do was calm down.

"What he bargained for and what he got when he married me was someone who taught during the day and was there to keep him company when he got home. What he ended up with was someone who was willing to work whatever hours were necessary to achieve my goals."

And so the marriage ended not so much out of bitterness but because they no longer shared the same values.

"I was never a woman's libber; I was oblivious to the fact that there were men and women and they got treated differently. I always just went ahead, worked hard, and succeeded."

This got to be more than some men could handle—dealing with a woman interested more in the bottom line than in the clothesline.

"Sometimes I would meet a man on a plane and he would ask what I was doing for dinner that night. We'd have a five-minute conversation and

I'd talk about the business I ran, and by the time the plane ride was over, he wouldn't mention dinner anymore."

A series of surveys beginning in the mid-70s showed clearly that men were becoming increasingly confused about how to treat women, and about how women wanted to be treated. A majority of both sexes said relationships between men and women were becoming increasingly tense.

Women were fighting their way up the ladder of success; sometimes they had to use the courts in that fight. Over twenty-four thousand complaints were filed against companies in 1974. Women no longer asked to be treated equally; they demanded it.

Mary lived in New Jersey and was one of those who filed suit. A good daughter of the Woodstock generation, she let the "old-boy network" in the company where she worked know it wasn't business as usual anymore.

Mary was a salesperson. One day her boss called her in and explained how she could get better accounts.

"He was very explicit about what he wanted," she said. "He didn't leave anything to the imagination." What he wanted was sex, and "he just kept asking and asking and I kept saying no and got the accounts nobody else wanted."

Sometimes she would be out on the road calling on customers and she would get a message that her boss had called. "I'd phone in and he would repeat the whole thing; he would describe in great detail what he wanted. I would say, 'I have to go,' and hang up."

She stuck it out for almost a year. "I kept thinking this can't be happening to me." But it was, so she quit her job and filed a lawsuit against her employer.

Mary was tempted just to forget it, chalk it up to experience, and get another job.

"I would go to bed at night and think he would do this to somebody else, so I guess I just felt a responsibility. It was wrong that he was doing it to me; it would have been wrong for me not to sue him and make sure he couldn't do this to other women."

Mary applied for unemployment but the first case worker she saw, a woman, told her: "He offered you a better territory; why didn't you take it?"

Mary appealed to the woman's supervisor, but he said Mary hadn't followed the proper protocol in taking action against her boss. "He told me I should have gone to the personnel director and filed a complaint. I told him I didn't trust anybody at the company by then but he said no." She was denied unemployment again.

Finally there was a hearing and she was called to the witness stand.

"Isn't it true that you wear very tight tube-tops to show off your rather large breasts?" the opposing attorney asked her.

Mary just looked down at her breasts, which are rather modest, shrugged her shoulders, and made a face as if to say, "Are you crazy?" The courtroom broke into laughter and she won a settlement.

She spoke on condition that her name not be used. Part of the settlement was that she not discuss her case publicly.

"That's how these guys hide," she said.

Soon after her hearing, another woman successfully filed suit against the same boss for exactly the same reason. The boss was demoted—not for what he did, Mary is convinced, but because he got caught.

One day Mary approached a waitress she had been watching in a restaurant. "Are you being sexually harassed?" Mary asked. Yes, the waitress said. Mary gave her some advice on how to handle it, and has done the same for many others since, becoming something of an ad-hoc watchdog for women's rights in the workplace.

"I think things have improved 100 percent," she said, "but it still has another 100 percent to go."

Jimmy Carter officially joined the presidential race in the fall of 1974, meaning he would be campaigning for two full years before the November 1976 election. This, infortunately, became the norm for future elections; the sheer length of campaigns would become another reason to turn voters off.

Here was a one-term governor from Georgia, a farmer (a peanut farmer at that), and a born-again Christian running for the nation's highest office.

Maybe that's the point: like Ford, Carter offered at least the hope of a new beginning. He was a fresh new face to a nation grown disenchanted with its politicians. Carter carried his own suitbag onto planes. He often stayed with ordinary citizens when he traveled.

But don't think he wasn't shrewd. As early as 1974 he often traveled with a cameraman and sound crew. Within a year his campaign strategists had thousands of feet of videotape from which to choose.

Jimmy Carter would be running against big government but Richard Nixon would indirectly play a key role. Gerald Ford's pardon of Nixon made him vulnerable.

Carter capitalized on other disappointments in the nation. In February 1975 ten thousand auto workers rallied in Washington for more jobs. Three months later tens of thousands marched.

These rallies were not all that different from the antiwar protests two years before—except that to the establishment these were good working people, or rather people who wanted to work, not "some damn Communist hippies," so they weren't gassed or arrested the way the kids were.

Violence did erupt, however, a few weeks later. On March 3, a Connecticut rubber plant was seized by Weathermen terrorists and blown up while three hostages were taped to a nearby tree.

Despite the continued terrorism of the Weather Underground, most of the activism of the 60s had died by now. Its leaders were either in hiding, like Abbie Hoffman, or were going about their lives.

About the same time, a study by the National Opinion Research Center revealed that only 14 percent of the nation's adults had confidence in the executive branch of the federal government, and only 17 percent had confidence in the Congress. Fewer than one in five of all adults felt the nation was heading in the "right direction," while 71 percent believed it was on the "wrong track." Less than half had confidence in organized religion.

Crime rates were rising, frightening whites more than blacks, although blacks were more likely to be the victims.

Inflation worsened, and in 1975 unemployment hit 9.5 percent, the highest since the Depression.

The U.S. could no longer dictate the world's economy. The Arabs had their oil and the Japanese were taking business away at home and abroad. And the Woodstock generation, now trying to move into the workplace, found itself struggling to get by.

Cynicism was growing among Americans. The divorce rate was inching up; half of all marriages now ended in divorce.

There was a lot of talk of "planned obsolescence." Items lasted only so long and then broke, so you had to get a new one. For a car it might be four years; a can opener five; a radio—you were in trouble as soon as you walked out the door.

You even had to look to Japan or Europe to get a decent car. "Let me get you out of that piece of junk," a Volkswagen dealer told the driver of a 1974 Ford who drove up to look at the new models.

Little wonder people, and particularly the Woodstock generation, started taking care of Number One.

If I can't trust the government, if I can't rely on the economy, if I can't even buy a damned car with any confidence, I'd better start watching out for myself.

The growing cynicism was compounded by the mobility of young Americans. More than half now lived farther than 200 miles from where they were raised. The family ties, the natural support systems, simply weren't there.

And the larger support system had all but evaporated. Long hair and a peace symbol weren't an automatic passage through a door anymore, even though they had opened many doors a few years earlier. Music, art, film, literature all failed to grab people, to break the Valium shell, to convince them that they could change themselves or their society.

It was the beginning of a narcissistic passage for the Woodstock generation, from the sharing and giving of the Us Generation to what came to be called the Me Generation.

Me Generation people bought expensive clothes and cars for themselves and manipulated personal relations to get what they wanted from other people. They became their own best friends.

The Me Generation was this letter to the editor of the *Kansas City Star*:

> Dear Editor:
> A friend of mine was given a ticket recently for parking in a handicapped-only parking space. That's not fair to the majority of people. If handicapped individuals can't make it an extra 20 feet, let them stay home....

The Me Generation was the Rochester, New York, businessman who wanted to break up with his girlfriend, but waited until after she took him on a free trip to Hawaii.

The Me Generation was drivers cutting each other off on the Santa Ana freeway in Los Angeles and flipping the finger to motorists who objected.

The Me Generation was the proliferation of college courses, seminars, and books on subjects like office politics that taught people how to claw their way up the corporate ladder with advice like "information means control." And so an executive from a New Jersey pharmaceutical firm started coming to work early so he could secretly read memos and mail addressed to his corporate rivals.

Many were shocked to see the Woodstock generation become the Me Generation, but it was because they hadn't seen the signposts along the way: the death of the generation's heroes, the failure of activism, Agnew and Nixon, the energy crisis, inflation, and the mindless isolation that was slowly turning into cynicism. And having grown up in prosperous times—therefore, unfamiliar with recession—many were scared they couldn't survive. For these reasons they turned inward, away from the Us, toward the Me.

The new attention to the self, to one's own ego, was evident in a dozen ways. One of the most obvious was on the dance floor.

Disco music emerged. The dance floor, once the site where hippies gyrated with wild abandon, became a place to show off through a rigid series of choreographed steps.

The movie *Saturday Night Fever* was a year off, but it caught the mood perfectly. It starred John Travolta, who by day was a gofer in a Brooklyn paint store and by night King of the Disco. He would preen at home before the mirror—his hair must be perfect, his tight shirt had to be neatly tucked with just the right number of buttons left open.

When he danced, even without a partner, people stopped to watch. He was a graceful peacock. He was somebody; not just the kid from the paint store. It wasn't important that the songs didn't say much; it was the beat and the moves that mattered.

It was mostly a white beat, and a corporate one. The music sounded as if it were stamped out of an audio cookie-cutter, repetitious without reason. Whereas the Woodstock generation had warily accepted the intrusion of synthesizers into its music, it now embraced a music built on electronics.

By mid-1975 there were more than ten thousand discos in the United States.

In April the legacy of Vietnam came home to roost. Saigon fell and Americans watched on TV as the mobs tried to barge their way into the American embassy in a desperate attempt for safety. They shook their heads at the sight of U.S. helicopters lifting off from the city one last time, with people frantically clinging to the choppers' skids, hoping, praying to hold on long enough to reach the U.S. fleet offshore.

Many didn't.

On April 30, 1975 the North Vietnamese flag was raised over the presidential palace in Saigon, now Ho Chi Minh City. The final cost of the war to America: more than fifty-six thousand dead, three hundred three thousand wounded, and over a hundred billion dollars spent.

But at this point few in the U.S. cared much. In the years ahead, the story of Vietnam would be told in movies and on television dramas. It would be portrayed more accurately than any other war—not only the bravery but the pettiness of the military; the corruption of the South Vietnam government, the drug use among American troops. But not yet. Now, the country just wanted to forget.

On college campuses—to the shock of the 60s activists—ROTC enrollment started to increase. This was the clearest sign that the next generation was turning from the activism of the 60s. It was not so much that the values of that decade were being denied as that they were being ignored or forgotten.

It was a time for things like mood rings—rings that changed color supposedly in response to how you were feeling at the time—and pet rocks.

Pet rocks were the invention of an out-of-work advertising man whose pitch was that a pet rock was better than a cat or a dog—it didn't need housebreaking. Each sold for $3.89 and came with a manual on the care and feeding of the rock. Stores sold out.

Citizen Band radios, CBs, were the biggest craze of the year. Applications for CB radio licenses in 1975 increased almost 600 percent over the year before. Over a million CB radios were imported from Japan during the first nine months of the year alone. A hit record, "Convoy," by C.W. McCall, told the story of a band of truckers traveling across America and, linked by their CB radios, on the lookout for smoky (the police) and for bears in the air (police helicopters). "Convoy" even became a movie, starring Kris Kristofferson and Ali McGraw.

Some sociologists made much of the significance of CB radios; more than a few thought them an outlet for a nation struggling to communicate with itself.

But in the end, CBs, pet rocks, and mood rings really signaled nothing but the idle playthings of a generation hooked on nothing. With nothing better to do with its time, it indulged in whimsy and fantasy, looking for some kind of kick, some kind of fix.

The entertainment industry understood that the nation was weary and needed to have its senses stimulated by plain old suspense and drama. And that's what it started churning out.

The watershed came in the form of a fish. *Jaws* is the story of a great white shark that terrorizes a quiet New England resort town. It shattered box-office records across the U.S. and created "Jawsmania" complete with T-shirts and inflatable replicas of the Great White shark. Shark fishing suddenly became a hot sport.

The top TV shows in 1975 focused on laughs: "Barney Miller" and "Welcome Back, Kotter." Norman Lear's satirical soap opera "Mary Hartman, Mary Hartman," starring Louise Lasser, displayed an offbeat humor rarely seen on television, as did another new show, "Saturday Night Live." The latter would have the more profound and lasting effect.

America's comedy scene, once so rich, had fallen on hard times. The death of variety shows removed one national forum; the passing of the popularity of comedy albums took away another.

Innovative comedy in the country was now localized—at places like Second City in Chicago. NBC's new, unusual live Saturday show would draw much of its talent from Second City—comedians unknown to most of

America, though not for long. The Not Ready for Prime Time Players would usher in a new era for its Woodstock generation audience.

The hippest thing to do on a Saturday night was stay home and watch the show. "Saturday Night Live" was outlandish and irreverent. Its early stars, including Chevy Chase (whose slapstick parodies of Gerry Ford's clumsiness were becoming legend), John Belushi, Dan Aykroyd, and Jane Curtin, would all retain a strong following after leaving the show.

Humor had always played a key role in the movement, but that role had now changed. A Lenny Bruce or a Mort Sahl—or an Abbie Hoffman—used humor to keep people involved in and outraged about events going on around them. Now the generation sat home, watched its show, had a good laugh—and further escaped from what was going on around it.

All around it bits and pieces of things emerged to remind the Woodstock generation of its past.

Mafia boss Sam Giancana was shot to death in the kitchen of his suburban Chicago home. In 1988, authors would speculate that Giancana was killed because of his role in a failed CIA plot to kill Cuban leader Fidel Castro in the early 60s. There were also stories that Giancana was killed to help cover up a Cuban conspiracy in the assassination of John Kennedy.

Much of the generation would forever disbelieve that Lee Harvey Oswald acted alone. Suspicion would always remain that the Warren Commission covered up a conspiracy. The Woodstock generation would forever relive the murder in Dallas. Each anniversary of his death was like an unfinished chapter in its life.

President Ford escaped death himself in 1975—twice.

On September 5, Lynette "Squeaky" Fromme, a follower of Charles Manson, was arrested after agents wrestled a gun from her hand as she approached Ford during a California appearance. Seventeen days later Sara Jane Moore fired a shot at Ford as he stepped out of a San Francisco hotel. Both were later sentenced to life imprisonment.

One of the most heart-wrenching stories of the year involved Karen Anne Quinlan, a twenty-one-year-old New Jersey woman who had been in an irreversible coma. After five months of keeping a vigil at her bedside, Karen's parents came to an agonizing decision: they asked the courts that her life-sustaining respirator be turned off.

The case sparked a nationwide debate over the right to die. It remains one of the most difficult moral issues of our time as technology in the medical field advances faster than our ability to make clear choices about how and when to use that technology.

For the first time, doctors could keep patients alive through artificial means. But whether they should do so and whether the quality of life that results should be considered in deciding treatment are questions at the center of a debate that caught fire with Karen Anne Quinlan.

It would intensify in the 80s when Elizabeth Bouvia, a cerebral-palsy patient, asked a California hospital to allow her to starve to death. In another case, the parents of a severely handicapped infant, identified only as Baby Jane Doe, would fight attempts to force surgery that would have prolonged her life.

In 1982 California would enact the nation's first right-to-die law, allowing terminally ill patients to refuse extraordinary life-prolonging treatments. A number of other states adopted the same type of law, and although they didn't end the debate, they gave people more of a say about how and when to die.

But Quinlan's was the case that brought these questions into the open. Her parents finally were allowed to remove her from the respirator—but, in the strangest turn of the case, Karen remained alive. She stayed in a coma for almost a decade before dying of pneumonia in a New Jersey nursing home in June 1985.

The 1976 presidential election was a year away, but the campaign was already in full swing.

The Democratic race shaped up as a fight between Jimmy Carter and Sen. Henry M. "Scoop" Jackson of Washington. They stayed pretty much neck-and-neck during the early part of 1976 but Carter clinched the Democratic nomination by winning the late primaries. The press no longer called him Jimmy Who.

Carter chose Sen. Walter Mondale to be his running mate as a way to placate the liberal end of the party. "It's now time to heal," Carter said in accepting the nomination. But the rifts of the Woodstock generation would not pass easily. Just a few weeks after his acceptance speech, Carter was booed by the American Legion for promising to pardon draft resisters.

On the Republican side, Ronald Reagan seemed to gather strength in the spring by winning four out of five early primaries. Ford rebounded in June by winning Ohio and clinched the nomination by winning New Jersey. Ford chose Sen. Robert Dole, of Kansas, as his vice presidential partner.

The Woodstock generation began to see politics as an intrusion into its life. Even the Olympic games, which were supposed to be free of this sort of thing, became tarnished by politics.

Little hint of this was brewing during the Winter Games in Innsbruck, Austria. The hit of the games was U.S. figure-skating gold medalist Dorothy

Hamill. Thousands of men fell in love with her and thousands of women went out the next day and had their hair cut in the suddenly famous Hamill "wedge" style.

But the Summer Games, held in Montreal, were marred by controversy: thirty-two nations withdrew because of political reasons and six Eastern European athletes defected. It would be more than a decade before another Olympics would be held without political controversy. And the Woodstock generation—which not too long ago had wanted to "bring the war back home"—now bemoaned the fact that politics was getting even more involved in their daily lives.

He-men and glamour girls were becoming popular again, a far cry from the social-conscious role models of ten years before.

The movie *Rocky* made a star of Sylvester Stallone. It is the story of an over-the-hill prizefighter—not a has-been but a never-was—who gets a fluke shot at the heavyweight championship and almost pulls off an upset.

"There ain't gonna be no rematch," battered champ Apollo Creed tells Rocky at the end of the film.

"I don't want one," Rocky answers.

He lied. *Rocky II, Rocky III,* and *Rocky IV* would follow.

And then there was the Farrah phenomenon. Only a few years earlier, Farrah Fawcett's biggest role was on a commercial for shaving cream. After "Charlie's Angels," her posters sold in the thousands and she was a regular on dozens of magazine covers. The generation felt no shame and sensed no irony in making a sex symbol one of America's main celebrities.

On July 4, 1976 America spectacularly celebrated its bicentennial. Tens of millions showed up at big celebrations and little parties across the nation. The national anthem was sung at daybreak at Fort McHenry in Baltimore, and Washington had a $200,000 fireworks display that entertained over six million people. But New York Harbor was really the center of the party.

The harbor was dotted with ships from thirty-one countries: tall ships, war ships, yachts, even rowboats. At night millions watched one of the largest fireworks displays ever.

Peter Max had decided to paint the tall ships. He could see much of the action from the twenty-six windows of his eighteen-room Manhattan home high above the Hudson River. He had set up easels at each window. Water colors were at one, pastels at another, inks at a third, color pencils at a fourth, and so on.

Peter painted a few, but was disappointed with the result. He couldn't see the details of the ships; they were too small. The tall ships weren't tall enough—not like the big liners and container ships he watched plowing up and down the Hudson.

Maybe I should forget about these things and do a big Statue of Liberty, Max thought to himself. He loved the Statue of Liberty and collected photos of it.

Peter took a big eight-foot canvas and started painting, oblivious to the hundreds of friends who had gathered in his home not only to watch the fireworks but to watch him work.

It was a glorious day for Peter Max. He listened with excitement to the story of the daring raid by Israeli commandos only hours before to free hostages held by terrorists at the Entebbe Airport in Uganda. He saw the excitement outside and gradually became aware that he was surrounded inside by friends and well-wishers.

When his painting of the statue was done, his friends could see it was done with broad, bold strokes, with a pride and emotion that perhaps only an immigrant could know.

Max, on July 4, 1976, was in the fifth year of a thirteen-year "creative retreat." He had achieved megasuccess in the Woodstock era, then things got too big, too crazy, too corporate. He had in fact become a corporation all to himself and this had got in the way of other things—his art, his peace of mind, his search for life. So he simply dropped out.

Peter Max and his art are synonymous with the 60s. In many ways he was the 60s.

Peter Max elevated posters to an art form. His brightly colored designs ended up on greeting cards, clocks, sunglasses, watches—he even designed a smiling sneaker that sold more than a million pairs.

When people today conjure up images of the 60s, very likely it's a Peter Max image: the doves and stars in brilliant bold primary colors, the flying people, the androgynous figures intertwined with boldly colored shapes, the psychic feeling throughout. His style did for art what the Beatles' *Magical Mystery Tour* did for music: capturing the acid-trip sensibility and free-flowing feel of the times.

The colorful, mystical feeling in his art reflects his almost magical childhood. Max was born in Berlin but moved with his family to Shanghai when he was only one year old. His introduction to America came in the form of the colorful comic books that he cherished: Flash Gordon, Buck Rogers, Captain Marvel, and Submariner.

Once a week he could hear American music on the radio and gradually the culture of the East, the temples and pagodas and the Chinese music and art, blended with his images of the West.

When Peter was ten his family embarked on another journey, to Tibet, and then went by boat to South Africa and Israel. By the age of thirteen Peter was studying astronomy at the University of Haifa with students a decade older. He loved to watch the stars at night, and they show up often in his work, as do the pagodas he played near during his youth.

He moved to New York at sixteen and studied for five years at the Art Students League. He studied realism and he still doodles in that style. But mostly Peter turned to expressionism. "I found expressionism more fun," he says, and it gave him more of an opportunity to inject his feelings and mood into the art.

There was another reason. Like much of the Woodstock generation, Max lacks patience. Realism "takes a lot of time to do a piece and I really want to see the rewards sooner."

Fame came quickly.

About the time he was selling three posters to future Woodstock creator Michael Lang, Max was helping a friend design a restaurant in Manhattan, the Tin Lizzie.

"What this restaurant needs is a good poster," Peter said. "It should be color; that's the wave of the future."

The design he took to the printer was a kaleidoscope of psychedelic images.

"You have any more of these?" the printer asked.

"Sure."

They negotiated a deal to produce them, a fifty-fifty split, without even leaving the printing press.

Peter ran home and got ten other designs and brought them right back.

The posters cost six cents to print and wholesaled for one dollar. Within nine months four million were sold. Twenty-two years later they brought $500 apiece, unsigned.

The money started coming in, but somehow it wasn't quite satisfying. Something was missing. Already he was starting to draw criticism as a mass-production artist, but while this criticism was surfacing, Max was dealing with other, deeper questions about himself.

He wanted to understand "Why is life? We know how it works but not why."

Peter created a collage and arranged the pieces on a five-foot-by-five-foot glass table in his home. He arranged and rearranged it, hoping that some combination would appear to give him a glimpse into the order of life. He even got a tall ladder and looked down on it from above, resting his head on the top of the ladder until his chin hurt.

The answers would start coming in Paris, while Peter was consulting on a movie.

The collage was still spread out in his home when a producer called. Something was wrong with the film. He wasn't sure what, but he wanted Peter to sit on the set for a week and help him. Peter said no.

"I'll give you $10,000 for a week," the producer said.

Peter said no.

"I'll give you $20,000."

Peter said no.

"I'll give you $30,000."

The answer was still no.

Finally, Max agreed, but only after the producer caught the next flight from Paris to New York and showed up at Peter's door at 3 A.M. and pleaded with him to change his mind.

A few days later he was at the Hotel Napoleon in Paris talking with the producer when he saw a distinguished-looking man with black robes and a beard walking toward him. He must be a foreign diplomat, Max thought, until the producer said, "Meet the swami."

Immediately, Max said, "something touched me."

Peter spent a week with Swami Satchidananda, talking and listening and learning about the meaning of life. Two years later the same swami would sit on a stage and talk to the four hundred thousand at Woodstock. And the end of the week Peter implored the swami: "Come to New York . . . New York needs you."

The swami said he would come but only for a few days on his way to Canada. Peter called up twenty-four of his best friends and they met the swami in Max's home. These were hard-driving advertising executives, businessmen, a few hippies. Everyone was mesmerized. After a few hours Peter called his friends aside and said, "How can we keep him here?"

The poorest of the bunch, a handyman hippie-type, threw four cents on the table; it was all he had. Then everyone threw money on the table—twenties, a few fifties. They put the swami up in a hotel room and he started giving classes. A few attended at first, then dozens, and then they had to rent a hall to fit everyone in. He touched on the order of life, about animals and people and the environment. Peter was enthralled. It's where he first became seriously involved in the ozone problem, and endangered species, issues he would work for later.

For Peter Max things started falling into place. He had always painted flying people; now he believed they were spreading the message of peace and love.

"As life goes on we harden," Peter said; "just as we get calluses on our hands and feet, our personalities get hardened." The swami helped soften those calluses.

Things were also falling into place for his professional life; in fact, he was becoming a cult hero. He was capturing in his work something that the Woodstock generation loved. And bought.

By 1971 he was big business. His name was on more than a billion dollars' worth of retail merchandise.

Critics complained that putting his designs on mass-produced products such as plastic radios or rainbow sunglasses diminished the power of his art. "It wasn't just for commercial reasons," he still argues. Max believed it was important to put his art within the reach of his fans.

Within a few years he was on seventy magazine covers and four hundred television shows. He was driven around town in a decal-covered 1952 Rolls-Royce, but he had no time for painting and he ended up doing much of his drawing in the back of a limo or in a hotel room.

"My life revolved around corporations, schedules. I just wasn't painting anymore," he said. "Life was crazy."

And then he just quit.

He made the decision while vacationing in Mexico. He was relaxing in a chair and watching the birds, and decided he needed to wind down his lifestyle a notch or two.

He gave up his Rolls and his entourage—he went from fifty-two assistants to five. Then he embarked on what Peter Max calls his "creative retreat."

Peter didn't stop working. He did stop traveling so much to promote his products and going to art shows and meeting with the press. He still painted and had some exhibits.

While the world wondered about his disappearance, he went to Woodstock—the town—and Europe and vacationed in Barbados, where he still loves to jet ski.

One day in Barbados he beached his jet ski to get a soda; he rode it right up on the beach, shut it down, and jumped off—almost into the lap of a woman sunbathing.

"Peter Max," she said. "So that's where you've been."

In 1974 he was commissioned by the U.S. Postal Service to design a ten-cent stamp to commemorate the World's Fair in Spokane.

In 1976 he completed a mural that still greets immigrants at 235 Mexican and Canadian border stations. "I wanted to create a cheerful picture that would say, 'Welcome to this incredible country.' "

That year he was divorced after ten years of marriage and two children, Adam Cosmo and Libra Astro, and that year he produced a book, *Peter Max Paints America*. The cover of the book was seen in a photo on the front page of the *New York Times,* sitting on Jimmy Carter's coffee table the day he won the Democratic nomination for president.

And, of course, 1976 was the year that Peter Max painted the Statue of

Liberty. The next year an assistant asked, "Aren't you going to do the statue again?"

"I thought it was a good idea," Peter recalls, "but I told him to order two canvases in case I screwed one up."

The first painting was fine, so Peter painted two statues. The next year he would do three paintings; the next year four; and then five until 1981, when he got a call from Nancy Reagan asking him to paint the Statue of Liberty as part of the Reagans' first Fourth of July celebration in the White House.

Peter was so proud that he rented rooms facing the White House in the Hay Adams Hotel for friends and family members invited to the event. He did six paintings between 8 A.M. and 9 P.M. on a forty-foot-by-ten-foot scaffold guarded by marines in their dress blues.

And then he resumed the creative retreat he had started in 1971. When he finally returned in the 80s, it was a new Peter Max, and a different America.

Four days after Peter painted his first Fourth of July Statue of Liberty in 1976, Richard Nixon was disbarred by the state of New York. But for Watergate, Nixon would still be president. Now, he couldn't even practice law.

Other prominent symbols of the Woodstock generation started disappearing. Liverpool's Cavern Club, where the Beatles first played, closed. The stage was cut into sections and sold.

A number of radio stations gave up hard rock as audiences dipped.

And the most important symbol of all—the generation's youth—was fading. The oldest members of the generation that once said "Don't trust anybody over thirty" were now turning thirty.

Mao Tse-tung and Howard Hughes and Mayor Richard Daley, of Chicago, all died.

The last U.S. convertible, the Cadillac Eldorado, was phased out. (Mao, Hughes, and Daley would not return, but the convertible would.)

On November 2, Carter won the presidential election. Democrats celebrated by symbolically opening a bag of peanuts. Ford actually won more states, but Carter's states had more electoral votes.

Carter was the first man from the Deep South to be elected president in more than a century. Ford blamed his loss on, among other things, his performance in the presidential debates.

In the second debate, Ford simply misspoke: "There is no Soviet domination in Eastern Europe and there never will be under a Ford administration."

"I would like to see Mr. Ford convince Polish-Americans and Czech-Americans," Carter responded.

A decade and a half later the president's mistake would be repeatedly cited when people recalled the Ford years, as if that were all they could recall.

CHAPTER FIVE

Hitting Bottom

Gordon Black first met Jimmy Carter in 1974 when he picked him up at the airport in Rochester, New York. Black's job was to drive Carter around that day and the next so he could meet people and speak and help their mutual friend Midge Constanza run for Congress.

For years, Black had been at the fringe of various movements here or there. He used to travel to La Honda and buy his marijuana from Ken Kesey but never got into the Kesey drug scene or the Prankster lifestyle. He protested against the war, and had traveled to demonstrations, but he never got down deep into the movement. Gordon was more of a theorist; so after he got his doctorate from Stanford he moved East to teach political science at the University of Rochester. And for a political scientist, it was a treat to spend a day and a half with the governor of Georgia, a man who asserted that he would be the next president of the United States.

"He was obviously very bright, and very, very warm," Black remembers. And so Black was eager, when asked in 1976, to prepare Carter's New York swing during a critical moment in his campaign for the Democratic nomination for president. It would be a busy trip: Buffalo, Rochester, Syracuse, Albany, Schenectady, and finally New York City.

"That was my first understanding, my first hint of the problems he would have later," Black said. "Jimmy Carter doesn't like people."

It's been argued, perhaps correctly, that Jimmy Carter was the smartest president since Thomas Jefferson. But it takes more than intelligence to run a country. Carter inherited a nation that stopped believing in its leaders. He would leave a nation that stopped believing in itself.

When Carter left office, 81 percent of all Americans felt the nation was in "deep and serious trouble," twice as many as when he was sworn in as president, according to a *Time* magazine poll. And fewer than four of ten adults, in a Roper poll, were optimistic about the nation's future.

The most affected was the Woodstock generation. Its optimism was the lowest of any age group. Its pessimism ran the deepest. In a real sense, the generation would hit bottom by the end of the Carter years. It would be looking for something, someone, to restore faith not only in the country but in itself.

For the first time, a deep sense of guilt, or shame, or embarrassment, or loss of face was infiltrating the generation's sensibilities. Clearly, the game had been lost: it had not changed the world. The Woodstock Nation did not overcome. It no longer even seemed to exist.

Although he believed in many of the same values the generation had grown up with—the primacy of civil rights and human rights highest among them—Carter didn't have the magic or the charisma to regenerate its flagging interest in these values. He had no poetry, no music.

Carter would preside over a time of diverse and seemingly insoluble problems: Americans were taken hostages and the nation was powerless to help them; a serial killer would strike fear in the nation's largest city; there would be a nuclear accident, mass suicide, environmental disasters. Each highlighted the sense of impotence, the feeling of helplessness, of the nation—and the generation. Finally, just ten years after Woodstock, the generation gave up the ghost; its spirit had fled.

It would recapture this spirit, in a different way more suited to a different time; but if the wake for the hippie movement had been held years before, the late seventies were its funeral.

Gordon Black thought he caught a glimpse back in 1976 of what would happen and why.

Black had worked for weeks setting up the trip, arranging the cars, coordinating the flights so that things would work like clockwork on the Carter trip. Instead of the considerate warm person he had met two years earlier, Black found the candidate to be cold and silent. And with the exception of Carter's press secretary, Jody Powell, Black thought the small clique of Georgians gathered around the future president was even worse: "They were arrogant, disorganized, and almost totally lacking in people skills; and here I was, doing this for nothing."

Black was with Carter for sixteen hours.

"I had spent two weeks of my time working on this, but not once during the day was there a friendly word or a thank you. In private, he was as cold as anyone I have ever dealt with."

Carter changed the minute he stepped off the campaign plane—waving to the crowds, shaking hands, smiling his famous toothy grin. Back on the plane, he was cold again, as if a veil had been drawn over him.

By the end of the day Black was brooding. Jody Powell, sensing something wrong, walked over to talk and Gordon unloaded on him about Carter, saying, "He is the coldest son of a bitch I've ever met in my life; ice would warm him up."

Powell walked away and Black could see him say something to Carter, who then turned, faced Gordon, waved, and flashed his toothy grin. At that moment Carter campaign worker Gordon Black decided to vote for Gerry Ford.

"I knew then," Black said, "that Carter liked humanity, but he didn't like people."

This dichotomy in Carter's character—his great caring for society, and his strange inability to connect with people personally—would doom not only his presidency but the hopes he carried for healing the nation.

Carter won the closest election of the century. When inaugurated on January 20, 1977, he promised to regenerate the spirit of trust in America. Then, as if to drive home his point, he surprised everyone by walking home to the White House hand in hand with wife Rosalynn and daughter Amy rather than using the waiting limousine.

Carter wasted little time getting started. Within a week after his inauguration he pardoned most of the Vietnam draft dodgers, allowing them to come home. Many had been living in Canada or Sweden since the war and this was Carter's attempt to start healing the wounds of Vietnam.

In March Carter hosted a call-in show—a first for a sitting president—and spoke to forty-two people during the program. It amused some in Washington that Carter was available to ordinary citizens of the nation but inaccessible to people in the nation's capital. The president and his aides frequently failed to return calls to even the most powerful congressional leaders.

Carter had been elected partially by running against Washington; and so his staff treated the rest of the government with a degree of the arrogance and disdain that Gordon Black had witnessed two years earlier.

For his own part, the president remained isolated behind his own palace guard—the Georgia mafia—and this helped spell his downfall in the years ahead.

It was over the selection of one of his friends that the Carter administration had its first, but not its last, crisis. Carter had chosen Georgia banker Bert Lance to run the Office of Management and Budget, one of the most powerful posts in the U.S. government, even though Lance was under investigation for violating federal banking regulations. The investigation uncovered more and more clear-cut evidence of wrongdoing. Yet, Carter continued to defend his close friend.

The press jumped on the story while Democrats and Republicans alike called for Lance's resignation or dismissal. Carter refused to fire Lance, even though he had campaigned on a platform of high ethical standards and promised not to tolerate even the slightest impropriety.

Lance resigned in September. He was indicted less than a year later.

Next it was revealed that several Democratic congressmen pressured

Carter to fire U.S. Attorney David W. Marston of Philadelphia because he was investigating them. Several congressmen were indicted, but to a growing number of people it seemed like business as usual in the White House.

To members of the Woodstock generation, it seemed like old news and it didn't matter that it was the grinning Jimmy Carter instead of the sneering Richard Nixon. Rather than make the scandals or the nation's problems a rallying point, the generation saw one more reason to shake its head, turn away, and forget about it all.

A new kind of "event" marked 1977, one that stimulated not forgetting, but remembering.

On February 1, more people watched the first episode of "Roots" than had seen any show ever. It ran for eight days and reached over a hundred million viewers.

Based on the family tree of author Alex Haley, "Roots" traced the lineage of Kunta Kinte, enslaved as a youth in Africa. It followed the struggle that he and his descendants waged against their slavery in America.

The show carried special importance for black viewers, and for members of the Woodstock generation in particular. It raised questions of racial pride, social injustice, and bigotry that stirred forgotten memories.

The lifetime of the Woodstock generation spanned the years of the most important civil rights struggle since the Civil War—from the freedom riders, to the Civil Rights Act of 1964, to the march on Washington, and beyond. This was a transitional generation in the history of the country; it was the last generation to grow up with Whites Only signs on bathroom doors. And although "Roots" certainly did not rally it to civil rights activism or anything close to it, the show at least nudged its consciousness.

Karen Howze watched "Roots" in San Francisco. She was working as a reporter for the *San Francisco Chronicle* and going to law school at the same time.

"It had a tremendous effect on all Americans," she said. "I knew some of the things it showed because family members had talked about it. But it was so poignant to have it right out there on television."

It struck Howze that millions of Americans, not just blacks like herself, were watching the show. It also struck her that this was a significant moment for television, which had finally matured to the point that it could take on such an emotional issue.

The miniseries remained as a new form of entertainment. The next year over a hundred million people watched the miniseries "Holocaust" on NBC. Dozens more followed among them "Shogun," the story of an English sailor in feudal Japan, and "The Winds of War," the saga of an American family and its entry into World War II.

Motion pictures were going through their own changes in 1977. On

May 1, *Star Wars* opened nationwide and was by far the biggest moneymaker of the 70s. The movie depicted a high-tech battle between good and evil for control of the Force, a mystic-religious energy in the universe. *Star Wars* also signaled the beginning of a more sophisticated approach to science fiction—state-of-the-art computer graphics, mechanical models, and glorious special effects.

Star Wars set records for merchandising. Tens of millions of dollars were spent on everything from scale models of spaceships seen in the films to detailed Darth Vader costumes.

But somewhere between the already-growing success of the slash-and-gash horror movies and the new series of gigantic-budget sci-fi films to come, the kind of small movies that carried big meaning for the generation were lost. *Harold and Maude*, *King of Hearts*, and the like would be all but squeezed out of Hollywood for more than a decade. It was as though the dark side of the Force had sneakily overwhelmed the good side of the Force, and Luke Skywalker was nowhere in sight.

There would emerge, by decade's end, movies dealing with serious social and personal concerns. But the big-budget blockbusters had captured Hollywood and would hold it hostage for years.

That same year, 1977, the government reported that the number of adults under thirty-five living alone had more than doubled since 1970. People in the Woodstock generation were getting married and having children later, and this was dramatically affecting not only the kind of housing people wanted, but also schools, more of which were closing; supermarkets, which began offering salad bars and single servings of food; and restaurants, which started booming, since no one wanted to cook.

This was growing evidence, though none understood it yet, that the nation was paying attention to the Woodstock generation, and would continue to do so. After all, Woodstock members were the heart of the huge baby boom. The nation's businesses, politicians, and institutions would continue to court them, cater to their whims, and indulge their fantasies. For a generation feeling powerless in the mid-1970s, it would grow to wield enormous power.

On July 13, 1977 New York City went dark. Nine million people were without power. For two days stores were looted and property vandalized—a sharp contrast to the famous 1965 blackout, which turned into something of a festival with people sharing and helping one another.

But New York was entering an even darker reign of terror. Somebody calling himself the Son of Sam was killing young people using a .44 caliber Charter Arms Bulldog revolver, opening fire at almost point-blank range with the most powerful handgun in the world.

The tabloids had a field day—"Where Will Sam Strike Next?"—and panic-stricken parents ordered their teenage sons and daughters to stay at home.

In July Sam wounded his twelfth and thirteenth victims. Then came a break in the case. A parking ticket issued near one of the shootings led police to David Berkowitz, a chronically depressed and paranoid loner from Yonkers.

Berkowitz later pleaded guilty to the Son of Sam killings, explaining that voices ordered him out into the street. He was sentenced to twenty-five years to life in prison. Six young people were slain in the year-long murder spree and seven wounded.

On August 16 the world was stunned by the death of rock-and-roll superstar Elvis Presley of a heart attack. He was found unconscious in Graceland, his mansion, and rushed to a nearby hospital where he was pronounced dead. The King had ballooned to 250 pounds and was a heavy user of drugs and alcohol. Elvis was one of America's most dynamic and successful pop musicians and within hours of his death there was a run on his records at stores across the nation.

For days, thousands of grief-stricken fans lined the streets outside his home.

Presley was a demarcation point for the Woodstock generation. He had been the King only to its very oldest members and went out when the Beatles and the British invaded.

Another passing of note: Volkswagen announced it would phase out its famous bug, the official car of the Woodstock Nation. It would start producing something called the Rabbit. The Beetle had been omnipresent in the 60s, whether in glorious Day-Glo colors or as just a plain old beat-up bug. It was cheap, efficient, and always reliable, and now it too would go the way of the peace button and bell-bottom jeans.

In music, the British punk-rock movement was sweeping Europe. The Sex Pistols and Sid Vicious represented the dangerous, outrageous spirit that parents would hate: an anti-everything message, a fuck-you attitude that made the Woodstock generation seem tame.

But in America the punk movement, with its purple-haired followers and antisocial lyrics, found a home only in small enclaves like New York's Lower East Side. A club scene flourished there with an energy unknown since predisco days. But this time, the Woodstock generation stayed home.

And they stayed home during the next wave of demonstrations in

Washington. These came from an unexpected source. Angry farmers rolled into the city in trucks and on tractors, blocking intersections and snarling traffic. It was the harbinger of a nationwide farm strike in 1978 to call attention to the grave economic conditions and federal bureaucracy that were forcing farmers into bankruptcy.

In March 1978 Carter would yield to the pressure and proposed increased federal aid to the nation's farmers.

The feeling of helplessness and impotence, the sense of being over-powered by events, spread throughout the nation, and the Woodstock generation. Billy Hayes had reason to feel free and strong—he had escaped from prison, from Turkey—but life after prison was leaving him, too, feeling overwhelmed and powerless.

Three years earlier Billy had got himself transferred to Imrali Island, a prison off the coast of Turkey. It was a step up from Istanbul; he could now leave his prison cell to swim, run, sit in the sunshine, and build up his energy.

Although Imrali had more freedom, it was still a prison, the guards still carried guns, and he could still get a bullet in the back if he tried to escape. But at this point, Billy thought, what the fuck? What have I to lose? They might shoot me but at least I'll be free.

"They're stealing your summers, man," a fellow prisoner had told him, "How many summers do you think you have left?"

Now the winter of 1975 would soon set in. The nights were already getting colder and the days shorter. Billy thought he could not bear even one more winter in prison, and he was facing twenty-five of them. If I don't do something soon, he thought, I'm going to lose something of myself that I'll never get back.

One day early in October he waited until a storm came over the island and then hid in a tomato processing plant until the sun went down. Carefully, dodging searchlights and staying out of sight of the guardtowers, he slid down to the coastline and into the water and stole a small rowboat belonging to a fisherman who had taken refuge from the storm.

Billy rowed most of the night. His hands ached. Finally he struck the mainland. Then he ran, hitchhiked, and bused his way to Istanbul.

He rented a room in a cheap hotel, dyed his blonde hair black, and shaved off his mustache so it would be harder for people to identify him. By now the police were surely searching for him. Billy was free, but he was still in Turkey and had to find a way to get out.

He took a bus to a town near the border where Turkey meets Greece and then a cab closer to the border. He waited until night, then waded through the mud and swam a river. Billy was now in Greece, where he was arrested again, this time by the Greeks, who said they could do one of three things: send him back to Turkey, throw him in jail, or deport him to some other country—like the United States.

The Greeks hate the Turks, so they deported Billy on the grounds that he was a bad influence on the youth of Greece. Twelve days later he was on his way home, the happiest "bad influence" in the world.

And then, Billy Hayes says, the really weird part of his life started.

More than a hundred reporters were waiting for Billy when he arrived at New York's Kennedy Airport on October 24, 1975. He had hoped for a period of decompression after five years of prison. What he got was a case of the bends.

"I became a media celebrity and things just snowballed," he recalls. "The media just swallowed me up and I went along with it."

Billy was a hot story. The news of his escape had spread and everyone wanted to interview him. Magazines sought his story, newspaper reporters called, television and radio requested interviews—everything, including book offers.

His lawyer screened agents and a book deal was signed. A movie deal was made only six months later and then a national tour to promote the book, *Midnight Express—The American Papillon: A Young Man's Escape from a Turkish Prison.* This was followed later by sixty days on the road to plug the movie.

He had spent five years in prison plotting only how to escape. Now there were breakfast interviews, luncheon news shows, late-night talk shows. People wanted his opinion on every subject under the sun.

"I felt like Marco Polo just back from Cathay," he said, "and everyone wanted to know what it was like."

And always the same questions: Do you have any regrets? Are you sorry? Would you do it again?

"All this was happening and I didn't know where my life was heading," Billy said.

He wanted to move on but he was stuck in the past.

The clincher came one night when Billy was walking through Times Square with his sister. Suddenly she stopped and pointed up in the air. There in lights over Manhattan flashed the sign: The Billy Hayes Story . . . *Midnight Express.*

"I had to get away from the fucking Billy Hayes and *Midnight Express* bullshit," Billy said, "so I loaded up my Volvo, put my bike on the roof, drove to Florida, and took a right toward California."

In Iran violent riots broke out against the rule of the U.S.-backed shah. Most Americans paid little attention at first and even less to the rantings of exiled Muslim leader Ayatollah Ruhollah Khomeini, whose dream was to install an Islamic republic in Iran.

Month by month the shah faced mounting opposition to his fifteen-year rule as more bloody riots swept through major Iranian cities. When four hundred thousand antishah protesters marched in Tehran, the U.S. government recommended that dependents of Americans leave the country. These events would lead to a monumental crisis, seemingly so distant at the time, in the United States, and to the greatest feeling of impotence the nation had ever known.

Environmental problems captured the Woodstock generation's sympathy if not its active involvement. In Niagara Falls, New York, emergency state and federal aid was pledged to residents of the Love Canal area, forced to leave their homes when dangerous chemicals leaked from an abandoned dump.

Families living in the area had been plagued by high rates of birth defects and miscarriages. It was a nightmare come true. For years environmentalists have been warning that the dumping of pollution and chemical waste would result in just such a disaster.

In August Carter declared Love Canal a disaster area and the families were evacuated. Some of the homes were boarded up and fenced off, a testament to the sins of the past.

Matters like Love Canal, "Roots," and a protest in Washington engendered the sympathy and anger of the generation, and fired its collective conscience. But repeatedly the members failed to take action and this continual habit of feeling angry but not venting that anger deepened and solidified their sense of impotence.

A few hopeful signs surfaced in 1978.

Women continued to progress in their battle for equality. Six were selected as the first female astronaut candidates, the federal government ruled that hurricanes would no longer get only female names, and a judge ordered that women reporters must be allowed into locker rooms at sporting events.

Still, the average woman was making only 60 percent of what the average man made for comparable work. Ironically, the Susan B. Anthony dollar was released that year honoring the famous suffragette and hardly anyone noticed.

The Camp David Accords were signed by Egyptian President Anwar el-Sadat and Israeli Premier Menachem Begin at a summit in the Maryland mountains. For thirteen days President Carter shuttled tirelessly between the two camps to forge an agreement that was to be a framework for peace in the Middle East. It was a highlight, perhaps the highlight, of the Carter presidency. His term was not yet two years old, but events were primed to move the administration steadily downhill. The nation was slogging into a period of disasters and near disasters.

The greatest tragedy occurred on November 17, 1978, when 911 followers of the Reverend Jim Jones committed murder and mass suicide at their temple in Jonestown, Guyana. Parents fed cyanide-laced Kool-Aid to their children and then gulped it themselves. Those who refused were shot.

A California congressman, Leo Ryan, had flown to Guyana to investigate reports that some cult members, many from the San Francisco area, were being held against their will. Ryan, his party, and some newsmen who tagged along were killed by Jones' followers as they tried to leave. Jones then ordered the mass suicide.

The nation recoiled at the horror of the photos of the rows of bodies, bloating in the hot tropical sun. It was the largest mass suicide of the modern era and few in the United States could understand the mindless devotion that moved over nine hundred people to follow their leader like lemmings to death.

Back in San Francisco murder on a smaller scale would, perhaps, leave a more lasting impression on the generation. Supervisor Harvey Milk and Mayor George Moscone were killed on November 27. Milk was the city's first openly homosexual elected official and a leader of the national gay rights movement. The killer was another supervisor, Dan White, the most openly antigay politician in a city where homosexuals had become a powerful political group.

Within hours more than forty thousand people gathered at city hall and marched in a hushed procession one and a half miles through downtown in a spontaneous outpouring of grief and gay pride.

Much of the generation was enraged at the killings. If the Woodstock generation was about anything, it was about the freedom of people to be themselves, straight or gay, black or white, Us or even Them. Now, again, someone with a gun had broken that commandment.

One of those most deeply touched was Jimmy Holloran. Jimmy, now a doctor and video producer in San Francisco, had interviewed Harvey Milk for a cable show. Milk was someone he respected and admired and he was so upset about the killings that he called his parents back in Washington, D.C., to see if they had heard the news.

Jimmy had withdrawn from his parents since moving to San Francisco.

He called rarely. He returned Christmas and birthday gifts unopened. Yet, he was so moved by Milk's death that he wanted to share his grief with his family. It would be a pivotal moment in Jimmy's life, a catalyst that would help him at last to come to terms with himself.

Jimmy had called his parents a few years earlier, finally to share with them the tortured secret he had kept for so long. "I've got something to tell you," he said. Then he informed them matter-of-factly that he was gay.

This was something that Betty Holloran had suspected but never mentioned. Now she promised to pray for Jimmy, pray that he would change.

"We were just horrified, embarrassed," his mother said. "The stereotype I had of homosexuals was just terrible. Effeminate men who hated women." That wasn't her son. Questions swirled in her mind.

Was it a sin? Was she at fault? What had they done wrong in raising their oldest child?

Betty bought every book she could find on homosexuality. She and her husband prayed for their son, prayed to God to heal him.

Betty also knew that Jimmy's admission lifted a huge weight off his shoulders; that being the oldest, being Catholic, being a role model was a very hard struggle for Jimmy, but not as hard as the struggle that had raged within himself.

Only a few friends knew that Jimmy was homosexual; old, close friends like Stuart Long, his companion at Woodstock, and Ed Mulholland, a buddy from Holy Cross who learned Jimmy was gay the night Jimmy got engaged to Diane.

"Diane called and said they were getting married," Mulholland recalls, "and then Jimmy got on the phone and said, 'I'm gay.'"

Even after moving to San Francisco Jimmy didn't totally accept the fact that he was gay. He lived a fairly straight lifestyle at first, even returned to seeing a psychiatrist, searching for an answer.

"What I should have done," he said years later, "was find a psychiatrist to help me accept myself the way I am and not try to change me."

He was angry with God for making him gay, angry with his parents because they couldn't accept who he was, and angry with the church because it didn't understand. Every once in a while he would think back to the day that as a teenager he confessed to a priest his thoughts about men. In return for his confession all he got from the priest was ridicule.

"It made me feel like the lowest form of life," Jimmy said.

Between 1969 and 1978 almost forty thousand gay men moved to San Francisco, most of them settling around the Castro Street area where Jimmy Holloran had moved. Many, like Jimmy, moved tentatively at first but gradually shifted from self-exploration to self-fulfillment. They had found an area where, for the first time, they were free to be themselves.

Tom Huster, a lawyer, met Jimmy in 1976 at a squash tournament. They became best friends. Still it was two years before Huster learned Jimmy was gay.

"He said he was playing on a softball team and I mentioned that I would like to play," Huster said. "Jimmy said they needed a second baseman and that's my position.

" 'What league is it in?' I asked.

" 'The gay league.'

" 'Are you gay?'

" 'Yes,' said Holloran."

Within a few years the fact that he was gay was the first thing people would learn about Jimmy Holloran.

Once, when the two friends went to a play, Huster introduced Jimmy to another lawyer who had also attended Catholic schools. They began comparing experiences.

"Jimmy started joking about how he thought about going to bed with this priest or that priest," Huster said.

Huster, who is not gay, was embarrassed. But he knew that after living so many years in a closet, Jimmy had become almost fanatic about being open in his life. "Becoming openly gay freed him from a lot of guilt and opened up a lot of possibilities for him. He became very content with who he was, very satisfied with what he was doing in his life."

It's as if Jimmy have moved to California with a piece missing and now it was restored.

San Francisco was a liberating experience, not just for Jimmy but for tens of thousands of other gay men. Being able to walk down the street, holding hands with another man; being able to have an intimate dinner in a romantic restaurant—these were things for which they could be taunted, beaten, or even killed in other communities. It was for this freedom that thousands of gays from across the nation came to San Francisco each year for vacation.

Jimmy talked about starting a tour company for them, hiring buses to take them around to the bars and restaurants.

Jimmy bought a small three-bedroom house and proudly tacked his old Woodstock tickets on the wall leading into the kitchen.

He played squash, then hurt his knee and took up tennis; still the great athlete, he quickly became an expert at that. He organized a gay baseball team. He loved to cook, and enjoyed having friends over, gay and straight.

He worked as a doctor at several hospitals, but practicing medicine was becoming a smaller part of his life. He hoped to give it up completely.

He acted in local plays and once met actor Rock Hudson. To millions, Hudson was the embodiment of the rough-and-tumble romantic leading man. Like Jimmy, and millions of other men in the 70s and 80s, Hudson lived a secret double life. Jimmy asked Hudson why he didn't come out of the closet, and Hudson said that would ruin his career.

Of course, Jimmy had lovers, a number of them. Early on there was Steve, a member of the University of California swimming team. They broke it off and Jimmy saw other men; almost all were younger then he. There was no long-term serious relationship, although friends felt he wanted one.

More than anything else, Jimmy became himself, and adopted a life-style that fit him.

"He was not your typical homosexual, if there is such a thing," said William Bradley, a friend and coworker. "He certainly wasn't your typical San Francisco gay man."

Jimmy didn't adopt the Castro look: jeans, workboots, flannel shirts, hooded sweatshirts, mustaches, and short hair. It was the same look you saw on Christopher Street in New York or at Dupont Circle in Washington, D.C.

In fact, Jimmy seemed to care little about what he wore. He really didn't think about it much, and friends wondered if he even owned a tie.

He drove an old car, a yellow Volkswagen, and eventually bought a van to make it easier to haul video equipment.

Jimmy became a prominent member of the San Francisco gay community but kept much of his past to himself. The people in California never heard the high school hero stories, his victories in sports, his academic achievements.

Jimmy liked to sleep late on Sundays, then sip capuccino and cook eggs Benedict for his friends. And he always liked to party.

"You could walk in on him anytime," Huster said. "He was a very open person."

By 1980 Jimmy was practicing medicine only about one day a week, using it just to pay the bills. Instead, he opened an independent video company, Shotwell Images Group, to create and produce medical and technical programs. Jimmy was finally doing something he enjoyed, something creative.

It was during the early 80s that he helped produce San Francisco's first gay television program, "Starlight Magazine." He also produced footage that was used in the documentary "The Life and Times of Harvey Milk." He was very proud of that.

He did much work for the University of California Medical Center, boring films on how to take out a gall bladder and the like. They paid the bills but weren't something Jimmy really enjoyed.

In the early 80s he also did some filming for the Shanti project, a support group for the terminally ill that would later open shelters for AIDS patients.

He enjoyed the community-oriented work and wanted to do more. Several AIDS videos followed, including one inside a clinic at San Francisco General Hospital. Jimmy spoke with several of the doctors there and got a thorough technical briefing on the growing magnitude of the AIDS problem.

"Jimmy was quite shaken," his friend Bradley recalls. "At that period of the early 80s every gay man I knew in San Francisco figured that if he didn't already have AIDS, he would be next. I got the feeling that's what Jimmy was thinking."

By the beginning of 1979 there were almost daily riots in Tehran, with protesters shouting "Death to the shah" and "Death to America." Americans were only now starting to focus on the problems in Iran. By the end of the year their attention would be riveted on Iran.

The last year of the decade was, in many ways, a difficult year. Unlike 1969, when Americans faced the nation's problems with boldness, Americans in 1979 felt powerless and turned away.

The shah left Iran in January, saying that he was taking a little vacation. Khomeini returned from exile two weeks later, greeted by millions on his arrival in Tehran. The government put in place by the shah fell and the newspaper daily printed lists of those executed.

On February 14 armed mobs attacked the U.S. embassy. Two marines were wounded and over a hundred people, including the ambassador, William Sullivan, were trapped inside for several hours.

Things weren't quiet at home either. In February Billy Carter attended a reception given by the Libyan delegation to the United Nations and was asked about Jewish criticism of his friendship with the outlaw Libyan state. "They can kiss my ass," Billy said. The president tried to dissociate himself from his brother's remarks.

On Wednesday, March 28, 1979, a tiny island in the Susquehanna River just south of Harrisburg, Pennsylvania, became the focal point of a worried nation and of the movement against nuclear power. And for the first time in a long time, the Woodstock generation stirred.

The Three Mile Island nuclear plant had problems with its cooling system and radioactive steam was released into the atmosphere. At the time it was the worst nuclear accident ever. Pregnant women and children within five miles of the plant were moved to safety and evacuation plans prepared for thousands more.

In Washington, D.C., Linda Lotz heard about the accident. She was from Harrisburg and her parents lived only nine miles from the plant. A friend who worked at a local news service called her regularly thoughout the day and read updated reports from the wire services.

Lotz was a twenty-nine-year-old activist working with an organization that was monitoring alleged civil rights violations by the FBI and the CIA. But suddenly, nuclear power became her overriding concern.

A few days before, Linda had seen a movie about a nuclear power plant gone amuck, and now she was worried about her family and friends living in the shadow of TMI's twin cooling towers. She tried to convince them to move, calling her brother, her parents, and then her sister, whose husband had worked building TMI.

"You've got to leave," she told her mother.

"There's been an announcement that there's only been a little problem," her mother said.

"No, mom, it's a major accident."

"I pleaded with them to leave," she recalls. "We offered them our home." But they all decided to stay.

Finally, Linda's sister called her back and told her to stop trying to pressure them to leave; they all felt safe.

The news was released a piece at a time and it wasn't until Walter Cronkite came on in the early evening that many people knew for the first time that TMI had more than a "little problem." Later it was learned that there was serious concern about a meltdown of the core in one of the plant's nuclear reactors.

On Saturday morning Linda's mother looked out on Interstate 83, the superhighway which runs near their home. The normally busy freeway was almost empty. That's when she realized how many people had done what her daughter had advised.

The following weekend, Palm Sunday, opponents of nuclear power held a protest on the steps of the state capitol, in Harrisburg. It was then that people watching the rally came to realize how dramatically different the antinuclear movement was from the antiwar protests half a decade earlier.

This looked more like a gathering of the PTA than a collection of long-haired hippies. Middle-class parents with children were carrying signs and locking arms. Experienced activists like Linda Lotz were also there, but most of the demonstrators had never been in a protest in their lives.

"That's one of the things about the movement as it evolved," Lotz said. "The movement had much more to do with people who were concerned about how this would affect their families and family lives."

She saw a high school classmate at the Palm Sunday protest. The woman had been a loner, never involved in school projects or clubs—"the last person in the world you'd expect to be involved in something like this," Linda said. But there she was, marching with her husband and newborn baby.

"When I saw her," Linda said, "I knew this had really reached into the heart of the community."

These were the members of the Woodstock generation who had never grown their hair long, or never protested against the war, or probably never even tried marijuana. Most had never spoken out before. Many, in fact, had never spoken in public. But in the next few years they would become impassioned advocates for their cause.

Because so many people were personally affected—through lower real estate values, or loss of jobs, or the health risk to themselves and their families—the antinuclear movement managed to gather some momentum in the late 70s when so many other movements were fizzling.

One group of women began an organization named the Middletown Mothers. Middletown is a small community just a few miles from the Three Mile Island plant. For years the members would meet regularly at one of their homes with an official of the Nuclear Regulatory Commission.

Lotz moved back to Harrisburg to become staff director of the Campaign to Stop the Restart of Three Mile Island, a coalition of antinuke groups. She stayed until 1985, only a week before the Nuclear Regulatory Commission approved the restart of TMI's second reactor. She moved to Los Angeles to work with the American Friends Service, a Quaker-sponsored group working on peace and justice issues. By the beginning of 1989 she was working to block construction of a planned nuclear plant in Southern California.

What was the lesson of Three Mile Island?

"Up until that time average people thought that industry and government were benign," she said. "TMI taught them that wasn't necessarily so."

A few months after TMI more than a thousand demonstrators tried unsuccessfully to shut down the New York Stock Exchange. Chanting "No nukes," they linked arms in an attempt to block the entrances. Later hundreds of thousands marched through midtown Manhattan.

The protesters and the issues they raised blocked several proposed nuclear power plants, and pushed the government to enact stricter safety regulations for the nuclear industry. The antinuke movement was one of the few things to truly touch the generation's soul during these years. Although most members would simply shake their heads and turn away, it was undeniable that the sleeping giant had stirred and raised its arm in protest, and that a nation had listened.

For a while at TMI there were worries that the accident exposed part of the reactor's nuclear core which could have lead to a tragedy of catastrophic dimensions. Ironically, that was the plot of *The China Syndrome*, the film that Linda Lotz had seen and that had been completed just before the Three Mile Island accident. The movie starred Michael Douglas, Jane Fonda, and Jack Lemmon, and the plot revolved around dangerous cooling problems at a nuclear power plant, problems that were kept hidden by a greedy corporation.

The China Syndrome also marked a mood in Hollywood once again to tackle serious social issues in a noticeable, if limited, way.

An Unmarried Woman, starring Jill Clayburgh, told women it was okay to be divorced. *Norma Rae*, with Sally Field, depicted the struggles of a union organizer in a southern mill town.

But more important, the Vietnam War was distant enough that the nation could start examining it in movies. *The Deer Hunter*, starring Robert DeNiro, won the Oscar for best picture of 1978, and *Coming Home* featured Oscar-winning preformances by Jane Fonda and Jon Voight. Both films dealt with the impact of Vietnam on those who fought and their families at home.

These were exhausting films for many in the Woodstock generation. The memories were still fresh enough and the emotions raw enough that viewing them the first time was emotionally fatiguing.

The nation had not yet dealt with its feelings about the Vietnam War, which would remain a festering sore in the national consciousness. These films raised uncomfortable questions about the war itself and the treatment of returning Vietnam veterans. But it would be years before the Woodstock generation could really deal openly with the war.

John Wayne died of cancer that summer, 1979, and the nation went through another strange period of mourning that pointed out the difference between young and old. As when Elvis died, many mourned; the Duke, the Great American Hero, had passed from the scene just when America needed a hero most. And, as when Elvis died, many in the Woodstock generation did not share in this feeling. John Wayne was the hero of the World War II generation, not the Woodstock generation. In fact, in some ways his militant, right-wing macho image symbolized things they despised.

By June less than one in three Americans approved of Carter's perfor-

Michael Lang rode about Max Yasgur's farm on his motorcycle, tearing down orders to stop working on the Woodstock festival site.

Photo by: Richard Gilbert
Twenty years later, Lang has hardly changed; and neither have his problems as he tries to solve last-minute glitches that threatened the second Woodstock.

Photo by: Henry Diltz
It was only by luck that Michael Lang found the natural bowl that instantly became home to the third largest city in New York State two decades ago.

Photo by: Henry Diltz
"By the time we got to Woodstock, we were half a million strong, and everywhere was a song and celebration."

Photo by: Henry Diltz
It wasn't until the final day that people could get close enough to the stage to actually see the performers clearly.

Photo by: Henry Diltz
The concert crowd formed the perfect organism: there was never enough food, and yet everybody ate.

Photo by: Philip Lerman
Once a *New York Times* rewrite man, "Hateman" moved to Berkeley to enliven the streets—
as he still does—with his message of true love: "I hate you! Have a lousy day!"

Jimmy Holloran was an All–New England baseball player at Holy Cross and played in the college World Series. Yet, he kept his secret life buried inside.

The mass card from Jimmy Holloran's funeral. His parents bravely spoke about his illness and wrote about his death.

Dr. James F. Holloran III

Born February 16, 1942

Died April 17, 1986

Peter Max and his art. He gave up his Rolls-Royce and entourage in the early 70s to concentrate on his art.

Max at the White House in 1981. He painted the Statue of Liberty on a platform guarded by Marines.

Max with Max (the one on the left is a photo): Twenty years ago his name and art adorned everything from sneakers to sunglasses; while Peter Max clothing is finding a resurgence, he promises that "it will never get as big as it used to be."

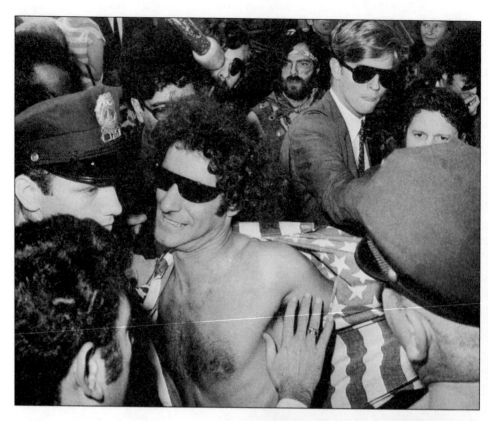

Bettman Archives
Abbie Hoffman in the famed shirt that often got him arrested for defacing the American flag: "I believe in the spirit of Abbie," said his brother Jack. "He was a real American patriot."

Photo by: Steven M. Falk
An Abbie for the 80s, fighting for his latest environmental cause: "This is my career. This is why I'm here on the planet."

mance in office. The president's ratings would further decline as people found themselves plagued by issues that affected their everyday lives. That was one reason why Carter's great social concern, his caring for the world, failed to capture the hearts and minds of the generation—the president talked about Afghanistan while Americans waited in line for gas.

In July gasoline became scarce again and many states returned to selling it on odd and even days. The annual inflation rate, which soared to 13 percent, contributed to a feeling of pessimism in the nation.

President Carter decided he had to talk to the nation about its problems and went on the air at 10 P.M. Sunday, July 15. The speech would be forever called his "malaise in society" speech. Carter never mentioned the word malaise, but that's the way it came to be remembered, and the way everyone felt when it was over.

Carter spoke of a "crisis of confidence . . . that strikes at the very heart and soul and spirit of our national will." And he added, "The gap between our citizens and our government has never been so wide."

Carter meant to inspire the nation, but his sermonizing style backfired. Watching the speech that night, people got a feeling of depression and impotence. Whose fault was it that there was a gap between the government and the people? Who the hell was president?

The Woodstock generation had never heard a president talk so bluntly and so openly about the problems facing the nation.

Two days later Carter called for the resignation of his entire cabinet and White House staff. He quickly reappointed all but a few who had come into his disfavor. Columnists and analysts called it a cheap gimmick and the resulting confusion within the administration was criticized by Americans and ridiculed abroad.

This was also the tenth anniversary of the Woodstock festival—and boy, did the generation need something to bring it back, some way to revisit the garden. There were those who tried to organize a reunion—a few thousand did show up in Bethel—but most of the Woodstock generation was simply too busy to notice.

Michael Lang didn't want a reunion. "I didn't want to do the 'Son of Woodstock.'"

Michael had gone to California shortly after Woodstock. "It took me about six months to find out I was a New Yorker." Lang said, and he came back.

He consulted on shows and festivals, booked some acts, and worked in the music industry he loved, using the experience he had gained from the Woodstock concert. This led to an offer from Paramount to run its record company, but Michael turned it down. He wanted to deal with music, not budgets.

Then, a couple of years later, he changed his mind. Like many in the Woodstock generation, the man who made it happen at Bethel felt it was time to start building something, and "I felt that a record company would be a good thing to build."

He started Sunshine Records with the Gulf and Western Company. "The whole thing was a surprise to me; I never thought I would be in business, I never wanted to be, and yet, there I was."

To his surprise he enjoyed it, particularly the music and the performers. One day a singer walked into his office with no appointment and no sample tape of his work.

"He just went to the piano and started playing," Michael said. It wasn't really Lang's kind of music but he felt the singer had talent, so he took him upstairs to a studio, they recorded a demonstration tape, and Michael offered him a contract that day. The unknown singer was Billy Joel, and Lang still has some of Joel's gold records mounted on his office wall.

Lang left Gulf and Western in 1976 and signed a production deal to work with independent acts and with promoters to set up concerts and festivals around the world—Germany, England, Canada—and across the United States.

Not long after he left Gulf and Western Michael met Joe Cocker's lawyer. Lang knew Cocker, of course. Joe had performed at Woodstock where his herky-jerky style prompted a fan to say, seriously, that he performed quite well considering he had cerebral palsy.

Cocker was looking for a new manager, the lawyer said. Would Michael be interested?

Michael agreed and has represented Cocker ever since, along with other performers off and on, and along with helping to plan and stage concerts and produce records.

Then came 1979 and many asked Michael, "What are you going to do for the tenth anniversary of Woodstock?" The answer: nothing.

Michael did have a recurring dream, however. It began in 1969, only a few days after Woodstock, when he was sitting around with Mel Lawrence and a few other people who helped put on the festival.

"What do we do next?" someone asked.

Slowly the idea evolved. What about a rolling Woodstock? We can put everyone on boxcars and when we get into towns the boxcars unfold into stages. We'll roll across America, from city to city.

Michael called it the Train.

The Train almost rolled in 1976 to celebrate the nation's bicentennial.

The ABC television network was close to sponsoring it, but the deal fell through.

We'll get it going sometime, Michael said.

Lang kept the dream alive. But years later he would come up with something even bigger.

Big things continued to happen in Tehran. On November 4 militant students seized the U.S. embassy again, taking sixty-three hostages. A few were released several weeks later but Iran threatened to hold the rest for a public trial.

Carter froze Iranian assets in the U.S. but beyond that appeared virtually helpless. Each evening on the news Americans watched the protests from Tehran and the students carrying banners that read: Khomeini Struggles, Carter Trembles.

There was a ripple effect. The U.S. embassy in Pakistan was destroyed and the State Department urged Americans in ten Muslim countries to leave as soon as possible. The U.S. embassy in Libya was stormed a few days later and anti-American protests flared in India, Bangladesh, and Turkey.

The U.S. was outraged but powerless to help the captives except to tie yellow ribbons around trees as reminders of the hostages and as symbols of their support.

Ronald Reagan and Edward Kennedy both jumped into the race for president. Reagan criticized Carter, saying the nation had lost confidence in its leaders—almost exactly what Carter had said four years earlier.

The hostage crisis would continue for more than a year. And during that period Jimmy Carter would frequently be referred to as the "fifty-second hostage." He remained for much of the time sequestered in the White House, guarded by the Georgia mafia, trying desperately to work his way out of the quagmire.

Finally he attempted one desperate gamble. Helicopters filled with commandos were sent to Iran to free the hostages. The mission was called off when several of the copters had mechanical trouble. The others landed in the desert to refuel. One of the choppers collided with a transport plane. It burst into flames and eight American servicemen died.

It was a fiasco, the absolute low point made worse by the fact that the Iranians released macabre photos of the disaster focusing on the scorched bodies of the dead American soliders. In one photo, a charred arm is seen reaching up as if pleading for help.

Imagine No More

When you hit bottom, there's nowhere to go but up.

The first tiny shift in The Force, the first symbolic hint of the road back up, came from an ecologist-activist-humorist by the name of Barry Freed. He was part of a successful campaign to save the St. Lawrence River, a man who sometimes seemed to resemble the on-the-lam Abbie Hoffman; he would turn himself over to the authorities.

Just days before, Hoffman's latest book, titled *Soon to Be a Major Motion Picture*, had been reviewed by the highly esteemed John Leonard in the *New York Times*. And the highly esteemed John Leonard seemed to like, almost seemed to miss, the on-the-lam Abbie Hoffman.

"In any other American age this Dennis the Menace might have been a Mark Twain or a Will Rogers," Leonard wrote. "He would never have been a Big Bill Haywood or a Walter Lippmann. He would like to be perceived as a cap of cyanide; he is thought of, instead, as a bag of pistachios. He didn't do much harm, and he feels bad for not having done enough."

Leonard even lamented not having Abbie Hoffman to talk to in person.

That review appeared on Monday, September 1, 1980. Two days later, he would have the "bag of pistachios" to talk to again. Freed—Hoffman— gave himself up after more than six years of hiding.

"When I was arrested, the war in Vietnam was still going on, Rockefeller's drug laws were just going into effect, and cocaine was considered the equivalent of heroin." Hoffman said at the time of his surrender. "I think a lot has changed since then."

It appeared to Hoffman that the get-tough 70s were giving way to a period that was funnier, looser. It was a good time to come back out into the sun, he thought.

Hoffman's sense of an opening-up society was no more accurate than Lenny Bruce's prediction two decades earlier that all those dope-smoking law students would become lawyers, and congressmen, and judges, and that they would legalize marijuana. It was not a cause they stayed faithful to.

For in the early 80s the nation, and the Woodstock generation, were interested not so much in "opening up" as in "getting away"—from the malaise, the boredom, the ennui, the problems of the 70s. Carter was a leader who spoke to the Woodstock generation's values, but did not inspire it to action; as a result, the generation was ready for a president who would move it—even if the values were totally wrong.

Nevertheless, the return of Abbie Hoffman symbolized the first hint of the reawakening of the sleeping giant that was the Woodstock generation. For once, one of the generation's own leaders was returning, instead of disappearing or getting shot.

Abbie Hoffman was forty-four years old at the decade's turn. Immediately it was clear that the jokester, the prankster, had remained faithful to his causes—and to his PR sense of the media: before Abbie's surrender, an associate reportedly called both the *New York Times* and Barbara Walters to arrange interviews.

He would return to his task and causes and even find new ones in the years ahead. He would go back to living modestly—although *modest* is a word difficult to apply to Hoffman—living in a converted turkey coop in New Hope, Pennsylvania. The hair, still flyaway, would become speckled with gray. A scraggly salt-and-pepper beard would frame a lined face. But what people would still notice first were Hoffman's eyes, still those laughing, infectious, happy eyes; the eyes of the child inside still following the electrical impulses of what he calls the "Rebel Gene."

Hoffman had been underground for almost seven years, but even while hiding Abbie couldn't change the habits of a lifetime. He was supposed to be keeping quiet; he was, after all, a fugitive from the law, still facing drug charges from the early 70s.

But Abbie Hoffman couldn't.

"I came back because I found myself always organizing people against some injustice." Instead of lying low, he fought censorship in Miami, corrupt military in Guatemala, and helped lead a movement to save the St. Lawrence River.

Living underground was a kind of therapy for Abbie. He learned who he was and what he was supposed to do with life and that he had the "Rebel Gene."

"So that's who I am; this is my job," Hoffman explains. "I'm supposed to do this. I discovered myself when I went underground."

Changed outside by plastic surgery, part of his disguise, and changed inside by the struggle of living underground, the happy hippie returned to do battle, Rebel Gene at the ready.

And there would be much to rebel against, and at least a few to join him. For as the decade dawned, so dawned the Reagan revolution.

Certainly, many in the Woodstock generation came to be enthralled by Reagan—even vote for him—thanks to his feel-good message and economic programs that put more money into their pockets. Others, like Hoffman, grew increasingly infuriated with him over the next eight years, seeing him as the president who dismantled social programs and civil rights legislation at every turn.

There were other tremors in The Force early in 1980. Among the sadder was the death, January 19, of Supreme Court Justice William O. Douglas. Very likely many at Woodstock, and many who subscribed to the ideals it represented, weren't paying enough attention back then to know that Douglas was their champion. Those who did remembered him as an ardent champion of civil liberties, a conservationist, and a defender of the individual's right to dissent.

When his tenure on the Court had ended several years earlier, it was after more than thirty-six years of speaking in a voice that the Woodstock generation never realized was so much like its own. Justice Hugo Black once said that his friend "must have come into this world with a rush, and his first cry must have been a protest against something he saw at a glance was wrong or unjust."

In July 1980 the shah of Iran died in exile in Egypt, bringing fresh hope that, finally, the American hostages in Iran would be released. Tehran quickly dashed those hopes, demanding that first the shah's family and fortune be returned.

The "most trusted man in America," Walter Cronkite, announced his retirement in 1980, making front-page news across the nation. Millions in the Woodstock generation had grown up watching "Uncle Walter" hosting the CBS "Evening News." There the generation first learned the frustration of Vietnam and the seriousness of Three Mile Island. Dan Rather replaced Cronkite in the CBS anchor chair, but not in the hearts of viewers.

College campuses had been changing. How much was shown in a poll by the American Council on Education and UCLA. College freshmen were now more interested in making money and achieving status than they had been at any time in the past decade.

It came as little suprise, then, that the *Berkeley Barb*, a leading underground newspaper of the 60s with a nationwide circulation, ended publication because of lack of interest.

But 1980 was an election year, and except for Iran most of the big news was coming out of Washington.

Teddy Kennedy—if nothing else, a hero-by-association for the Woodstock Nation, and one of the few voices left for the kinds of issues they cared so strongly about so many years ago—was already slipping behind President Carter in the primaries, and would soon fall by the wayside.

But Carter was having trouble in Washington. A proposed jobs bill, which would allocate $2 billion more for out-of-work young people, stalled in Congress for fear it would worsen inflation. Carter lobbied for it in a January 23 press conference, saying that jobs were a more crucial problem than inflation. Just two days later, however, the Labor Department reported the largest increase in inflation in thirty-three years.

Jimmy never was one for good timing.

Ronnie was.

Picture the scene in America, 1980. The country was tired, tired of tensions escalating with the Soviet Union after the invasion of Afghanistan, tired of the grain embargo, tired of Jimmy's malaise, tired of inflation, anxious about a recession and unemployment, and fed up with its politicians in general.

So many foulups occurred it was impossible to keep up with who was screwing up where. The rescue attempt of the American hostages in Tehran turned into a tragedy. An underground nuclear missile silo exploded; fortunately, no radioactivity was released. About the same time, U.S. nuclear forces went on alert against a potential Soviet strike; the Soviet attack turned out to be a simple computer error.

Miami was the scene of three days of riots sparked by the acquittal of four police officers charged with killing a black insurance executive. More than a dozen people were killed and hundreds injured. Property damage hit $100 million.

A U.S. senator and seven congressmen were caught in the net of the FBI's Abscam sting—and again, the nation watched its institutions deteriorating on TV. Abscam, short for "Arab Scam," was a two-year investigation by the FBI. Secretly made videotapes caught the lawmakers accepting bribe money from undercover agents posing as Arab sheiks in exchange for political favors.

The press, given a high-voltage charge by Watergate and made even more cynical in the intervening years, attacked the story vigorously, airing many of the details even before the trials were held. This time, however, the public turned on the press.

In a 1980 Roper poll only one in five Americans expressed a "great deal of confidence" in the press—down sharply from the Watergate years. Even Ralph Nader spoke out against the information on Abscam that was leaking to the press: "In the minds of millions of people these guys are guilty and they haven't even been charged."

Maybe the nation was just fed up with years and years of bad news. Or maybe it saw the press becoming increasingly aggressive and perhaps a little unfair. Certainly, there were those in the media who were becoming concerned about the growing fixation of reporters and editors on ferreting out bad news, even the most minor bad news, not for the public good but because it was seen as a path to promotion or media stardom.

Ronald Reagan had great timing.

And never was his timing as good as it was on February 23, 1980.

A debate scheduled between Republican frontrunners George Bush and Ronald Reagan was stalled because of confusion over whether the other Republican candidates should be allowed to join in. Bush and Reagan had paid for their own debate without including the others.

Finally the debate was about to begin, and Reagan tried to explain to the crowd what the confusion was all about.

The moderator tried to cut Reagan off. The moment was tense. And in the first great "sound bite" of the 80s, Reagan introduced the Clint Eastwood style the nation would later come to know so well.

Angry, jaw set, he turned toward the moderator: "I paid for this microphone." Digging in his heels to the cheers of the crowd, he spoke directly to it: "I thought some explanation was due you."

More cheers.

The moment, the momentum were lost for Bush—perhaps the nomination. No one would remember that the main argument between Bush and Reagan was over a proposed tax cut. Everyone would remember the tough guy from the West.

You could almost hear the strains of the guitar playing, the credits rolling for the western movie that Reagan would bring us, starring, of course, himself, and Nancy as Miss Kitty. You could almost see him pulling out his six-guns and mowing down the bad guys. He was creating an image: no bullshit, decisive, a man of action.

It was an image for the 80s. Even the Woodstock generation was swept away.

A week later Gerald Ford asserted that Reagan could not win, and hinted he might be available. "Every place I go and everything I hear, there is the growing, growing sentiment that Governor Reagan cannot win the election," said the former president.

There was a growing, growing sentiment all right. Reagan locked up the nomination exactly eighty-eight days later.

John B. Anderson, a Republican congressman, thought he saw a counterforce also, particularly in the Woodstock generation, which was fed up with Carter but, perhaps, not ready for Reagan's conservative brand of government.

"Too many people in our nation are disillusioned with the prospective choices our party structures are offering." Anderson said that April in announcing his campaign as a third-party candidate. Anderson, too, would be lost in the onrushing Reagan Revolution.

Reagan had great timing.

The national malaise spread like the ashes from Mount Saint Helens, which had erupted in May.

The nation's Olympians felt politics intrude into their old world, which was supposed to be safe from politics and national self-interest. President Carter proposed a boycott of the 1980 Summer Games in Moscow to protest the Soviet invasion of Afghanistan, and the U.S. Olympic Committee went along.

This was particularly galling to a nation that just a few months earlier had thrilled to the winter Olympics in Lake Placid, New York. The United States' victory over the Soviet Union on its way to a gold medal in hockey, combined with speed-skater Eric Heiden's five-gold-medal performance, had touched off patriotic celebrations across the nation.

At a bar in Rochester, New York, patrons avidly following the winter Olympics illegally intercepted the network feed of one of the ice hockey games so they could cheer the U.S. team live.

At Radio City Music Hall, in New York, the audience interrupted a performance of Snow White and began singing "The Star-Spangled Banner."

But thanks to Carter's boycott, there would be no shouts of "USA…USA" during the summer Olympics.

"They've gone against what they stood for," said an angry Bill Rogers, the great marathon runner, "which was not to allow any racial, religious, or political pressures to affect them."

But Rogers was ignoring the fact that the political pressures were affecting everyone.

In July 1980, President Carter proposed the reinstitution of draft registration. One would think this should have sent electric shock waves through the Woodstock generation. What did we fight for? What did we march for? But the response from the protesters of yore: No thanks; we gave in the 60s.

Of course, the entire Woodstock generation didn't feel that way. There were some protests: sit-ins in Hartford and Boston, a march in 100-degree heat in New York. The *New York Times* reported a conversation at the main New York post office between a protester and a registrant that sounded right out of another era.

"Do you want to go?" Linda Owoie said to John P. Mele as he started writing out his name in block letters.

"It depends on what it's for," Mele answered, continuing to fill out his form.

Owoie: "Any war is bad."

Mele: "Not if it's against fascism and dictatorship."

Owoie, jabbing a finger at Mele's registration card: "This is fascism right now."

Although some cries of "Hell no, we won't go" rang in the streets, something was missing. For one, the main rallying cry of the 60s—"One-two-three-four, we don't want your fucking war"—no longer applied. There was no fucking war. And this is a key to why the generation became less active in causes: having seen the monster in the 60s, and having slain the dragon of war, all else seemed a bit washed out, colorless.

The issues that would come now, and later—draft registration, homelessness, acid rain, even the nuclear threat—failed to grip the nation with the same intensity. Even though some sins of the past had caught up with us, the generation paid little heed. By now 710 families had been evacuated from Love Canal in Niagara Falls, New York, where a toxic waste dump was endangering life. Ripples of protest over Love Canal continued but created no strong, lasting environmental consciousness.

For years the United States considered itself big brother to the world. Now a foreign missionary, Mother Teresa, was visiting the poor in New York City.

The Woodstock generation was experiencing the same feeling that people who have been in space talk about: after such exhilaration nothing seems to measure up. The inability to experience pleasure is called anhedonia. For the Woodstock generation there was what might be coined anrabia—the inability to experience rage.

And there was more than that. In many ways, the Woodstock generation had grown up a little too much to see the world in black-and-white terms anymore. The protests over Carter's draft registration were tinged more and more with shades of gray—in the hair of the ex-Woodstockers and in the arguments they put forth.

In fact, the key debate over draft registration was whether women should be included. While feminists staunchly opposed the prospect of the draft at all, they cautiously backed the idea that if there was such a draft it had to include females. This was great fodder for anti-libbers like Phyllis Schlafly, who saw the argument as proof that backers of the Equal Rights Amendment wanted to draft women and put them in the army alongside men.

This was, of course, not what feminists meant at all. But the argument became muddled; there were challenges to registration on the grounds of sexual discrimination. It became a constitutional question.

If the Woodstock generation was somewhat lacking in political spirit, the young people of the 80s were devoid of it altogether. A national survey by *The World Almanac* that year sought out the heroes of Young America. The number one hero in the United States of America was actor Burt Reynolds.

Burt Reynolds!

He was followed by actor Steve Martin, skater Eric Heiden, and actors Eric Estrada and Alan Alda. Only one woman made the top ten—young TV star Kristy McNichol. The only nonentertainers in the entire top thirty were astronaut Neil Armstrong, writers Alex Haley and Judy Blume, and "Peanuts" creator Charles Schulz.

No business leaders, no scientists, and certainly no politicians.

This was a generation primed for a new hero and one was on the way. It would love Ronald Reagan, and follow him back to a conservative, straight, Eisenhower-like nation. He would free us from depression even as the hostages would be freed from Tehran on the day Reagan became president, after 444 days of captivity.

There is no overstating the importance of the hostage crisis on the nation's psyche. Yellow ribbons were hung from trees and poles across America. At noon every day hundreds of radio stations played the national anthem to honor the hostages. Every night Dan Rather ended the CBS "Evening News" by announcing the number of days the hostages had been held captive. A few hours later Ted Koppel brought us "America Held Hostage."

President Carter continued to be held hostage, too, sequestering himself in the White House for much of the time, adding to the feeling of impotence. In the end, it was the hostage crisis, more than anything else, that primed the nation for Ronald Reagan's tough-guy conservative message.

In music, different movements were afoot, traveling in directions that were anything but conservative. Ironically, they would be totally misunderstood by the older generation—the Woodstock generation now bore that title.

The musical movements were the remaining fragments of punk, the never-ending roar of heavy metal, and the now-emerging, intriguing new wave.

With the snowballing growth of commercialism in the music industry in the 80s, it was becoming virtually impossible for a new band without clear and immediate commercial potential to get a record out. Still, some groundbreaking music managed to thrive.

The punk movement was not really a success, except in its influence on other music. The prototype 70s punk band, the Sex Pistols, were much more successful in England than in the United States. But in the 80s the refreshing rebellious spirit of their music was cited as an influence by straight rock-and-roll bands like the Rolling Stones, whose song "Shattered" would carry the pulsing punk rhythms.

The punk bands were bands a parent could hate. They had been born in revolt against the mind-numbing disco beat that couldn't offend anybody. Punk kids were the outcasts, the fringe, the nerds. They were not the mainstream kids, the kids on the football teams.

It was a music that did not attract the Woodstock generation, although its fuck-you attitude carried an anti-establishment ring that might have had some resonance.

What the Woodstock generation would mistake for punk—and one of the things that drove it away from punk—was heavy-metal music. Heavy metal was very different from punk and would remain strong through the 80s. It was a white, male, WASP, middle-American music, whose audience was mostly under 20.

The message of punk was political, a message of anarchy and changing the system, whereas heavy metal was as regimented as IBM. It had a strict neo-Nazi dress code of tight leather and chains. And its message: Party hardy.

The rebellion of punk was a rebellion against society. The rebellion of heavy metal was a rebellion against going to school when you could be out getting drunk.

Women were absorbed into the punk movement. Heavy metal was sexist, seeing women merely as objects of desire.

Punk was a thunder-drumming British-born movement. Heavy metal was a screeching-guitar American-born movement.

Punk was nihilist. Heavy metal was fun.

Those who charged that heavy metal was antisocial and satanic had been fooled by heavy metal's put-on. It was strictly a commercial act. "Any of these groups that make a passing reference to Satan wouldn't know the devil if he bit them," said rock critic Edna Gundersen. "The heavy-metal musicians are rejected by the punk crowd as selling out."

But out of punk music would come an artsy, intellectual, creative sound called new wave. Its words were more challenging, its melodies more complex and innovative.

It would give some alternative to the middle-of-the road pop-rock that still dominated in the early 80s. For five years new-wave music had grown: Talking Heads, Blondie, the Ramones, the Cars, the Police, Devo. It was smart. It was interesting. It broke new ground.

For the most part, though, the Woodstock generation stayed with what was safe. A few years later it would discover these bands, especially the Talking Heads. For now, it puzzled over punk, ignored heavy metal, and failed to catch the new wave. The generation listened to the ballads and pop that flooded the airwaves and charts; listened to the safe, catchy tunes of Genesis and Yes; and wondered why no one was making creative music anymore.

The tastes in music reflected the tastes of the times. The Woodstock generation had lost its ability to take chances, musically, politically, socially. It was looking for security and stability, something strong and safe to believe in and be guided by. It got it.

On November 4, Ronald Reagan beat Jimmy Carter in a landslide of such magnitude that Carter began his concession speech at 9:50 P.M. Eastern Standard Time—even before the polls were closed in several western states.

A key moment of the campaign had come in Cleveland a few weeks earlier, when Reagan queried Americans during a debate: "Ask yourself, are you really better off than you were four years ago?"

The answer, the election results showed, was a resounding no.

The liberal fire of Woodstock had been suffocated by the realities of life, and would be nearly extinguished by the conservative wave of Ronald Reagan. Despite what the hippies of the 60s hoped, the bomber jet planes did not turn into butterflies after all.

And those who didn't believe it then, felt it deeply a month later. The generation was just beginning to re-create itself in a new, tougher 80s image. But one massive shock remained.

Although the election of a conservative, strong-defense president may have sounded the political end of the Woodstock generation's movement, it's spiritual end would come December 8, 1980 at 10:45 P.M.

The sound of four gunshots echoed off the buildings on West Seventy-second Street in New York City. They echo still.

The Dolphins were playing the Raiders on "Monday Night Football." Between plays, Howard Cosell interrupted with an announcement.

The Woodstock generation was dumbfounded, got up, walked across the room, and called itself on the phone.

Because of the time of night, many missed the news. But a sad telephone network was born, long and tentacled and reaching to the far corners of the country. The telephone sounds frightening and urgent when it rings late at night, and the calls that night were filled with fright and urgency as well.

"Hello?"

"Hi. It's me."

"What's the matter?"

A long pause.

"My God, what's the matter?"

"I just heard on the news. John Lennon is dead. Somebody shot John Lennon."

The calls continued into the night. A generation raised on the deaths of Kennedy, King, Kennedy, and so many others knew the difference between murder and assassination. This was assassination. And this generation knew that assassinations change the lives of everyone who cares. Forever.

Those who had been watching the football game suddenly realized that they would forever remember this moment, and forever remember it imbued with the annoying nasal hyperbolic babble of Howard Cosell. It bordered on a humor that even Lennon might have appreciated.

Then the next realization hit: the Beatles would never get back together.

It was an embarrassingly selfish thought, like realizing that for ten years you had harbored a secret wish to see the Beatles together one more time, as though that would bring back not just a group but something more, something you'd lost along the way. And now it wouldn't happen. Ever.

And so the calls went on into the night. People needed to communicate with those they had grown up with, listened to Beatles records with, spent allowances together on Beatle singles and lunchboxes and Beatle magazines and buttons. People who were there when you wanted to grow your hair long and your parents said no and you did anyway—the first sign of rebellion.

These were people who knew that your favorite Beatle—everyone had a favorite—used to be Paul, but in the 70s you tired of his silly love songs. People who knew how much you hated Yoko because you thought she broke up the Beatles.

The Beatles meant more to the Woodstock generation than, perhaps, any other single group, singer, politician, event, notion, book, movie, slogan, photo, T-shirt, poster, lyric, or hand gesture. They transcended the Us and Them split of the generation.

The Beatles had come onto the American scene in the pivotal year of 1963. With their hair that then seemed long—and seems so neat and tidy in retrospect—with their music, and their spirit, they ushered in an age with such command that even when they broke up, shortly after Woodstock, they remained an integral part of the generation's consciousness.

And as they grew, their music changed, and it was this music that led the generation through its changes. More than any other album, "Sergeant Pepper" was the music of the decade. More than any other individuals, the Beatles were the voice of the decade.

Dylan was more thoughtful, but so damned confusing. The Stones were more raucous, but better suited for a party. The Beatles' lyrics were pulled apart, played backward, and argued about incessantly. Was Paul dead? Did Lucy in the Sky with Diamonds stand for its initials, LSD, or, as John always insisted, was the name simply taken from a drawing his son Julian brought home from school?

And under their endless cascade of images, of tangerine trees and marmalade skies, sat four men with public personalities as distinct as those of the Four Horsemen of the Apocalypse.

Paul was the cute one, Ringo the funny one, George the quiet one. Paul would take us on happy pop-song trips through the 80s. Ringo would act, and sing, and always make us laugh. George would get heavy, and make us think about Bangladesh.

And John?

John, with his marvelous quick wit, his love of the absurd, added the darker side of the Force. In so many of the songs that Paul would give a pop lilt to, John would add a counterpoint of irony and black humor. Paul would write: "We can work it out." John would add the bridge: "Life is very short, and there's no time...."

John was the intellectual, the Thinking Man's Beatle, the poet, the peacenik, the radical.

The soul.

That is how it went, on those telephone lines on that cold December night. People now in their late twenties, early thirties, and suddenly feeling very old, gathered in front of the Dakota—John's apartment building on Central Park West—where he had been shot.

Many would sneer at the generation for pouring out such emotion over a mere singer, for even daring to equate his death with the deaths of the true leaders of the time. But they did not understand: this was not the death of a singer.

This was the death of youth.

They were drawn to the Dakota by a need to feel, physically and tangibly, a part of an event that had killed something inside them as well.

First on the scene were eyewitnesses to the shooting, then people who had been a few blocks away and heard the shots. By midnight people were coming from all over the city. More than a thousand people, some crying, some dazed, some singing John's songs, first one person, then groups:

Imagine all the people
living life in peace
You may say I'm the dreamer
But I'm not the only one

I hope someday you'll join us
and the world will live as one.

And the sadness, of singing songs of hope and peace and realizing that
the voice had died, brought tears anew. All along the streets around the
Dakota, people began hugging, and praying, and chanting: "All we are
saying is give peace a chance."

In the days that followed, people struggled to understand what had
happened and to understand why John Lennon's death meant so much to
them. The generation now understood the outpouring of emotion from
their older brothers and sisters when Elvis had died. But they understood
that this was different, too, because Lennon was not merely the King of
Rock and Roll; Elvis would always retain that title. Lennon was something
more. The Beatles were something more. The 60s were something more.

The next day, radio stations across the country and in cities around the
world—from Rio to Belgrade—turned to all-Beatles programming. "American Pie," a song Don McLean wrote about Buddy Holly's death—another
death in another time—was borrowed to help express the moment:

I can't remember if I cried
When I read about his widowed bride;
But something touched me deep inside
The day the music died.

Details began surfacing about Mark David Chapman, the man charged
with killing Lennon. Most ironic, and most discussed, was the fact that he
was carrying a copy of *Catcher in the Rye*, a book considered a seminal work
for the generation. J. D. Salinger's fascinating tale depicts a confused youth
trying to learn what coming of age is all about.

The shooting also touched off a national call for handgun control.

Outgoing President Jimmy Carter paid tribute to Lennon: "His spirit,
the spirit of the Beatles—brash and earnest, ironic and idealistic all at once—
became the spirit of a whole generation."

And many said the spirit of this brash, earnest, ironic, idealistic generation died on that hard day's night.

For some, it had an opposite effect.

Ken Kesey had been watching that Dolphins-Raiders game, and had
learned the news from Howard Cosell. A few days later he was in a bar with
journalist Hunter S. Thompson, who was in Eugene to talk to a journalism
class at the University of Oregon.

Thompson wondered aloud when it might be his turn for an assassin's
bullet; Lord knows he had "pissed off quite a few citizens in my time."

"But you've never disappointed them," Kesey said.

Still, Kesey was disturbed. Unlike Lennon, he had stopped nourishing his own idealistic fantasies somewhere along the line. What would Lennon think of him, when the revolutionary roll is called up yonder, if he had failed to nourish a fantasy or two?

This is the effect that Lennon's death had on Kesey. It reminded him of the importance of pie-in-the-sky revolutionary fantasies. Kesey had a fear of emptiness, and Lennon's death reminded him of that fear: reminded him that if you fail to nourish your fantasies, they grow cold.

So in spite of his own wish to avoid the crosshairs of notoriety, an idea popped into Kesey's head. "Maybe," he said, "it's time to talk a little sky-pie again."

In New York crowds continued to gather at the Dakota. Some thought about what Lennon had meant to them. Some thought about what he had meant to their generation.

John Leonard wrote in the *New York Times* of what it meant to understand that the Beatles were now and forever torn asunder: "Not quite so obvious . . . is the weird sense of betrayal many of us feel . . . because, somehow, they seem to have let us down.

"They seemed for a time . . . to be the perfect commune imagined by the 1960s when, the fever told us, politics and culture coincided and were transubstantial. Thanks, we needed that. And then they split. They had no right to do so. We lived on the joy of their ensemble. Happiness is not a warm gun."

There was no funeral. The following Sunday, at Yoko Ono's request, there was a ten-minute silent memorial. No one knows how many gathered all around the world; the largest gathering was in Central Park, near the building where Lennon had lived and died.

By noon more than a hundred thousand had gathered there. At 2 P.M., the appointed hour, a sad, thick silence descended, punctuated only by the whirring of police and news helicopters above.

David Colton, a reporter for the Westchester-Rockland Newspapers, was in one of those helicopters. He wasn't sure what he was supposed to write, or why he was there. He had been through a lot in the eleven years since attending Woodstock. He had married, and he'd struggled, and tried to survive. He had worked as a garbageman, and got into journalism late. He was starting to do well. He had seen liberal idealism become pragmatism and the Me Decade and the beginnings of yuppiedom, and wasn't sure where he fit into it all.

Now he was in a helicopter over Central Park—an amazing thing, even with nothing going on—and he didn't write a single word in his notebook.

Instead, all he could think of was what had happened to him, and how he wasn't in the crowd, participating in the moment of silence, but in a helicopter, outside the event, covering it.

"There was always something special about Us, about the first babyboomers, and the first TV kids, and the first Howdy Doody kids, and the first Davy Crockett kids, and the Kennedy kids, and the first generation to put its head under the desks for A-bomb drills.

"There was something new happening and even when we were kids, we knew it. The teachers, and our parents, would tell us we were different, we were special.

"And there I am in this helicopter. I just remember how transcendent a moment it was. John Lennon, of everyone, was the person who touched me deepest, always. Who spoke what I was thinking. And his death really upset me. But my job was to cover it. And it was a distancing. It was when I realized how distanced I was from our generation. How I had moved on.

"And in a way it was good that I wasn't down there. In a way it was good that most of our generation wouldn't be down there, most of our generation would be doing something else."

John Lennon's death was the demarcation line in the road back up from the bottom for the Woodstock generation. That tragic moment taught so many members of the generation that, indeed, they were moving on; that the past was past, the future lay ahead, and it was time to learn what that meant.

The day he died Lennon had been at a radio station giving an interview for RKO General Radio Network. The interview would be played many times in the days after his death. He talked about "Double Fantasy," the album he had done with Yoko, as a fresh start for him, a new beginning after years of problems with drugs, music, his children, his life. He talked about many things. But the words that would be played over and over from that interview were these:

"We're either going to live or we're going to die. If we're dead we're going to have to deal with that. If we're alive we're going to have to deal with being alive.

"The thing the 60s did was show us the possibility and the responsibility that we all had. It wasn't the answer; it just gave us a glimpse of the possibility—and in the 70s everybody's going nah, nah, nah, and possibly in the 80s everyone will say, 'Okay, let's project the positive side of life again.'

"We all survived Vietnam or Watergate, the tremendous upheaval of the whole world. It changed. We were the hit ones of the 60s. But the world is not like the 60s; the whole world's changed. I am going into an unknown future, but I'm still all here. And still, while there's life, there's hope."

CHAPTER SEVEN

A Reason to Believe

In the 1968 play *Little Murders* a city is terrorized by random gunfire. There have been 345 unrelated, unmotivated homicides in six months. The main characters are an idealistic, strong young woman and a cynical photographer who is incapable of emotion. She rekindles his idealism, and at that moment becomes victim 346.

In the end, the photographer and the woman's family become inured to the violence—by participating in it, buying a gun and picking off passersby from their window.

Author Jules Feiffer could not have known how prophetic his play would be in portraying the psychic trauma of the Woodstock generation.

After Kennedy, King, and Kennedy, after the deaths of civil rights activists Goodman and Schwerner and Chaney, after Vietnam and Kent State, after Janis and Jimi and Jim, and finally after John Lennon, the Woodstock generation, like the family in the play, had become numbed by violence. And afraid to make heroes anymore.

The generation became unable to feel any but the strongest, most intense emotions. As it moved into the Reagan years, it was not so much tired as spent.

There would be more killing, much more, and in frightening new arenas. The killing became more random, more senseless; its motivations more blurry and weird.

Pope John Paul II was shot on May 13, 1981 as he rode in an open car through St. Peter's Square in the Vatican.

Someone began killing small black children in Atlanta; twenty-eight would die before Wayne Williams, a music promoter and talent scout, was arrested.

The next year, in October 1982, someone would kill randomly by spiking the painkiller Tylenol with cyanide. Johnson and Johnson took Tylenol off the market, but seven people died in Chicago and a rash of copycat poisonings occurred in Michigan and California. And in California, drivers started shooting at those who cut them off on the highway.

The generation would be momentarily stirred by each killing; then it would sink back into its numbed state.

The tears shed for John Lennon would be cathartic, but they would not break this stupor. In fact, the mourning for Lennon may have been the Woodstock generation's last good cry.

The years had buffeted the nation like a long, cold rain. Now, Ronald Reagan was offering shelter from the storm.

In the same hour that Reagan was inaugurated, on January 20, 1981, the fifty-one Americans who had been held hostage in Iran for 444 days were released. Reagan was swept into office on a platform of tax cuts, decreased power for the federal government, increased power for the states, and a strong national defense. In truth, he was swept into office on the strength of seeming to be the last man in America who genuinely believed in the American Way, who sincerely felt that, by golly, this was a great country, and that if only everyone knew it they would be fine. He was not merely going to preside over the nation; he was going to heal it.

The Reagan Revolution swung into full force almost immediately. He ordered a freeze on federal hiring and government regulations. Then he announced a plan to cut the federal work force and tie welfare to work requirements.

Those who thought he could be tamed—those who thought he would be disastrous for social programs, for the poor, for single mothers, and figured they would be able to shield the neediest from his budget-slashing ax—were stunned at the swiftness with which this old man could move.

They stood by like the bad guys at the bar in one of Reagan's old western movies, and got the smirks wiped off their faces as he whipped out his pistol and fired six perfect shots at them.

Six more shots would ring out soon; fortunately, the aim was not perfect.

On March 30, 1981, Reagan was emerging from the Washington Hilton Hotel, after a speech to union delegates of the AFL-CIO.

Reagan and Secretary of Labor Ray Donovan had driven to the hotel from the White House together, and in the limousine Donovan told Reagan an old New Jersey joke about a local politician appointed to be superintendent of weights and measures. On the first day, reporters asked the politician, "Sir, how many ounces in a pound?" "Hey," he protested, "give a guy a chance to learn his duties."

Soon it would be Reagan's time to learn his true duty: to inspire a nation.

Walking out of the hotel through the VIP exit, he raised his arm in that grandfatherly wave. Suddenly he was crumbling, shot in the chest. Press

Secretary James Brady was lying on the sidewalk, blood oozing from his head; a police officer lay next to him. A man named John Hinckley was pinned to the ground by Secret Service agents, and the nation prepared for its mourning ritual.

Not again, the nation sighed.

This is how absurd things had become. Someone of the Woodstock generation—Hinckley was thirteen at the time of Woodstock—had tried to assassinate the president. Why? To win the heart of actress Jodie Foster, who had once starred in a movie about a man, driven crazy by life, who plots to shoot a presidential candidate.

But Reagan would not die.

He broke the cycle of America's practiced mourning ritual, adding to his myth, and making him seem bigger than life. His shooting recalled all the other shootings, all the way back to JFK—only this time, the Big Man rewrote the ending.

"I hope you're all Republicans," Reagan quipped to doctors just before they operated to repair the bullet's damage.

"I forgot to duck," he explained to Nancy.

"All in all, I'd rather be in Philadelphia," he jested after surgery.

Here was Reagan, not cynical but grinning at death. Laughing at it!

Somehow, Reagan's survival came to symbolize a renewal of the nation's spirit. And for a generation whose spirit was sorely sagging, a chord was finally struck.

It may have introduced the wrong song—this was not the president who stood for the things people sang about at Woodstock. Nevertheless, Reagan would bring that sense of renewal. These were tough times. Renewal was enough. It was shelter from the storm.

The resurrection of Ronald Reagan recalled the grail legend of the Fisher king. In the legend the king was ill and the country barren. Only by healing the king could the country be made prosperous. And Percival went off in search of the holy grail, to make well the king and restore health to the land and the nation.

And now Reagan, just a few days after being shot, was cheerily walking out of the hospital, refusing even a wheelchair. The king was well again, the land would be rich again, the crops would grow, and prosperity would be restored.

The generation not only believed in Ronald Reagan, but desperately needed to believe in him. He would say the homeless were homeless because they wanted to be, and there was almost no hunger, and ketchup was a vegetable—whatever the king said they believed because, after hitting bottom in the Carter years, they needed desperately to.

Well, maybe not the ketchup part. But the Woodstock generation did fall behind the king. It wasn't the issues that were important now, but the sense of confidence and belonging that the generation longed so deeply for. Belonging to something healthy and happy and prosperous and free.

For the first time in four years a majority of Americans polled said they were "generally optimistic" about the nation's future, and the shift was most dramatic among young adults—the Woodstock generation. The number of people who felt that the nation was finally headed in the right direction increased by more than half.

It's not that most generation members—or even a slim majority of them—agreed with what Ronald Reagan was saying. But they liked the way he was saying it—the positive style, the optimistic tone, the sense of confidence. In fact, most members of the Woodstock generation, in those same polls, disagreed strongly with Reagan on almost every specific issue facing the nation. Yet they voted for him and thought he was doing a good job. For the first time since Watergate, since the boring years of Gerry Ford, since the depressing years of Jimmy Carter, he gave them an excuse to feel good about something again.

Later, Reagan would become a central figure for activists to rally against. Then the generation would begin to emerge, to once again fight for the causes and issues important to it.

But in the early 80s Reagan was a central figure for the generation to rally behind.

Before you can change the world, you have to believe it's changeable, and the Woodstock generation had stopped believing that long ago. Ironically, its reemergence started with Ronald Reagan's breaking it out of its stupor, replacing its feeling of impotence with one of strength.

National Review saw this as Reagan calling a nation of believers back from the edge of cynicism.

After Reagan's return from the hospital, he gave a televised address to Congress. *National Review* wrote:

"Reagan has had the skill to make his revolution appear to be simple common sense. 'Our government is too big and it spends too much.' Ovation. Massive public support. Four standing ovations from Congress. Reagan's political momentum appears to be irresistible. Peering gloomily over the president's shoulder in the upper-right-hand quadrant of the screen, Speaker (Tip) O'Neill's rotund countenance said it all. The settled assumptions of half a century were being tossed into the wastebasket."

The generation didn't fall behind Reagan en masse. The opposition remained loud and boisterous in those first years.

In *Jules Feiffer's America: From Eisenhower to Reagan*, Feiffer wrote that "Ronald Reagan . . . is how we might like to picture ourselves if we were packaged for a commercial: easy, manly, outrageous, gracious, humble, good-humored, patriotic. Unlike Jimmy Carter, he is very much larger than life. . . . I suspect that we will survive him out of dumb luck. And for a while, at least, we will have learned his lesson: nostalgia is dangerous as a philosophy of government."

After Reagan's first State of the Union message, in January 1982, Democrats responded by challenging his revolution on national television. His tax cuts, his revamping of the government, his proposals to turn over to the states those messy annoyances like food stamps and payments to poor families with dependent children, were a travesty, they said. An embarrassment to a nation that prided itself on caring about the individual.

They said his theme was not happiness but "unfairness"—to the poor, the old, the farmer, the small businessman.

The Democrats brought on regular citizens; one elderly woman said she liked President Hoover better than Reagan because "he was blunt and he was what he seemed, and this one is charming and he beguiles you."

He beguiled all right. And the children of the Woodstock era needed some beguiling.

Reagan rolled back environmental protections in the name of jobs, he cut taxes in the name of stimulating the economy, he vetoed housing bills in the name of reducing the deficit, and they ate it up like an Alice B. Toklas brownie, and it made them feel just as good. Hell, better.

And in the coming years, when Reagan delivered on some of his promises, and the economy surged, and unemployment dropped, the nation was practically giddy.

At this point a true change in the Woodstock generation set in. The name for the change wouldn't be coined for a while; it had to evolve.

YAPs, the generation was called at first, for young aspiring professionals. This name did not stick, perhaps because it conjured up an anti-Semitic connotation; it sounded so much like JAPs, a derogatory name, an acronym for Jewish American Princess.

Then came "yumpies," for young upwardly mobile professionals. But that didn't quite do either. Woodstock members were, in truth, not very upwardly mobile. The economic times didn't allow them to move easily above the financial status of their parents. Their parents owned homes and put their children through college; this generation would struggle just to attain the same level.

"Yuppies" was the term that would stick—young urban professionals. Certainly they were young. They appeared to be urban—they were moving back into the cities, renovating old townhouses, gentrifying neighborhoods. And many were professionals—lawyers, journalists, condo converters.

They were also white and heterosexual, which fact spawned the need for terms like buppies (black urban professionals), guppies (gay . . .), puppies (pregnant . . .), and the like.

In reality, yuppies formed a very small part of the generation. As in the 60s the cameras followed the relatively small group of hippies so closely that it seemed that all their generation were flower children, that everybody must get stoned; so now the media focused so intensely on this small group that it seemed that the whole generation was yuppified, that everybody must get cloned.

And yet there was some truth to this. The incredible exposure in the media and in advertising turned the yuppie image into one of success, and thousands of nonupwardly mobile nonprofessionals jumped on board the bandwagon.

By 1984, when a *Newsweek* cover declared it the "Year of the Yuppie," the change had solidified irrevocably.

There would come C. E. Crimmins' *Y.A.P.—The Official Young Aspiring Professional's Fast-Track Handbook*, which noted bits of the jargon this generation created—like "interface," for communicating with another person or a computer. *The Yuppie Handbook* represented a desire in the mass media to chronicle the yuppie movement, and an even more fervent desire by marketers to sell things to it. And did yuppies buy!

Rolexes and condos and answering machines and VCRs and espresso makers and pasta makers and everything from designer cheese for their shelves to designer diapers for their babies. An estimated two million Walkmans were sold in 1981 alone.

A dress code slowly formed—natural fabrics, styled hair and button-downs for men, power suits and pumps for women.

An ethic also slowly formed—one of achieving, striving, and buying. Suddenly everything was work: working hard and working out and working within the system; working mothers and working relationships; working the phone and working the room and working the nightshift.

This change would come in a year filled with a puzzling mix of events. When the newspaper *USA Today* started up on September 15, 1982, it had two deaths to report from the day before—Princess Grace of Monaco, and Bashir Gemayel, president of Lebanon.

The paper made the death of the movie-star-turned-royalty its lead story, and placed the account of the assassination of the central Middle East leader inside—an America-first decision that perhaps reflected the me-first interests of the generation it was trying to woo.

It was impossible to escape the yuppie influence. The image was everywhere, from news magazines to American Express commercials.

Brad Blanton, a clinical psychologist, watched the change in the Wood-stock generation. While many puzzled over the road from hippie to yuppie, he had ideas about why the change was happening and what problems it might produce.

Blanton knew what he was talking about. Now he treated yuppies. Back then he was a hippie.

At the time of Woodstock, Brad Blanton was almost thirty and a veteran of the civil rights movement. He didn't go to the concert; he had a one-year-old daughter and was into being a father then, a traditional role for a man who had lived a fairly untraditional life.

He was born in Virginia and ran away from home and moved to Texas as a teenager. He did acid before he smoked marijuana, did peyote with the Indians, and learned from both. He believed in telling the truth.

The truth got him fired from Miami University in Ohio. Blanton was teaching the cognitive theory of psychology, and teaching a lot of what he learned on LSD: there is a difference between what is actually going on around you and what your ego is telling you is happening.

He began advocating that students take acid and smoke dope, instruction not appreciated at a good ROTC school, and he was soon on his way out.

An ashtray that now sits in his office comes from Mendocino, California, where he spent a month living on a school bus after being kicked off campus. It was part of his own Rolling Thunder Review, six months of traveling around the country in that school bus, with his daughter and wife. Eventually they formed a commune back in Ohio near Antioch. The community lasted four months, and two of the three couples got divorced—"another great attempt to redo the world that didn't work," he said.

But they were wonderful times for him, times of exploration, of liberation, of experience. On acid, he was forming the basis of the therapy he would use later: don't trust your mind, trust your experience. Learn to tell the difference.

"Following the experience" took him to Bear Creek, off Highway 1 near Big Sur in California. About a dozen people were living there, sometimes more. They lived without clothing, swimming in the creek and sunning on the rocks and getting lost in the woods and reading.

The work they did consisted of drawing lots to see who would don clothes that day and walk to the highway and stand with a sign that said, simply, Food. Cars with hippies would stop—they always stopped; this was the early 70s, after all. The hippies offered food and drugs, and they hung out and talked and got stoned for a while. In the evening whoever had drawn the day's duty would trek back to the creek with the daily offerings.

This would seem like panhandling to those who grew up later. But this was not begging; these people were not homeless. This was called sharing, and they were called a family.

And the sharing was an important thing to do. At rallies people would put out their hats and say, "If you have money, give. If you need money, take." And you would take and give money and somehow everyone came out all right.

So the sharing took place, and as the sun sank, Brad, who had drawn the duty that day, trudged back to camp.

"As a matter of honor, as a pledge, we would open up everything and dump it into a pot," Brad says. "All the dope and all the food in one pot, and we'd stir it up and scoop it out and eat it and see what happened.

"Some nights, I don't know what happened. One night I think we had an orgy. I'm not sure. I remember I came a few times, but I don't know who with."

Years later, sitting in his office in Washington, D.C., speaking with a southern twang, he laughed, loud and hard, the gutteral laugh coming from a deeply remembered experience, deeply remembered joy.

What happened? What happened to all of "Us"? Why did people stop living like that? And for God's sake why did he leave Bear Creek?

"Well, after a while, after I went back and took a shower and put on some clothes, I really felt good," he says. "It does get a little bit old and you get tired of freedom. It's too much work. It's human nature: when you get tired you want to rest."

A popular metaphor of the time was the story of the monkey and the bottle. The way you trap a monkey, the story went, was to find a big bottle, with a neck just wide enough to put a walnut inside. The monkey puts his hand into the bottle, and grabs the walnut. Now he cannot pull his hand out, because while holding the walnut his fist won't fit back out of the neck of the bottle.

That's what happened to Brad Blanton. He got trapped just like the monkey. For him, the walnut was a shower. For others, it was something else, but always something small, some little walnut.

For some of that generation, raised in nice middle-class homes, it would be nothing more than the desire to cop a good, hot, steamy, soapy shower. For others, maybe clean sheets, a good meal.

Once trapped, there would be new needs: a house to keep your shower in, a room for the bed with the clean sheets, a job to make the money to pay for the good meal. And later, a bigger house, a softer bed, a better job.

Walnuts.

Whatever Brad Blanton's walnut, it brought him back, and he framed his doctoral degrees on his wall next to a sign that says "You're only young once, but you can stay immature forever."

People came to him with what were called stress problems, a term that came into vogue in the late 70s. Poor people were crazy; middle-class people had stress.

Stress is the yuppie disease, and Brad Blanton taught yuppies to deal with it through yoga or autogenic relaxation or polarity therapy.

Exercise came into vogue, but yuppies didn't even exercise right. They saw it as one more occasion for competition.

So when Blanton counsels yuppies—lawyers, doctors, journalists—he counsels them based on a key theory: the conflicts of adulthood parallel the conflicts of adolescence.

Yuppies are "perennial adolescents," he says, "They want status. They all want to be rich, and they're all very concerned about other people's expectations. They're perennial adolescents, because materialism has allowed people to remain in adolescence for a long time."

In fact, the emergence of the yuppie personality, and the way the generation hooked onto it, revealed a generation in search of an identity in the early 80s.

"If you were working in a fucking law firm and they were making you kiss their ass for seven years before you could even be considered for partner, and you were working seventy, eighty, ninety hours a week—they got that out of you because they had you sold on the idea that you might not know who the hell else you were, but by God you knew you were a lawyer."

That sense of identity, that sense of belonging, had been missing for generation members since the early 70s. Now they found that the sense of belonging could be purchased—by buying into the yuppie image, they were becoming part of it.

Statistically, yuppies continued to make up a very small portion of the baby boom; they would be the minority-that-seemed-like-a-majority, just like their hippie ancestors. Later in the decade, studies would show that less than 4 percent of all babyboomers would make more than $35,000 a year. More than a third would earn less than $10,000 a year. Asked to describe their lives, babyboomers were the most likely to say their lives were getting harder, least likely to say they were happy, most likely to say they were having marital problems.

But the yuppie image, as opposed to the yuppie reality, became thoroughly pervasive. It formed the new Us and Them of society. And in Ronald Reagan's America, yuppies got to perceive themselves, once again, as the Good Guys.

The simplicity of the images we retain—of Reagan revitalizing the country and yuppies revitalizing themselves—belies the complicated swirl of activity of those first two years of Ronald Reagan's America.

Spiro Agnew resurfaced; a court ruled that he did take bribes. Billie Jean King resurfaced, admitting that she had a lesbian relationship with her former secretary, Marilyn Bennett.

In a great metaphor for the lingering malaise of the Carter years, sinkholes in Florida started sucking things back into the earth. Cottages, imported cars, and campers just disappeared, sinking from their own weight into a land unable to hold up under the strain any longer.

And one main issue of the 80s continued to grow in strength and visibility: hundreds of thousands marched at a nuclear protest in Central Park in June 1982.

"Gee, it's just like Woodstock," many said. But they were wrong.

At this and other demonstrations of the time, ex-hippie onlookers expected the rebirth of hope, the rekindling of the good old liberal spirit of caring and sharing. They saw hundreds of thousands marching against the nuclear arms race, and thought that surely this was a sign, surely the tide had turned.

Surely not.

There were some victories for liberals. In September 1982 the Senate defeated a proposal that would have restricted abortions—but only the most optimistic (and there were a few of those around at the midpoint of Reagan's first term) thought that winning such a battle meant the end of any war.

It was a time of technological explosion. *Time* magazine's Man of the Year was the computer. And Woodstock members, for the first time, started to feel a little old. For it was not they, but their children, who would grasp the new technology and feel comfortable with it.

For every member of the Woodstock generation who tossed a career aside for advancement into the field of computer programming, two were found who thought it a mystic science. To be sure, they put computers into their homes, and learned a few things on it, like how to write a book, but their offspring mastered the science and moved it along.

There were other technological advances of the time, all striking once-familiar chords in the hearts of the generation. The first shuttle launch took place on April 14, 1981, echoing the national pride of the moon landing just before Woodstock. And in the same December week that Dr. William DeVries implanted the first artificial heart in the body of Barney Clark. Charles Brooks, Jr., became the first person executed by lethal injection.

A lethal injection also killed John Belushi, one of heroin and cocaine. He was found dead in a rented Hollywood bungalow in March 1982. It would be wrong to call him a hero of the Woodstock generation—in fact, the generation was making few heroes anymore—but he was certainly their darling disaster, their beloved wildman, the king of crazy.

Ever since he had burst from the Chicago comedy scene to national prominence on "Saturday Night Live," Belushi was—well, different. A legion of late-80s comics owed him a debt for the barriers he broke in comedy: not in the topical sense of a Lenny Bruce, but for the sheer energy and dangerous anything-goes edge to his style.

His rubbery face, his ear for dialects, his apparent delight at smashing and screaming his way through sketches, made him frighteningly funny. His audience was wide: his character of Bluto in *Animal House* set the standard for the beer-swilling campus cutup movies of the 80s. His super-hip teaming with Dan Aykroyd as the Blues Brothers had a multiethnic appeal—besides, the music was damned good.

But mostly he was famous on the exploding New York comedy scene. For a while, just before his death, the hippest place to be was anywhere Belushi was doing cocaine.

Cocaine was enjoying its heyday in the early 80s. It was the yuppie drug of choice. It was everywhere, in the workplace, in nightclubs, on airplanes, on Wall Street, in Hollywood. The party was in the men's room stall. Cocaine had the double attraction of making ordinary people feel extraordinarily brilliant, good-looking, alert, exciting, and sexy. Because it was extremely expensive, possessing it was an instant status symbol.

It was the perfect drug for the Woodstock generation's newest incarnation because it didn't make you tune out; it made you feel incredibly plugged in, wired into everything. Even when Richard Pryor nearly killed himself when a freebase cocaine mixture exploded and burned him severely, the generation did little more than laugh (a common joke at the time was to run a Bic lighter along a tabletop, and ask, "What this? Richard Pryor jogging!").

When *Wired*, the book chronicling Belushi's drug use, was published two years later, Belushi's widow, Judy Jacklyn, would be furious at author Bob Woodward. She felt that he had not portrayed the man she knew and loved, but simply told a drug story.

She may have been right. But Woodward, whether by accident or intent, had seized upon the element that would have the most enduring impact.

A jaded generation could not long remain shocked that another of its celebrities had succumbed to drugs. But as the story of Belushi's death unfolded—of the wild parties, of who was and wasn't there, of who stuck that needle into his arm—a pin burst a balloon that had floated over the generation for so long.

It didn't happen right away, but John Belushi's death would be the beginning of the end of the generation's love affair with drugs. Cocaine would remain immensely popular, for a while. But its relatively positive image at this time—a wild, partying image of working hard all day and tooting up all night—would begin to sour for the Woodstock generation.

A drug paranoia, the likes of which hadn't been seen since the generation's youth, would grow. And the generation itself would participate fully in the antidrug movement.

Over the next few years, athletes and celebrities and just plain folks would all do antidrug commercials. Nancy Reagan's Just Say No to Drugs program would swing into full gear.

Some found this refreshing, a healthy sign that the generation was cleaning up its act. Others lamented having to fight the fights of the 60s again, to hear again calls for extremely harsh sentences for the simplest drug possessions—rather than funding for badly needed treatment programs and education. Either way, the furor following John Belushi's death was the beginning of the generation's finally coming to terms with its own drug habit.

Toward the end of 1982 the Woodstock generation heard other echoes of the 60s. Unrest in El Salvador, and what appeared to be Ronald Reagan's growing militarism, gendered echoes of Vietnam for the babyboomers. Reagan had sent twenty additional advisers—the same term used originally in Vietnam—and $25 million in military aid to El Salvador.

Author Barbara Garson, in a 1982 essay, recalled the taunts she'd heard as an antiwar protester in the 60s.

"What are you freaks gonna do when the war's over, huh?"

"If it weren't for the war you rat finks would be out of business," she responded.

Now she saw herself reliving that. She wrote about her bone-wearying frustration with a nation that just doesn't seem to have learned anything from Vietnam. On the eve of an El Salvador demonstration in Washington, she wrote:

"To stop just one war you have to mobilize so many people, so often, for so long. And when the war is over, what have you got? You've got the peace you needed to move forward in the first place, only everyone's exhausted.

"For most of my friends, the 70s brought five or six years of well-deserved rest and recuperation. The recuperation was used to find steady jobs, to find steady families, or to learn to live without either.

"Perhaps I lack stamina. El Salvador is only my second time around, but even as I board the bus for today's march on Washington, already I'm worn out. I'm tired of fighting against intervention There. I want to be fighting for basic change Here."

There appeared no question that America seemed to have forgotten Vietnam. Or, more precisely, had blocked it out. Ten years later the war was still painful to deal with, to talk about.

But the emergence of a new wave of books and movies and stories and scholarship about Vietnam was starting in full swing in the early 80s, and the war seeped slowly back into the public consciousness.

There was no doubt that a key shift in The Force, a change in the Woodstock generation's consciousness, a key milestone on the road from hippie to yuppie and beyond, came in the early 80s as America rediscovered the Vietnam War.

Of course, even before the war was over, Vietnam was being examined and reexamined. Since even before the publication of David Halberstam's *The Best and the Brightest* and Frances FitzGerald's *Fire in the Lake*, two 1972 bestsellers, the public had engaged in the argument over the war.

But never like this.

The change was visible on two fronts. The first was the college campus, where suddenly the Vietnam War was being taught as history to students who weren't born when America began its involvement.

The new Vietnam scholars on campuses across the nation were getting to the heart of what actually happened in Vietnam, and why. They were "challenging some of the most cherished beliefs of both the right and the left," wrote Fox Butterfield, a *New York Times* correspondent in Vietnam between 1971 and 1973.

Among the new findings in the early 80s:

• That Lyndon Johnson wasn't the warmonger many thought, but reluctantly sent troops to Vietnam for fear that if he "lost" South Vietnam, Congress would not pass his Great Society programs.

• That both hawks and doves were wrong about the Communists in Vietnam. Whereas American administrations didn't understand that the roots of the Communists' appeal ran centuries deep for the Vietnamese, antiwar critics overglamorized the Vietcong.

• That the 1968 Tet offensive, considered by most Americans as a major setback for the United States, was actually more devastating to the Vietcong; the losses they suffered were so great they had to be replaced by North Vietnamese regulars.

• After Tet, while most Americans had given up on the war, the United States position became stronger and support for the Communists was undercut by American firepower.

• The antiwar movement was not as much a force in ending the war as many thought; it was the cost of war, not the public sentiment, that prompted Lyndon Johnson's decision in March 1968 to deescalate the war.

For the Woodstock generation, hippie and nonhippie alike, these arguments raised strong emotions. They were fighting words, and cut to the quick. No one in the movement could ever believe that the antiwar movement didn't stop the war. Those who served in Vietnam laughed bitterly at the notion that Tet was a victory for the United States.

The college campus, however, was not the major front where the rediscovery of the Vietnam War was taking place. Not in the hearts and minds of the Woodstock generation.

The bitter wounds that the war left, the divided nation that remained divided and sickened, needed healing. Replaying the battles, reviewing the strategies, reassessing the movements and their impact, rearguing the worthiness of the Vietcong—none of these would serve that purpose.

The major front involved the horrid treatment of its returning veterans, and the unresolved need to understand what the war meant—these were the matters that surfaced now.

Two major controversies of 1982 would start the nation, and more personally the Woodstock generation, on its path toward grappling with these key issues.

One began when Ronald Reagan declared that Vietnam was a "noble cause." Nothing more infuriated the generation that found the war despicable and fought against it. Noble cause? Fighting against the war was the noble cause, they said.

And, they believed, if Reagan could call Vietnam a noble cause, we were doomed to repeat the mistake, in El Salvador, or God knows where.

The controversy over his statement coincided with the second and larger controversy that year, over the building of a memorial to Vietnam veterans.

On the most sacred ground in the nation, at the nation's town square, near the memorials to Lincoln and Washington and Jefferson, a monument was to be built the like of which this country had never seen.

Even before ground was broken on March 26, 1982, the nation debated the memorial designed by Yale architecture student Maya Y. Lin. Paid for by private donations, it would consist of two long black slabs arranged in a V-shape and inscribed with the names of the fifty-six thousand Americans killed or missing in Vietnam. Some would hail this as a perfect, fitting tribute to the Americans who made the ultimate sacrifice; others would deride it as a black hole in the ground that was not so much a memorial as a tombstone.

There was no clear division between those in favor and those against the monument. Vietnam veterans themselves were deeply divided. Even when the design was modified, to include a statue of three soldiers standing near the wall, the intense emotion was not quelled.

When the monument was opened to the public, in November 1982, the emotion welled up and overwhelmed anyone who came near. Whether you loved or hated the monument, whether you found it appropriate or inappropriate, it was impossible to get near it and not be moved, deeply, disturbingly.

The monument's walls form a little protected cove of land, and along the walkways at the monument, within that cove, tens of thousands of people reverently moved.

They would go to a book near the walls, and look up the name of a loved one. It told them where to find it on the wall. And they would find the name, engraved in the shiny black wall, and they would touch it, and they would cry. And cry. And veterans came and hugged each other, and people who had protested the war, and ridiculed these men when they returned home, would hug them, and cry.

The nation's capital was awash in emotion and argument. Veterans and ex-hippies and ex-straights and people who felt any connection to the Woodstock generation, from the parents who lost children in Vietnam to the marines who fought there to the curious to the cynical, cried and fought and argued over the war and its meaning, over its survivors and their treatment, and over the fundamental underpinnings of the generation itself.

And a wound began to heal.

In those early days, as America finally began to decide what it thought of the war, the heartfelt issues were: How would America remember the war? How would America deal with the men who fought it?

What began to happen was, the war was separated from the men. It was not the war that was memorialized here, but the men. It was not the war we were asked to make peace with, but the men. The Woodstock generation was not apologizing for having resisted the war; but it was beginning to apologize to the men who had fought it and for the way they treated them when they came back home.

Gary Stoces knew how poorly Vietnam veterans had been treated when they returned home. He had separated the men from the war long ago.

For him, the nation's sudden embrace of its Vietnam veterans had a hollow, bitter ring. "It's like, people are telling me, all is forgiven. Well, who in the hell are they to tell me I'm forgiven? Nobody's ever asked me whether I forgave them."

Gary Stoces was one of the originals. Early in 1965 the first ground troops saw combat in Vietnam. Gary landed in Vietnam on May 10, 1965, his twenty-fourth birthday. The first song he heard, coming out of a transistor radio, was "What a Day for a Daydream."

Life alternated between periods of boredom and intense activity. You read, you hung out, you went on patrol. You were always tired, because it's hard to sleep when it's 105 degrees. You were always wet, from the rain or sweat. You were never dry in that country. You didn't have jungle boots, unless you got them on the black market. There were ammunition shortages. And you were always pissed off in the infantry—that's just the mindset.

The confusion, the absurdity, the lack of any clear sense of purpose, the restrictions the soldiers were under—all began to weigh on him. Then came Operation Starlight.

Stoces, a platoon sergeant, recalled this first major ground operation of the war: "We're doing a hammer and anvil—you chase the bad guys into a line. You are the hammer, and the idea is to drive them into the anvil.

"Most of my platoon got it. It was very strange; it was the first time the marines had seen combat since the Korean War. There was utter chaos. A lot of senior NCOs got it; since they were the only ones with experience, they were doing jobs that were theoretically beneath them, but they had to do them because nobody else knew what the fuck they were doing. We were the hammer—but we got hammered."

What was it like to have your fellow infantrymen dying all around you?

"It didn't shock me. You didn't really have time to worry about it until later. It happened so fast. There's the initial fear, but then all of a sudden adrenalin just kicks in and it just takes on a whole strange thing.

"Time does a funny thing, it just expands and contracts. If someone was timing you, you could probably beat (track star) Carl Lewis. But your perception is that you have lead weights tied to your feet, you're running in slow motion."

Back at the base, Stoces felt protected and invulnerable—he had made it through. But he also understood it was the simple luck of the draw that got him out alive.

And then it was back to the routine: sitting around, getting soaking wet, going on patrol, and sitting around some more. But cynicism began to creep in, and Stoces started to become antiwar.

Not like the protesters back home—he had little respect for them. He became antiwar because "it was stupid. You started asking people, What is our mission? And I'm not talking seize-and-occupy-hill-84. But what is the overall mission of the United States in Vietnam? And you know what I found out? Nobody could give me an answer.

"And the minute you start putting people in a life-and-death situation without giving them a reason—what they're expected to give their life for—it's just bullshit.

"The average GI had no idea what was going on over there. And with thirteen months of that, it just takes on an atmosphere of some perverse survival training."

He returned to the States, was stationed at Quantico, Virginia, for a while, and then got shipped back to Vietnam through a glitch in the military bureaucracy that only a cynic such as Stoces could love.

"You're going on embassy duty," he was told.

"But that's volunteer."

"You just volunteered."

So Gary found himself back in Vietnam, a sergeant in charge of security at the ambassador's house in Saigon. The war was becoming more and more absurd to him, the reasons for being there more and more vague. He disliked the embassy duty: "At least up in the jungle you know who your enemies are."

One afternoon in 1967 he was driving past the Brinks Hotel in Saigon, a building used as bachelor officers' quarters. He was driving behind a garbage truck; the truck had no muffler, and the noise was annoying. In the truck were Vietnamese garbage collectors heading up to pick up the trash at the hotel. An MP blew his whistle at them; maybe they didn't hear it because of the muffler.

The MP opened fire on them.

At that moment, by mere chance, an MP vehicle came around the corner armed with an M60 machine gun. The MPs in the vehicle saw the shooting, and they too opened fire, catching the garbage truck in a crossfire.

"As soon as the first shot was fired, we dove out of the jeep, myself and a platoon commander, just dove out. We're pinned down, and the MPs are blowing the living shit out of this truck. And now there were garbage collectors who weren't going to collect the garbage from the Brinks Hotel. Absolutely fucking absurd."

Stoces was a marine, and he was doing his duty, but it became harder and harder. Saigon became "a city of one-legged men, all these Vietnamese soliders, missing legs, missing arms.

And beggars, thousands and thousands of beggars. "We were creating something like twenty thousand refugees a month, and they're all winding up in Saigon. And that's gonna really make the people love the United States.

"You go in and you napalm them on Monday, you run a search and destroy on them on Tuesday, you give them soap on Wednesday, you burn their fucking rice crop on Thursday, you give them bulgar wheat to eat on Friday, you have to write your report on progress on Saturday—and then you can't understand why these people don't like you. It was insane. It's just crazy."

Crazier still, to him, were the public executions. "You want to draw a crowd? You would not believe how many people turned out to watch somebody die. Even in a war zone. They would take people, tie them to a stake in a public square, and shoot them. You know why they stopped? Because it would tie up traffic; too many people came with cameras to take a picture of some guy die."

And so was born the cynic. And it came to pass that the cynic and the vice president of the United States had a little chat.

Hubert Humphrey visited Vietnam in 1967 and was staying in the ambassador's building. And one night his air conditioner caught on fire.

The wiring in the building was old, French, and complicated, and the Secret Service agents, feverishly trying to figure out how to turn the damn thing off, were unable to. With smoke billowing out of the machine, Stoces ran into the room, located the right switch, and turned it off.

Humphrey sat up in bed. Stoces marveled first at having found the only man he'd ever met who slept in pajamas in the tropics. Then he marveled at how composed Humphrey was. Wakened from a dead sleep by smoke billowing into his room, he sat up in bed, and decided he would like to talk with Stoces.

Asking about Stoces' service record, he mistakenly concluded that Gary had volunteered for this duty, and began discussing the war. Finally, he asked Stoces about his own support for the war.

"Frankly, no sir, I don't support the war," Stoces replied. "I'm here and one advantage is I'm making $650 a month tax free, and right now I'm not getting shot at. I didn't volunteer to come here. I volunteered to go to Moscow, and I ended up in Vietnam."

Humphrey asked him about his feelings about the antiwar movement back home.

"I don't care if Norman Mailer marched on the Pentagon; it doesn't change anything," Gary said. "I'm still here. I don't care whether the government likes whether I'm here, or you like whether I'm here. With all due respect, I'm still here."

Gary finally left Vietnam in 1968. Airline flight attendants talked about the haunting feeling on flights bringing soldiers home. The soldiers cheered as their plane left the ground, then nobody spoke for eighteen hours. They sat and drank in silence.

Gary's flight was like that. And his return to the States was stranger still, for it was the night Martin Luther King was assassinated. His own homecoming, to Washington D.C., was into a night of riots and smoke; soldiers with rifles were everywhere. He felt he was back in Vietnam.

"My god!" he thought. "We brought the war back home!"

And in a way he had.

One night sometime later, Gary visited an old friend. They had known each other before the war and the friend was an ex-marine. Now the friend was speaking what many were speaking at that time, especially in the wake of the My Lai massacre.

"I was called a Nazi, a war criminal, by a guy I had considered my best friend. He's pulling out articles from the *New York Times* about the use of napalm. I got up and left. What am I going to do? If I belt the guy it confirms every suspicion. I was shocked. And I was hurt."

Worse was the day-to-day isolation. "You felt like an outsider. I really didn't feel like we belonged in this society. It was nothing anybody would say, but it was the looks, like 'dogs and soldiers keep out.'"

Still in the Marine Corps, Gary wore his uniform around the city. He got into hooking rugs, and often visited a hippie yarn shop.

"I go in in uniform, these people are looking at me. After a while they saw me going in so much, buying yarn, they couldn't believe it. They just couldn't believe it. I wasn't a baby killer. It was like, for a marine you're a pretty nice guy. Like they had expected me to bayonet them or something.

"I didn't talk to a lot of people. You could go into a bar, and you had the military haircut, and people would just shun you. There was a slogan in those days: Women say yes to boys who say no. Then the rumor somebody started: that people coming back from Vietnam had this incurable strain of VD, the Red Rose. Everybody in the world's getting laid except veterans.

"You were very wary. You'd go into a bar and sit in the corner. You just didn't trust these people. It's a hell of a way to come back into your own country."

His circumstances strained his relationship with the woman he was seeing. She wanted to go out, he wanted to stay in. He didn't like her friends and they didn't like him.

The lasting effect of it all, he will realize years later: "I'll never trust an American politician again. Never. I don't vote. I don't trust organizations. That's why so many Vietnam veterans aren't members of the Vietnam Veterans of America. Veterans just don't trust groups anymore.

"It's the cynicism. I do not know many uncynical Vietnam veterans. I think it was Mencken who said the true cynic is the guy who, upon smelling the flowers, looks around for the casket. I know a lot of guys like that. I'm like that, pretty much. You just don't trust many people."

And so, as the Vietnam Memorial was unveiled in November 1982, Gary viewed what was happening with a mixture of anger and resignation. He heard a nation getting ready to forget the lessons of the war. He heard a nation ready to make the same mistakes.

"They took the best army that this country has ever put on the battlefield, and they wasted these kids. They just fucking wasted them— every one of those names on that wall. Joseph Brodsky, the poet, has a line from one of his poems, 'Build a monument to the lie.' I don't mean to take anything away from the people whose names are on that wall. And I have no objection to the monument. But that's the thing—build a monument to the lie."

The following spring Stoces was sitting outside a neighborhood pub. A bicycle rider went by, and Gary watched as he was hit by a car going full speed. The rider was thrown thirty feet through the air.

"I just sat there. Theoretically, yeah, I should have run out there and used all my military training, my first-aid training. But I felt like, fuck him. And it was kind of odd to me that that was my attitude. It doesn't make me happy, but it'd be the same if it happened today."

Maya Lin understood cynicism. A mixture of cynicism and idealism had fought for control of her life, ever since she was a child growing up in Athens, Ohio. She had always liked animals more than people; people were always screwing up. Even though she lived in the city, woods were nearby, and there she spent much time, gaining a great respect and love for nature and its ways.

While her cynicism made her feel that people were always screwing up, her idealism made her believe she could change that. And a dozen years later she would be a more integral part of the country's own battle between cynicism and idealism than she could have imagined on those long, warm summer days in the woods.

Maya was nine years old Woodstock weekend. She spent that weekend in the woods, walking and playing, oblivious to what was happening in upstate New York. Maya's parents were from mainland China, and their children inherited some of the parents' remoteness.

So, it's not unusual that war protests and the like were alien to little Maya. As she got older, the issues that interested her tended, say, more toward stopping whaling than stopping the war. The first political action group she associated with had nothing to do with the generation's protests going on in the nation, but with the dangers she saw in her own world: she circulated petitions to stop steel-trap hunting in Ohio.

By the time she reached Yale a sensibility had started to form that was more Eastern than Western, and, strangely, much more Japanese than Chinese. Japanese architecture tends to respect its site, tends to flow with its site, whereas Western architecture tends to dominate the site.

Three incidents joined by strange happenstance set Maya on the course that would bring her to the national limelight.

One was the junior year she spent in Denmark taking an intensive course in Danish architecture. By chance, she was studying a part of Copenhagen that happened to be a huge cemetery. How different from an American cemetery, she thought. Because space was so dear, cemeteries couldn't be set aside the way they were in America, and this cemetery was like none she had ever seen back home. It was more a park than a cemetery; the dead took their place among the strolling, mingling living.

Second, upon her return, she and a few other students designed a course on funereal architecture, and got a professor to lead the course. One of the projects was to design a memorial for World War III.

Finally, there was the poster. One of the students saw a poster for a design competition. The competition was to design a memorial for the Vietnam War.

She had studied war memorials for the project, she had studied funereal architecture for the course, but she had never studied the war.

"I felt that my opinions and my judgments about the war weren't important. I felt very strongly that it's not so much a war memorial as it is a memorial to those who were killed," she said. "I wanted to focus on those who had served and those people who had died. It should be about the people, not the politics."

Of course, the politics began to intrude immediately, even before her design took shape. A professor tried to argue her out of taking part; he had been a vehement antiwar protester, and he felt any involvement in memorializing the war would be morally incorrect.

She argued back just as strongly. "If you take such a perfect idealistic stance and you wait until the world is better before you create your work," she told him, "then you'll never be creating your work. I really believe what you do and create has to make the world a little better."

Maya had a few things clear in her mind: that politics had no place in the memorial; that the memorial should be about people and should help people get over their grief; that the memorial should respect the site; and that she herself must remain neutral.

"We in present-day society have kind of bottled up a lot of emotions," she says. "To really get over a death, you have to allow yourself a sense of mourning, which means you have to accept that they have died. We in today's society tend to shy from that. Especially with the Vietnam War, we just bottled it all up. So I wanted to aim the design toward a very honest notion of the acceptance of the loss, the death."

That is how Maya Lin arrived at her elegant design. To this day it remains a place both very real and very cathartic; to touch the wall is to understand, to feel the wall is to feel the loss. It is a place filled with tears and ghosts, with pride and anger and acceptance. It is a healing place.

But the maelstrom of argument over the design swirled. Maya kept her own counsel, knowing that her feelings had no place in the discussion. But she was angered and amused by those who tried to paint her as an antiwar type.

"I am a generation beyond those who protested for or against, so my opinion isn't so much an opinion as a reaction to that time. The design is neither denigrating nor mock-heroic. It's very honest. It doesn't judge. It looks at one very simple price.

"I didn't want to do anything that would make someone whose name is on that wall literally turn over. There are people on that wall with 180-degree opposite opinions. I didn't think it was my right to make an opinion to stand for all those people."

She wanted a memorial that would help heal the nation, that would bring together people from both sides of the great rift. She wanted to be a bridge. The first night she visited the memorial, she knew it had worked.

A Vietnam veteran was there, towering over her, six feet eight inches of rage. He appeared to be drunk. He was yelling at her and cursing her, going through his catharsis right in front of her, she hoped, as he called her an elitist artist who was trying to hurt and denigrate veterans of the war.

Others ran to call the cops. Maya stood and talked to him.

"This was meant for you, believe it or not," she told him. "What you're going through, and even though you're kicking me for it, you're going to feel better for it."

She was shaken by the incident; it was her first experience with the way people would experience her art. To hell with those who saw it as an antiwar memorial, she thought. This wasn't about which side you were on. This was about healing. And it was working.

Perhaps because she never became part of the Woodstock generation's protest and angst, or because art gave her an outlet for her need to create change, she was able to stay idealistic—to lose her head while all about her were keeping theirs.

Today, she works out of her home in New York City, and has a gallery uptown. She's involved in the renovation and restoration of a home in western Pennsylvania, is creating a public sculpture for New York's Penn Station, and is creating a civil rights memorial for Montgomery, Alabama.

In creating public art, she feels she can help create change—and that keeps the cynicism just outside her door.

The contrast between Gary Stoces' cynicism and Maya Lin's idealism formed the challenge for the Woodstock generation as it moved through the 80s and into the 90s. Some remained cynical; some retained or regained their idealism; most struggled between the two.

For Maya, the attempt to remain idealistic, and to bring some of that idealism to the Woodstock generation, was not a futile task:

"There's always hope. I don't think we're going to be perfect, but that doesn't mean you don't strive for perfection. I don't believe we're just on this planet to eat and sleep. We've got to do something more than that."

CHAPTER EIGHT

A Time for Choices

By now the Woodstock generation was beginning to emerge from its reverse-cocoon: the free, multicolored butterfly of the 60s was becoming the caged, sober caterpillar of the 80s. The shared experience of assassinations, Vietnam, Watergate, Tehran, and the rest implanted a deep cynicism about politics and institutions.

But there was another experience members of the Woodstock generation shared. They have always followed the media, and they have always been followed by the media. They were the first TV babies, and the first to see themselves on TV.

A common memory of people in 60s protests was attending a rally, such as Earth Day, and then going home to watch themselves on the nightly news.

As the Woodstock generation began to rise again over the next few years, its renewal would be, at first, more emotional than practical. It would feel itself changing and feel itself becoming more involved, even though its actions may not have shown it.

The Woodstock generation "cocooned" during these years, spending more time at home and less outside. And television responded. As events of the world unfolded in their own homes, in living color, people sometimes felt the emotion of these events as if they were really participating in them. They sat and shook their fists at Ronald Reagan or George Bush or Gary Hart, or news reports on homelessness, or corruption, or antiabortion protests, or social-security cutbacks. And they became angrier than they had been since the 60s.

The anger made them feel involved. The only problem was, they really weren't. The only action many of them took was to reach for the remote control. There was an inward change, but not an outward one.

Eventually the anger would turn into real action, at first over issues that affected people directly. Workplace issues, like day care and equal pay for women. Or issues that affected their homes, like toxic waste dumps, closing schools, or highway construction.

But not yet.

160

Now, only the first hints of the emergence of the Me Generation were observed. People were beginning to care. They weren't doing anything about it yet, but at least they were beginning to care.

And television was at the heart of this change.

The generation was used to having its daily routine turned into a news clip or, in the case of Woodstock and Watergate and dozens of other events, a movie. It was a generation with the sensibility of a movie star: always ready for a closeup.

The Woodstock generation was watching TV while TV was watching the generation, and the generation was watching TV watching the generation. The effect was like a mirror-in-a-mirror-in-a-mirror.

But beyond that, television became not just a vehicle for social voyeurism, but, for many, a vehicle through which they made the choices about what to do with their lives.

The choices of a teenager in the 60s, before Woodstock, were "street choices," decisions you made by seeing and talking with people in the real world. Join the rallies or attend class. Smoke dope or don't. Go to Vietnam or go to Canada or join the National Guard. Play football and drive a Chevy, or play Frisbee and drive a Volkswagen.

Chevy may have marketed to straights, but certainly Volkswagen didn't market to hippies. Hippies drove bugs not because commercials showed hippies driving bugs, but because of things they saw and heard on the street.

But in the 80s, would-be yuppies saw a TV-created image they could connect with in almost every commercial or magazine ad. And, glued to the couch, they let advertising and programming, not the street, guide their choices.

Marketers of products and politicians and promoters of social causes came to understand that if this generation could watch a program like "Family Ties" or a jeans commercial and say "That's me!" and buy, then it could also watch an anti-apartheid rally or a political commercial and say "That's me!" too.

The importance of television in their daily lives grew by leaps and bounds over the next few years. By the late 80s it was a rare family event or reunion that didn't include someone with a video camera. People would gather around their television sets during the reunion itself, to watch what they had taped moments before. In one family, the father brought his small children to the hospital the morning their baby sister was born; before noon, they were back home with a videotape. Visitors who asked what it was like for the children to see their baby sister for the first time were instructed to watch the tape.

So, products and politicians and ideas began to be marketed at the

Woodstock generation, partly because they finally had some money, and partly because of its fascination with recognizing itself on television. The generation's locus of decision-making became the home within the home: the television set.

The nation changed in many other ways during these years. The changes were real, out-in-the-street changes. But the Woodstock generation was slow to take part, largely because it would watch on TV and feel itself already taking part.

"We are badly detached from history," said Abbie Hoffman. "We're disappearing into our fantasy world, and television is the perfect medium for that."

And television was the perfect medium for Ronald Reagan. He proved this during a week in October 1983, one of the most traumatic weeks in the lifetime of the Woodstock generation.

Concurrent events thousands of miles apart, in Lebanon and the Caribbean, shocked even the most apathetic. In a period where even the most horrible of news began to seem commonplace, they touched the generation to its very soul. If there was ever a week to rekindle the fires of the 60s, this would be the week. Liberals and conservatives would vie for the generation's soul like a devil on one shoulder and an angel on another.

The year 1983 was filled with the issues of the 60s played out in the fashion of the 80s. That year critics asserted that Reagan's policies were demeaning and harmful to women, and cries of "gender gap" sounded as loudly as calls for women's liberation in the 60s. It was the year two hundred thousand marched on Washington to commemorate the twentieth anniversary of Dr. Martin Luther King's famous march. It was the year the nation battled over aid to El Salvador and a Soviet fighter plane shot down a Korean airliner full of people.

But for one week there were only Lebanon and Grenada.

At 6:22 on the morning of October 23, 1983 a truck carrying twelve thousand pounds of dynamite sped toward the U.S. Marine Headquarters in Beirut where American "peacekeeping" forces were stationed. Security guards opened fire, but it was too late. The truck exploded with such force that it rocked buildings throughout the city. In the headquarters 241 marines were killed, some by the force of the blast, other buried under the charred metal and concrete.

The nation was stunned by pictures of marines trying, with their bare hands, to dig out comrades, sitting dazed on the rubble, or standing with their heads bowed, weeping. For the first time since the Vietnam War, the

Woodstock generation opened its newspapers to see columns filled with the names of dead American servicemen.

Two days later, more than two thousand marines streamed ashore in the darkness onto the tiny Caribbean island of Grenada. They stormed the government house and captured an airfield that Ronald Reagan said was being built by "Cuban thugs." He argued that American students there were in danger because of a growing Communist influence, and that several Caribbean nations had come to him desperately asking for help.

Death and despair followed the first event; victory and pride followed the second. Those who saw Grenada as a macho response to Lebanon caught the spirit, if not the sense, of the week. For these were two events totally unrelated but thoroughly joined; they had nothing and everything to do with each other.

The nation was caught in a tornado of information, of recrimination, of emotion, of argument. Senators, congressmen, journalists, pollsters, and neighbors screamed and jostled and tried to make sense of it all.

Were we right to have our boys in Lebanon?

Were we wrong to invade Grenada?

If the initial response to Lebanon was unified grief and anger, the initial response to Grenada was a conflicting mass of patriotism and ridicule. After leaving office, Reagan would say that Lebanon was the low point of his administration, and Grenada the high point.

The arguments over Lebanon were whether we should have been there in the first place, and whether we should retaliate. The argument over Grenada was whether we should feel pride—especially after the Jimmy Carter years—in a victory, or whether we looked ridiculous in picking on some construction workers on an airfield in a tiny country. The arguments were heard from the halls of Congress to the street corners of America.

Even before Lebanon and Grenada, those who opposed Reagan and his policies had tried to enlist the support of the Woodstock generation by identifying Vietnam with El Salvador and Nicaragua. The May 1983 *Progressive* was indicative of this call:

> We've been watching dreadful reruns recently in Central America. Once again the United States is committing its power, its prestige, and its military might in a Third World civil war, this time not in Vietnam but in El Salvador . . . The temptation is to switch channels, tune out, turn off the set. But these aren't reruns; they're real. The demonstrations that spread more than a year ago to protest U.S. intervention in Central America need to be organized again. The phone calls need to be made, the letters sent, the petitions signed, the pickets formed, the marches begun.

During that fateful week in October, the emergence of Ronald Reagan's gunboat diplomacy excited that cry to a bellow. The parallels to Vietnam were numerous. Lebanon represented the highest number of American casualties in a single day since 246 servicemen were killed at the start of the Tet offensive in 1968. Grenada was the first place since Vietnam where the United States had committed troops to a major attack.

The American media were excluded from covering the Grenada invasion. Some believed that would anger the Woodstock generation, if not for the apparent violation of the First Amendment, then at least for depriving it of watching the invasion live on TV.

In contrast to Grenada, Lebanon didn't fit in with Ronald Reagan's new tough-guy image that was making the nation feel good about itself. The pullout could be seen as caving in to terrorists.

On Grenada, William Buckley ridiculed the liberal fury: "It is discouraging that so many voices are raised to say the most irrelevant things . . . Surely the salient point is that with minimum loss of life we have rescued a little island in the Caribbean from a monstrous tyranny whose script was being written in Moscow and Havana."

Which path would the generation choose? The outrage of the left? The practicality of the right?

The decision would shape the nation for the rest of the decade. But it wasn't the magazine columnists or the analysts that swayed the answer.

It was a great night of television.

Ronald Reagan decided to calm the fury, and on the night of October 27, 1983 went on TV to talk to his people. It was a stirring, passionate speech showing none of the faltering confusion he had begun to exhibit at press conferences. Calmly and confidently, he described the proper response to Lebanon: we will mourn and we will rage, but we will stand tall. And he outlined a scenario for believing in Grenada:

"We got there," the president said, "just in time."

In the end, it wasn't the logic of his argument that won over much of the Woodstock generation. It was the beauty of the image he offered.

For a generation seeking its adult image, here was the capstone: it's all right to be, as Reagan called it, strong. This was not America getting involved in "straightening out local messes." This was America standing up for liberty and truth and the rights of people, in this case, Grenadans and our own American college students.

And the generation bought it. It did not buy the argument; it bought the image. Surveys later showed that the children of the 60s retained their basic mistrust of government, of military involvement, of public officials and politics. But that night they bought the image, the sense of strength, the sense of belonging. Mostly, they bought Ronald Reagan.

To gauge the power of Reagan's speech, pollster Tony Casale conducted two surveys, one just before the speech and one after. Before the speech, 39 percent of the American people agreed with Reagan's decision to send the marines to Lebanon. After: 53 percent did. Before: 48 percent said keep the marines in Lebanon. After: 59 percent agreed.

Approval of the Grenada invasion rose from 48 percent to 68 percent.

And the greatest swing occurred among those people in the Woodstock generation.

A shift in The Force had taken place. Like the Fisher king, Ronald Reagan was healing the nation.

But Abbie Hoffman still believed that power belongs to those who take it. And, having been brought into the great fight over the Delaware River by a citizen's group called Del-Aware, for which he was working as a dollar-a-year organizer, it was time to take it again.

Having copped a plea and done a short jail sentence for the drug charges that drove him underground, Abbie was ready to be Abbie again.

The Philadelphia Electric Company, in the middle of one of the most historic and beautiful areas in the Northeast, decided to diversify and get involved in the water business. It proposed to build a pump, take water from the Delaware River, and send it forty miles away, in part, to cool a nuclear power plant.

But the area had a poor people-to-water ratio already and the Delaware River carries much historic weight. The pump would be located just a dozen miles from where George Washington crossed the Delaware to attack the Hessians during the Revolutionary War.

"So it's a river war," Hoffman said, "in the sense that Mark Twain said, 'Whiskey's for drinking, water's for fighting over.'"

He would be involved in more than a half-dozen such wars through the 80s, but said, "This is the toughest."

Del-Aware brought Hoffman in after losing its case in federal court. Many of its members were ready to give up.

"I was intrigued," Abbie said. "I had come through this area on a speech to Lehigh University and had seen the Dump the Pump signs, and I would come to their meetings. I saw Republicans, Democrats, young, old, people from Woodstock, people from the town, the postmaster was there, people who had supported the war."

Hoffman agreed to join the fight, just as bulldozers were coming to the site of the Point Pleasant Limerick Pumping Project.

"It was incredible to see thousands of people waving American flags and singing 'America the Beautiful'—on our side!"

Within two weeks, Hoffman and a fellow organizer had the whole county involved. "As I said before, I'm not the brightest organizer in the country, but I am the fastest."

Hoffman was doing what he did best—nuts-and-bolts grassroots organizing, with voter referenda, and door-to-door canvassing. At the site there was guerrilla theater—people dressed as American revolutionaries and bearing signs saying Don't Tread on Me—and there were people camping out for weeks. The battle began to turn around.

"It was like I was underground again, with CB handles and communication networks, using runners, riders on horseback. You're talking to River Rat One—that was my handle."

A voter referendum showed opposition to the pump growing. And there were signs that pro-pump forces would be thrown out of county office in the next election.

There were, however, some setbacks. As the years went by, some of the fighters could no longer afford to live in Bucks County, growing each day thanks to its location about midway between Philadelphia and New York. Development had driven up land values and the cost of living.

There were threats of lawsuits that scared off some of the new generation of antipump forces. And a judge warned the county commissioners that they would be held in contempt of court if they didn't allow the pump to be built.

"The utility company is more or less having its way," Hoffman said. "It's winning. It's not won this battle yet, but it's winning. And people sit around and wait for the bump in the night."

The bump in the night?

In the 80s a parallel issued faced the area. The beautiful, rural community around New Hope had been taken over by the same kind of development and cluster housing that so many communities are plagued with. The developers faced little opposition much of the time.

Abbie attended a meeting about one such development, at which the builders discussed preserving the land's beauty, promising golf courses, landscaping, ice rinks, gently sloping lawns, and new trees.

Hoffman got up to speak and, of course, it was fire and brimstone.

"A rural area is not golf courses and ice rinks and theme parks," Hoffman said. "Rural IS, it doesn't have to be landscaped, it just IS!

"And now American Legion people, DAR, are saying 'I never in a thousand years thought I would stand up and agree with Abbie Hoffman, but I do.'"

So Hoffman fought on. He owned almost nothing. It helped, he said, in his line of work, because then he didn't have to worry about losing everything in a lawsuit.

And he dealt with the anger of the people around him, anger over development, anger over a water tower, anger over the pump. He worked to channel that anger into organizing.

And occasionally he heard some angry people talking about blowing up the pump.

The bump in the night.

Did he think anyone will really blow it up?

"Well, you know life is a soap opera. I've had people who are devout Quaker pacifists tell me they're going to do it, and I've had people trained in demolition squads in Vietnam—we call that the barroom strategy.

"Whether it happens or not—I'm liberal arts, it's out of my control. Will it happen? I don't know. I've never been at this stage in a battle. I've usually won 'em all by now.

"I will say this: In order for the planet to survive, there are going to be acts of ecoterrorism."

Hoffman, as the years wore on, developed a comfortable relationship with even the local police. But Abbie says that if any really serious shit goes down, he would be the one to take the rap.

"If while we're talking you hear a loud bang, and the pump owned by the Philadelphia Electric Company blows up, I'm gone. It would take me about fifteen minutes to leave home. That would be the police signal to come and get me."

And so, in small ways, the battles of personal freedom and saving the ecology went on. And in larger ways, the values of the Woodstock generation were re-emerging, as Ronald Reagan prepared for his re-election campaign.

It was 1983, the year that Karen Carpenter died of a heart condition brought on by anorexia nervosa, an eating disorder, little understood then, in which people literally starve themselves to death.

Psychologists would come to understand this disease as one afflicting people who feel they lack control of their lives. Sufferers subconsciously believe that if they can't control anything else, they can control their own bodies.

They become slaves to their own self-image. It is a disease to which the Woodstock generation, with its media-manufactured model images, would be extremely susceptible. In particular, the disease would afflict white women of the Woodstock generation.

That was 1983, the year the nation noticed how bad its schools had become. The National Commission on Excellence in Education called the United States "a nation at risk," saying its education foundations were being eroded by "a rising tide of mediocrity."

This set off a national campaign to improve the schools. And many of the back-to-basics programs that were instituted ran counter to the open-school, progressive-education ideas encouraged by the Woodstock spirit two decades earlier.

The Woodstock generation would be blamed for having encouraged experimental education, but they never influenced the school system the way they had intended. In the early 70s, 25 percent of all college graduates were in teacher education programs. But most found they could not get jobs in teaching; with the end of the baby boom there simply wasn't as much need. Some of the best would not wait in line for teaching jobs; they found employment in other fields—and the quality of education suffered.

In 1983 Sally Ride made history. She was the first U.S. woman in space. More than two hundred thousand T-shirts were sold bearing the slogan Ride, Sally, Ride.

Interior Secretary James Watt, defending the composition of an advisory group on coal leasing, said, "We have every kind of mixture you can have. I have a black, I have a woman, two Jews, and a cripple." Watt would apologize, but his comments widened the rift between the Reagan administration and minority groups.

Watt also tried to ban rock groups such as the Beach Boys from the nation's Fourth of July celebration on the Mall in Washington, supporting instead Wayne Newton. It was all too much. In October Watt resigned under heavy pressure.

Reagan announced his controversial Star Wars program, which he said would build an invisible shield against nuclear attack. The president also spoke against abortion, but the antiabortion movement assumed a militancy that he had not urged, with firebombings of abortion clinics and the kidnapping of one abortion-clinic owner in Illinois.

A sizable segment of the Woodstock generation opposed Ronald Reagan. Some were descendants of the freaks and radicals and liberals and hippies and yippies of the 60s and they were growing, if not larger in number, at least stronger in conviction.

Writing in November 1983, Sidney Lens, senior editor of the *Progressive*, summed up the position that faced the 80s radical: "Good people . . . are eager to send Ronald Reagan packing in 1984 . . . But how are we going to do it?"

Lens argued against the beliefs of radical friends that an activist had to support John Glenn or Walter Mondale, or anybody with a chance of unseating Reagan.

"We should not succumb to the notion that voting is the decisive form of political action," he wrote. "There is more serious and significant political work to be done. We can hold a vigil at a federal building to protest U.S. intervention in Nicaragua or Lebanon. We can sit in at a senator's office to demonstrate our opposition to Euromissiles or the MX. We can march and mobilize. . . . Those of us who seek real change will practice politics . . . in the streets."

And people were taking to the streets. In perhaps the most inspiring moment of the times, for those who believed in liberal causes, a Jobs, Peace, and Freedom march in Washington that August brought two hundred and fifty thousand people to the site where Martin Luther King led the historic civil rights march twenty years earlier.

This time there were many themes, many causes: antinuclear activists and peace activists marched with those arguing for gay and lesbian rights. Ousting Reagan was a unifying theme, but rekindling King's dream was the unifying hope.

It was a mélange of general 60s sentiment and specific 80s causes: Pete Seeger sang of Ronald Reagan ("This old man, he plays seven, big business is in hog heaven") and Bill Cosby spoke (calling him "Ronald Dancing Mouth") and Coretta Scott King presided (assuring the morning crowd that the slain civil rights leader "will still be marching with us today") and Dick Gregory, and Andrew Young, and the Reverand Joseph Lowery ensured an echo of the past as marchers attempted to set a tone for the future.

As the crowd chanted, "Run, Jesse, Run," imploring him to join the race for the presidency, the Reverend Jesse Jackson exhorted them to action, calling the disenfranchised a David that could defeat the Goliath Reagan if it would only pick up its slingshot:

"David has unused rocks just lying around. In 1980 Reagan won with a reverse coalition of the rich and the unregistered. Rocks just lying around. Reagan won in Massachusetts by twenty-five hundred votes. There were sixty-four thousand unregistered blacks. Rocks just lying around. . . . Our day has come. March on. . . . From the outhouse to the statehouse to the courthouse to the White House, we will march on."

Mickey Berra was one of the people inspired. Things were going well for him. He had worked as a grip on many motion pictures—from *The Exorcist* to *Three Days of the Condor*—and was making a comfortable living.

Mickey was twenty-nine in 1984. It had been a long road from Petersburg, Virginia, where he had grown up, a "poor white boy in a tough little town." Petersburg was the headquarters of the carnival, and between the carnival and the army base were gambling houses and whorehouses.

Berra's father died when Mickey was three years old; living with his grandmother and hanging around the carnival toughs, Mickey quit school after the fifth grade to head out with the carnival. By the time he was eighteen he was getting into trouble with the law.

Mickey was white, but only to one voice in those years would he listen.

"I was growing up, I was poor, Martin Luther King was very inspirational to me. This guy meant something. He represented what I was for—to get a fair shake. I was looking for a way out. He was talking for the people, instead of for business."

Mickey's life began to straighten out. He started getting decent jobs and stopped getting into trouble with the law. But he knew that most of the people he grew up with weren't as fortunate.

"I'm a lucky guy. I had people help me out. I'm not as happy today as I once was, because I don't see it being that way for everybody. Most people just don't have that chance."

This was what turned him toward Jesse Jackson, who, for Mickey, spoke in a way he had longed to hear since Martin Luther King died.

"I think Jesse Jackson is a brilliant guy. He talks for the people. He's talking about things that little kids need to hear, not things business needs to hear, not what people out there gut-fucking each other need to hear."

Supporting Jackson meant taking some abuse along the line. His wife, who is Jewish, doesn't agree with him; the split between Jackson and the Jews was a thorny part of the Rainbow Coalition. Others, however, would be more abusive.

"I have had people call Doctor King a Communist when I say he's my hero. I've had people say Jesse Jackson was a racist, or whatever. I don't believe it."

An easygoing man with tousled hair and a boyish smile, a talented and dedicated worker, Mickey had little trouble finding work. And his work, one afernoon during the 1984 presidential campaign, brought him face to face with Ronald Reagan.

Working as a grip for a production company, Mickey was part of a crew putting together a twenty-minute segment to be used as part of the opening at the Republican National Convention. There were two days of shooting at the White House, and two at Camp David.

On a patio at Camp David, Reagan was sitting at a table, Nancy at his side, a TelePrompTer just off-camera on the table in front of him.

Reagan began reading from the TelePrompTer. And then, suddenly, he began talking about something else—whatever topic popped into his head.

"Reagan just kept wandering off into space," Mickey remembered. "The cameraman would look at me, and the TelePrompTer man would look at him. Nancy reached over to Reagan and said no, that was the other thing they were discussing earlier. And we'd start all over."

Reagan struck Mickey as a nice man, kind of harmless, but certainly not fitting his image of a leader.

But a leader he was. And the Woodstock generation still followed.

Reagan started dismantling anti-discrimination programs that helped minorities get jobs. Yet many whites, some of whom even marched in Washington for Jobs, Peace, and Freedom, sat by; it was a different issue when those ideals conflicted with their own careers.

It was this conflict—between wholehearted belief in social justice and equality and the instinctive reaction to pull back when such issues affected their lives, their jobs—that would persist in the heart of the Woodstock generation for some time.

And many resisted making this choice. The Woodstock spirit remained a sleeping giant inside them.

For those in the Woodstock generation who did not embrace Ronald Reagan, there were other candidates to strike a chord in their long-lost idealistic hearts. But none would be able to create an image strong enough or lasting enough to truly move the generation forward. Besides Jesse Jackson, there was Gary Hart, called the perfect candidate for the yuppie generation—good looking, camera-friendly, idealistic on social issues but with an overlay of practicality. He was an environmentalist from Colorado who sounded like an intellectual from Boston.

Perhaps the most important candidate for the Woodstock generation was not a presidential candidate, but his running mate. Walter Mondale, former vice president, would eventually rise to the Democratic nomination more through default than through carving any great new vision. But his vice presidential choice, Geraldine Ferraro, a tough-talking politician from Queens, New York, generated waves of awe and excitement.

The first woman on a major presidential ticket, Ferraro brought a blend of street-smarts and humanitarian ideals that drew many from the Woodstock generation to her Democratic team. But disclosures of shady dealings by her husband John Zaccaro, a New York real estate entrepreneur, and the ultimate weakness of Walter Mondale meant that her influence would be short-lived.

Also on the scene was former astronaut John Glenn, who had the psychic appeal for the Woodstock generation for having been one of the first men they called a hero.

The movie *The Right Stuff* was coming out then—author Tom Wolfe's history of the start of the American space program. Glenn was portrayed as Mr. Clean Marine, eager to "give 100 percent" for NASA and his country. Some thought it would enthrone him as a demigod of 60s valor for an 80s election. The movie did credibly well, but Glenn, espousing the most middle-of-the-road values possible, did not.

The timing was perfect for another film, *The Big Chill*, the ultimate yuppie movie. It was the story of seven friends from the 60s, who had lived some unspecified radical life at the University of Michigan, reunited by the suicide of one of their friends. They spent a reunion weekend together, to listen to 60s music and evaluate what had become of themselves and their generation.

One was going to be a lawyer defending the poor; instead, she ended up representing the rich. Another, who was going to teach ghetto kids, became a writer for *People* magazine.

The film infuriated the true activists of the 60s. Pauline Kael warned in the *New Yorker* that "anyone who believes himself to have been a revolutionary or a deeply committed radical during his student-demonstration days in the late sixties is likely to find *The Big Chill* despicable."

Still, the film was a big hit and spawned several albums of "Big Chill" music and a number of movie imitators.

Notwithstanding, the movie was vague about just what the seven actually did in the 60s; they occasionally referred to some unspecified "revolutionary" activity, but more likely they were among that larger group who attended the rallies and mouthed the slogans and did little else.

That, in fact, is a fair representation of the Woodstock generation as it really was, rather than as it likes to believe itself to have been.

The film's message was that the 60s weren't really about issues, but about good feelings and togetherness. And to recapture the 60s, you didn't have to become politically active at all. You just had to recapture the feeling.

An earlier low-budget film, *Return of the Secaucus Seven*, had a similar radical-reunion plot but dealt with the very personal feelings of 60s radicals coming to terms with ideals lost and ideals retained. The message many took away from *The Big Chill*, however, was not about the issues of the 60s, but about that sense of belonging.

"I felt I was at my best when I was with you people," one character says to her friends.

Activists from the 60s through the 80s complained the movie trivialized their lives.

The Big Chill was one of those movies that went beyond the movie reviewer's realm; reporters were dispatched to talk to people about the movie. But the media missed the point entirely; much of the makeup of any newsroom at this time consisted of early-thirties members of the Woodstock generation holding down straight jobs. And so the reporters and the yuppies talked and they all felt very good, and the stories that appeared in the papers were very positive.

Sixties music returned to the airwaves, in part spurred by *The Big Chill* and in part the result of good marketing strategy. By 1984 a majority of babyboomers were in the buying years, and advertisers wanted to reach them. Oldies stations had been around since rock and roll was old enough to be called oldies; but now, new neo-oldies stations would bow to the generation. They played Aretha Franklin through Elton John and Crosby, Stills, Nash, and not-so-Young.

This recalled the lament Abbie Hoffman made about the Woodstock concert all those years ago: if the only message is in the music, then the message will be lost.

And it was true, while some messages were falling on deaf ears the band played on.

Somehow Ronald Reagan had brought the country through Lebanon and Grenada feeling good, and somehow the Woodstock generation had reconciled its differences with its past and was feeling good, and even the economy—showing sharp recovery from the recession—was feeling good.

It was spring 1984 and Ronald Reagan declared it "Morning in America."

All that summer the nation felt very good about the Olympic games. The city was Los Angeles, the state Euphoria. And rather than douse the spirit, a Soviet boycott (retaliating for the U.S. boycott of the Moscow games in 1980) only enlivened it. Run by Peter Ueberroth, the games even turned a profit.

Gymnast Mary Lou Retton and diver Greg Louganis were the new love children of this generation, and the luminaries of these perfect games, which gave little thought to the Soviet Union or to Cuba or to the other countries that refused to show up.

The remaining 60s radicals said this was also how their generation was acting toward El Salvador and Nicaragua—giving them little thought. But the activists were hard to hear over the cheering Americans watching the gold medals pile up and chanting, "USA! USA!"

A few months later that chant would change to "Four More Years! . . . Four More Years!"

Reagan's reelection was more of a coronation. So strong was his hold on the nation that Walter Mondale lost in a landslide. No matter that Washington, D.C., was frozen solid for his second inaugural and most of the festivities were moved indoors; it was Reagan's self-declared time of renewal. And much of his support came fron an unusual source.

A new generation of college students was hitting the books, saying no to drugs (but saying yes to alcohol at a soaring rate), and, most of all, saying I Love You to Ronald Reagan.

The big issue for the students then was the drinking age. A movement was afoot to raise it. Older Americans, and particularly those from the Woodstock generation, were becoming increasingly concerned about the epidemic of drunken driving. Drinking and driving had always been a problem. But now, the children of the 60s had teenagers and they looked at things from a slightly different perspective.

Tougher drunk-driving laws were passed; parents formed groups like Mothers Against Drunk Driving and lobbied state legislatures to raise the drinking age.

The kids took to the streets, but with almost no help from the Woodstock generation that had fought and won a similar protest twenty years earlier. Their argument then was: "If I'm old enought to fight a war, I'm old enough to drink." But in the mid-80s there was no war.

America's new youth lost this fight, but they were drawn to Ronald Reagan, who offered them grandfatherly assurance, moral rightness, and economic prosperity.

Johanna Neuman, a reporter for Gannett News Service, watched the kids fall in love with Ronald Reagan as the president hit the campaign trail in 1984.

Her first stop with Reagan was on the campus of Bowling Green University. The fact that the students idolized this man struck her as very strange. But the fact that she was there herself, and would later cover the White House during Reagan's second term, seemed stranger still.

Johanna started college in 1967, at Santa Cruz in California. It was a campus designed to deter student unrest, one of those idyllic college creations of the 60s—a pass-fail system with stringent evaluations, a terrific student-teacher ratio, and a setting of majestic redwoods and mountains in the California sun.

But she was chafing to be where the action was, and the action was at Berkeley. It took awhile for the emotion to turn into action. But one day there was a student meeting; there had been a surplus of funds, and now a debate ensued on how to use them. One proposal was to purchase the necessary hardware to allow reception of FM radio stations—the audio home of the hippie movement, the place to hear Arlo instead of the Archies.

A student stood up and told the crowd, "If I wanted FM radio I wouldn't have come to Santa Cruz." Johanna's blond hair whipped behind her as she turned her head toward a friend. "We're leaving," she said. Johanna transferred to Berkeley.

Which is how she came to be involved in a protest against the man she would later cover as president. Reagan, as governor of California, was also chairman of the Board of Regents of the University of California. He came to Berkeley in 1970 to defend a decision not to allow Eldridge Cleaver to speak on campus.

Johanna took her place in the march, lending her body but not her voice to the angry crowd. "I remember many boos and catcalls and great anger about the issue on campus," she says. "Berkeley was the birth of the free-speech movement, so free speech was a mantra.

"I do recall thinking that he (Reagan) held his own through the boos, but I was not anywhere near charmed, as I am now. I was not a loud protester; I was a silent partner. I never got up on a soap box, I was never arrested."

Johanna still has all the Dylan albums made in those years, and she loved listening to Crosby, Stills, and Nash at an antiwar protest. But in a way, it was impossible to be of that age and not be involved in the music. Especially with beautiful blond hair and a name like Johanna—which led so many to ask her:

"Johanna? As in visions of? You're not the mystery girlfriend Dylan wrote the song about, are you?"

Of course she wasn't. But while the music did hold magic and meaning for her, it was the message, not the music, that was important.

Johanna was at Altamont, with the Stones and the Hell's Angels and the death. This gave her a bad feeling about music as a part of the political movement.

"I saw myself then, as now, as a political person, and my interest in the movement was its political ramifications. I listened to all the music. But unlike some of my friends, who were Grateful Dead junkies, that wasn't my part of it. I was never rebelling against Frank Sinatra."

The politics may have been part of what attracted her to the man she ran away with after college. Ten years her elder, he was a true revolutionary, a veteran of the free-speech movement at Berkeley. He taught American history and specialized in blacks in the Civil War period; and was a buddy of Huey Newton, an acquaintance of Bobby Seale, and something of a hero to Johanna Neuman.

They moved across the nation to live in Owego, near the State University of New York at Binghamton. Her man was excited by Johanna's generation, the Woodstock generation, this younger generation of radicals. But, he also found the members terribly naive, and he became increasingly disillusioned with where the nation was heading.

"I remember he said to me on New Year's Eve of 71, he wasn't at all sure he wanted to live into the 70s, the Me Decade, as we came to call it.

"And a few months later he killed himself, with a note that talked about his disappointment in the revolution, and about how he just couldn't go on in this atmosphere."

The reasons for suicide are never clear. He had been a "red-diaper baby," his father a Communist in the 30s, his mother a disciple of avant-garde dancer Isadora Duncan. They had marched every Sunday for the Rosenbergs, the radical couple charged with spying and later executed.

His parents mellowed with time; his father became an academic, and his mother taught dance. But Johanna came to believe that the tension of having such a radical activist background to live up to may have played a part in his decision to take his life.

By then, Johanna was twenty-one years old and angry.

She wrote a letter to Huey Newton, arguing that the radicals had to put down their guns, that violence would come to no good, that it would only hurt innocent people, people like the man she lived with. Newton wrote back, telling of the power of a gun for people who feel unempowered.

But the tragedy of her lover's suicide left Johanna changed in many ways.

"I had determined never again to depend on anyone else to put a roof over my head," she says. "I had been raised in a home where a career was expected of me anyway, but this underscored that I didn't want to depend on a man."

She enrolled in journalism school, and spent the next decade immersed in building her career. Eventually, she found herself in Jackson, Mississippi, at a newspaper she had heard was trying to turn itself around from a sorry past.

Having missed the civil rights movement, she used this as an opportunity to catch up on some things. She learned during her two and a half years in Jackson that everything in life is not black and white. There are many shades of gray.

"I saw all the ambiguities that come in a state like Mississippi where the white establishment could not be gentler with their black neighbors, but then marched into the legislature and voted down every bill that might help them.

"The wonderful ironies of daily life, in what to me was basically a foreign country, helped me grow up, and see that human beings are very complicated. They are not all evil or good, that we all have pieces of both in us."

With this more rounded, less hard-edged language and thought, she moved on to Washington, and then to Harvard on a fellowship.

Johanna began covering the White House during the Republican Convention in 1984, and then it was off on the campaign trail and on to Bowling Green University with Ronald Reagan and his theme of Morning in America.

"This is the first time I had seen Ronald Reagan at a campus since I had protested against him at Berkeley fourteen years before and I was quite shocked. First of all, the men were very clean-shaven, with close-cut haircuts. They were muscular men in T-shirts that showed their biceps, they had been working out, and they're screaming 'USA! USA!' with their fists in the air.

"And then Reagan came on, and said something like, just say no, and they all screamed. They loved it. They applauded it."

But the greatest shock came during the question-and-answer period. A beautiful nubile woman of nineteen stood up to ask Reagan a question. She gave a girlish, sexy, bosom-heaving sigh and purred: "I have a question but first I have to say—you look greeeaaatttt."

"I just sat and stared at that girl," Johanna says. "I mean, this is the oldest president in American history, who when I was in college I thought was a fascist, and this woman had this sexual feeling, this nineteen-year-old had a thing about this seventy-five-year-old. And it was an image that was underscored every time I have been with Reagan at a campus."

Johanna has never spoken with Reagan about their long-lost connection. Her reluctance to mention it comes partly because Reagan has said, "I remember when they marched into my office barefooted when I was governor."

"I feel that if I told him he would then see me as barefooted."

But the long road from Berkeley to the White House still feels, to Johanna, as a continuous and connected one.

"I was mostly political then and I'm mostly political now. People recall how I used to dress—in every manner of hippie tent—and now I've become something of a clotheshorse so I spend Saturdays at Bloomingdale's.

"I suppose you could argue it's the same emphasis on clothes, just a different solution.

"I'm sure people look at me and see a yuppie. I have a Cuisinart. But what does that mean? I'm a card-carrying member of Amnesty International. I care deeply about human beings and what happens to them. By outward standards I'm part of the yuppie class. I have a cleaning lady. But basically my sympathy lies with the underdog. My sympathies are still with the have-nots, even though I am a have."

Johanna Neuman's job, covering the White House for the largest newspaper company in America, makes her reluctant to discuss some of her more political activities outside of work. But how she has changed, and the ways she has stayed the same, say much about the Woodstock generation.

"I look back and think of myself then as an absolutist," she says, recalling the 60s. "The world was black and white. You're for us or agin' us. There was no compromise. That's what made us feel so wonderful—that virtuousness that frankly you can only have if you're eighteen or nineteen years old. Never again do you feel so sure of life.

"The chords still play in me when I hear the music of the impoverished or the have-nots, but my vote has changed. I think the one element of my own development is an enormous cynicism about the process."

A few years after Bowling Green she married Ron Nessen, the presidential press secretary who defended Gerald Ford's coordination.

"That cynicism is the one thing that allowed me to marry a Republican. We are both quite cynical about the difference between process and ideology. Will Rogers once said, 'Anyone who has great respect for sausage or the law should never watch either being made.' In the end, it's all political compromise."

Still, Johanna doesn't dismiss the idealism of the 60s.

"It was a wonderful thing. That movement got the country out of war. And it is still prevailing on the mindset of the country, in that no one wants to go to Central America to fight communism. It's not a small accomplishment, what we did."

But what the Woodstock generation was going to do now, that was another matter.

It was in this period that antinuclear activism became stronger on the national scene. It was buoyed by such matters as Reagan's strengthening of the military, the deployment in England of American cruise missiles, and the growing call for a nuclear freeze.

Television mightily aided in giving this movement national exposure. "The Day After," a horrifying, apocalyptic view of the aftermath of a nuclear holocaust, riveted America's attention. For weeks before it aired, parents debated whether they should let their children watch it, and if so, how to explain it to them afterward.

Group viewings were arranged at churches and schools and counselors were brought in to help people cope with the painful emotions the film was sure to elicit. The National Education Association sent out its first-ever national alert, suggesting that children under twelve not be allowed to watch and that older children see it only with adults.

A starkly worded memo circulated in the New York City school system, summing up the dilemma facing schools across the nation: "ABC's intention in presenting it is to educate the public about nuclear war. However, the scenes of terrible destruction, people being vaporized, mass graves, and death from radiation sickness may NOT be helpful or educational for children and young people. This is not just one more horror film. Adults can confidently tell youngsters that ghouls and vampires don't exist, but the threat of nuclear war is real."

The White House, wary that the film would heighten fears over Reagan's arms policies, arranged for Secretary of State George Shultz to be interveiwed on TV immediately after the movie was shown. Shultz tried to turn the film into a public relations boost, saying the movie portrayed "a vivid and dramatic portrait of the fact that nuclear war is simply unacceptable."

But the controversy surrounding the film provided the nuclear freeze movement with a huge platform—and tons of free advertising.

The freeze movement had been building since the early 80s; a 1982 rally drew an estimated million people in New York City.

The week of "The Day After" was a busy one for David Cortright. As national director of the Committee for a Sane Nuclear Policy, one of two major antinuclear arms movements of the period, he was giving speeches and organizing groups to watch the film. And generally doing what he had been doing for a long time.

Since Woodstock, in fact.

David Cortright was in New York on Woodstock weekend. At Fort Hamilton. In the army.

David was from a conservative, working-class Catholic family. He had gone to Notre Dame and hadn't thought much about the broader social issues that others in the generation were screaming about.

Then came the draft.

At Fort Hamilton he talked to soldiers returning from Vietnam and "realized something was very wrong." He began associating with GI peace activities. It is little remembered that there were peace movements even on military bases.

David "began circulating petitions among my fellow GIs, all wishing we could be at Woodstock, and trying to make a little bit of a Woodstock happening within the army."

David wasn't sure what to do with his life, but knew he had been turned off by the military and turned on by the notion of organizing against war. "That set me on a course for my life," Cortright said.

"I would continue to work to prevent future Vietnams and prevent nuclear war, and try to see if the world couldn't order itself a little more rationally."

Cortright and other anti-Vietnam activists were instrumental in beginning the antinuke movement. As the 80s wore on, the movement became more popular.

Movements against the United States' policy in Central America were for hard-core activists. The protest against nuclear weapons, however, was a bit more middle-of-the-road, easier for people to get involved in. By 1982 more than ten million people across the USA had voted on various freeze referenda, according to Cortright's figures, and a thousand grassroots groups had sprung up across the country.

"A lot of people who had been involved in Vietnam, and then turned back to more personal concerns when the war was over, came out of the closet in the early 80s when the freeze came along." But many of them, David knew, lacked the deeper commitment necessary to remain active over the long haul. But it was a start.

The Woodstock generation had trouble remaining committed to issues because there was no issue—not even the threat of nuclear war—that touched people as personally as the Vietnam War did.

"I think there was certainly something about the Vietnam experience. It was much more searing and profoundly disturbing, and therefore more deeply motivating than the experience around the freeze," Cortright said.

"There were hundreds of guys who were getting killed every week. Our whole generation had to deal with this thing. That's obviously a much deeper and more powerful experience than what a lot of people felt in the early 80s: 'Oh, wow! Nuclear war really could happen, that's scary, maybe we can do something about it, let's get involved in the freeze.'

"It's obviously an important issue, but it's always more abstract."

But with hundreds of thousands—perhaps millions getting involved at least to some degree in the nuclear freeze movement, "The Day After" formed a timely milestone for the Woodstock generation.

Thousands of calls poured in to nuclear freeze groups around the country after the show. But the response would not last.

Nevertheless, this was a time for choices. The generation had broken its stupor with the emergence of Ronald Reagan; those who agreed with his policies as well as those who didn't discovered a newfound energy through his message of strength, his image of well-being. Now the question was, What would people do with that energy?

The antinuclear movement would be the first breaking-off point. A whole new breed of deeply committed activists—some with roots in the antiwar movement, some not—evolved as a tight, core group.

Most Woodstock generation members, however, did not make that choice, and haven't—at least not yet. Buoyed by the feel-good philosophies of Ronald Reagan, they turned toward enjoying themselves and the trappings of the good life that Reagan had made popular again.

The mid-80s saw the explosion in home video recorders. In the first five months of 1984, 2.3 million VCRs were sold, up 86 percent from the same period a year earlier. It was estimated at year's end that seventeen million recorders were whirring away in homes across the nation, seven million more than a year earlier. This was the year that the Supreme Court ruled you weren't breaking the law if you taped a show like "Hill Street Blues" at home.

It was also the year that stereo television and high-fidelity VCRs hit the market—the technology that would make the home-entertainment tidal wave possible. Stores like 7-Eleven and even U-Haul got into the video rental business, previously populated almost solely by independent operators.

Video in a different form had another important impact on the Woodstock generation. MTV had been broadcasting since the early 80s, but finally came into its own during the middle of the decade. The music industry wasn't yet at the point where it couldn't produce a hit record without a video, but it was getting close.

With perhaps the exception of long-standing stars like Bruce Springsteen, the early 80s were devoid of megastars in the music field. There were no performers that "everybody" was listening to.

The video boom of 1983–84 changed all that. The first performer to really successfully marry music and video was Michael Jackson. His "Thriller" video launched the revolution (or the video revolution launched "Thriller"); sales of the album topped anything previously seen.

Jackson also broke the white stranglehold on the music video scene. Michael was followed by other black performers. Tina Turner and Prince, for example, each had a major impact on the video boom.

Television created a mass audience that allowed stars to pop suddenly into national prominence, to reach everyday folk on an enormous scale. Cyndi Lauper and Madonna were perhaps the first two true VidKids—Lauper with her crazy, funny, funky, playful style; Madonna with her flagrant, sexy, skimpy-underwear appeal.

They may be what saved the Woodstock generation from becoming like the businessman in *The Big Chill*, refusing to play anything but 60s music. For the first time, the generation began to show interest in the new music.

The video boom made Cyndi Lauper and Madonna and Michael Jackson as ubiquitous as a *USA Today* box, as accessible as *People* magazine.

Whereas the mainstream music of the early 80s was safe (whitebread pop of the Yes, Genesis, and Foreigner variety), the video explosion brought thrills, musically and visually, to this national audience.

Jackson's video success—with "Billie Jean" and "Beat It" accompanying "Thriller"—gave birth to another phenomenon: the megatour. The Jacksons Victory Tour, held in giant stadiums across the country, gave rise to similar gigantic shows throughout the decade.

Without doubt, teenagers were the main target audience of MTV; in fact, a separate video channel for the slightly older set came around about this time. But MTV was where the action was, and where that national unity in music listening came about.

There was also a sad irony in this. The last time "everybody" listened to the same music was the late 60s. Now, that unity materialized not because of the content of the music, but because of the money behind it, the money that fueled the music-video machine.

There were other side effects of the video boom that were nostalgic reminders for the Woodstock generation. In the 60s, it was still possible for a little garage band on an independent label to attract a huge national following: the Grateful Dead, for example, thrived through the 60s and 70s (and much of the 80s) before it ever had a hit on the charts.

But the need for a video to promote a song shut the lid on that. Suddenly, there was not just the cash investment needed for the album, but also the bigger price tag for a video to consider. Backing only the safe and the clearly salable became even that much more attractive.

Not that many risks were being taken in music before, but taking risks now became virtually impossible.

"I can't think of the last hit single that didn't have a video," rock music critic Edna Gundersen said. "You just can't do it anymore. It just comes with the territory."

But this also meant that someone like a Janis Joplin would not stand a chance. There was just too much emphasis on image, on looks, on attractiveness. The need for packaging made Madonna drop her trashy look for a *Vogue* one.

"That's the thing that's selling," said Edna. "It's hard to distinguish now between the commercials on MTV and the videos. They're pretty much just cloning themselves, but it's revolutionized music."

Prince, for example, was always a critical favorite, and had some success, but the movie *Purple Rain* turned him into a megastar.

By the the end of the 80s Prince, Jackson, and Springsteen were still mining new territory, but the general mindset in the music industry was to play it safe, go with what works.

"It's the 'American Bandstand' line," Gundersen said, "it's got a good beat and you can dance to it. Clean, crisp, pop-sounding material that doesn't really offend anybody."

But at least a connection between the Woodstock generation and new music—a connection lost for many years—had finally begun to form. As the nation moved into the second term of Ronald Reagan, rediscovered the Vietnam War, and witnessed the full blooming of the yuppies, that connection would become important.

And as the generation made its choices, the music would once again nudge it along in the right direction.

CHAPTER NINE

The Road Diverges

Do not mistake nostalgia for rebirth. Do not mistake remembrance for renewal.

As the Woodstock generation moved toward the end of the 80s, it was carried back toward the past. But that nostalgia would prove fertile ground from which rebirth and renewal could spring.

"Nostalgia is a form of depression for society," said Abbie Hoffman. "It means they don't want to face the future and they can't deal with the present, so let's look to some bygone era for our styles, our music, our identification."

But the nostalgia of the 80s also prompted people to remember their 60s values and strengthened the fetal heartbeat of change within the sleeping giant of the Woodstock generation.

The conditions were ripe for a reawakening of the spirit: an Eisenhower-like president and a 1950s conservative wind blowing across the nation; an economic prosperity, or at least the appearance of prosperity; and a growing feeling of restlessness, visible only in fragments here and there, but a restlessness nonetheless.

And gone were the stupor and the malaise of the 70s. In its place were the first faint signs of a rejuvenated, reawakened generation.

When the 80s began, the generation was turning away from its youthful values: freedom, commitment, faith in one's own ability to change the world. As the 80s end, those long-dormant values call louder and more passionately to the generation. And the generation began to respond.

Or so it appeared. The question remained: What would happen to the Woodstock generation? Would the cynicism built over a decade and a half smother that renewal?

Or, as the *Washington Post* asked in 1986: Is "Doonesbury" less funny in the 1980s, or are we?

Artist Garry Trudeau had just returned from a hiatus; and when he came back, his characters moved from Walden Commune into the real world. And his readers, a solid chunk of the Woodstock generation, were less than universally enthusiastic.

"For almost fifteen years the main characters have been trapped in a time warp," Trudeau wrote before taking his two-year break. "My characters are understandably confused and out of sorts. It's time to give them some $20 haircuts, graduate them, and move them into the larger world of grownup concerns. The trip from draft beer and mixers to cocaine and herpes is a long one, and it's time they got started."

So as his characters changed—as Mike Doonesbury became an ad exec, Mark Slackmeyer joined National Public Radio, B.D. got drafted by the Los Angeles Rams, Zonker won the lottery and became a Lord—the comic strip's political commentary became more direct and bold.

Suddenly, Trudeau's characters made news themselves. Again and again, newspapers canceled his strip because it was "offensive" or too political. From an imaginary anti-abortion film called "Silent Scream II: The Prequel" to barbs thrown at targets ranging from Frank Sinatra to Santa Barbara's anti-homeless policy, the strip was constantly in the middle of the news.

"Maybe the answer to the 'Doonesbury' puzzle is that it's hard to be a gentle, liberal satirist in the 1980s," wrote David Ignatius, associate editor of the *Washington Post*, bemoaning the unfunniness of the strip. "In these conservative times, a fighter for liberal causes like Trudeau undoubtedly feels embattled, and perhaps also out of step with the national mood."

Trudeau allowed his characters to move into the 80s, but they retained a fierce connection to their liberal past. And this is the first key to understanding what was happening to the Woodstock generation. While the values of the 80s beat within their hearts, the values of the 60s beat there too. And this began to create an inner conflict.

In psychology, this is cognitive dissonance: actions and values sometimes conflict and people feel uncomfortable and unhappy.

And so it was with Trudeau's readers. Even those who agreed with his politics were annoyed at the intrusion into their entertainment. Again, the message was getting in the way of the music.

But the message was heard, nonetheless, and produced a discordant note; a feeling that something was out of balance, even as the old values started to murmur and bubble.

A feeling, buried deep inside, bubbled in many—that they could change the world. For some, their first instinct was to ignore the feeling; it was unsettling. But the way to eliminate cognitive dissonance is to make a choice. Choices were made, and they launched the Woodstock generation in a new direction, but on many different paths.

One path lead to the workplace.

A most underreported phenomenon of the 80s was that people were leaving their jobs and the security of corporate life in droves and heading off on their own. Americans, most of the Woodstock generation, were starting companies at a rate five times faster than at the beginning of the decade.

Increasingly, young adults had felt out of place in the business world they had joined. So, they tried to create a new one.

In the 60s the battle was to change society. This time around, for some, the struggle was on a personal level—to take control of their own lives.

At first glance, this seemed to be a mere extension of the yuppie dream: to own a business so as to make *all* the money.

But that wasn't the case. For one thing, surveys showed that most people who went to work for themselves made less money, not more, during the first few years. It frequently meant struggle and sacrifice.

They made the jump not so much for greed as out of personal need. A 1986 survey showed that most workers who changed jobs did so for money, a bigger salary. A survey of entrepreneurs about the same time showed that being their own bosses was more important than money; it enabled them, they said, to control their own lives.

And it didn't make much difference whether you were talking to someone in a pinstripe suit running a multi-million-dollar business or a guy running a small video rental shop. Each talked about two things: freedom and commitment.

David Ransen started his own company during the 80s. Like many Woodstock entrepreneurs, it was something he never expected to do.

David was at Woodstock—sort of. He went to Bethel a few days before the music began. He had been traveling with some friends, and they heard something good was coming down at Max Yasgur's farm.

David hung around, had a good time, and met some neat people. But he was due in Boston and decided to head off. Upon hearing the news about Woodstock on the radio that weekend, and upon viewing the pictures on a motel TV, he couldn't believe he had left.

He had a feeling of being-there-but-not-being-there—not all that different from his feeling at Clark University the next year. David didn't consider himself a hippie but felt a strong sense of belonging to those who did.

After college, David taught at Worcester Alternative School, one of the country's early attempts to create a different school environment. "They turned all the rules upside down," David remembers. Every rule in the school was arrived at by democratic vote, and every student and faculty member had a single vote—on issues from attendance rules to dress codes to whether there would be written exams.

David believed in alternative education and he was proud of how rarely the students took unfair advantage. But in the long run he was disappointed. The school knew what it was moving away from, but not where it was going.

He went to Cornell University, got his doctorate in 1979, and took a teaching job at Tulane University.

"At the time, my ambition was still to 'clean up Dodge City.' I felt like I wanted to do something about the education system. I thought it was awful, and I thought children were the answer and the hope."

He liked his new job, training teachers. But the institution required that he do other things; publish and gather prestige. After a year, he left.

David went through a few more jobs, each a little more distant from teaching the children and changing the world through them. He worked as a liaison between computer gurus and the educational researchers for the state of Louisiana and then went to New Jersey, where he took a bureaucratic job in the state's Department of Higher Education.

This was where David Ransen made his choice.

His job was not satisfying. Worse, he had become part of the bureaucracy.

So David struck out on his own.

"I certainly didn't quit my job and go into my business for money, because I was making what I considered to be very good money, and they kept throwing raises at me every six months. I wasn't expressing myself, I wasn't using my potential, either for my own benefit or society's."

David began doing consulting work—using the computer knowledge he'd picked up along the way—writing computer software for his clients. Some of the jobs were more satisfying than others, like the programs he developed for a company compiling information about cancer cases to figure out the best treatments for certain kinds of cancer. Others just paid the bills.

There were tough financial times, but he decided to move beyond working for one client at a time—just selling his hours. He wanted to create a product, something he could sell.

It started by accident. The woman he lived with was a sales representative for a computer company that needed a better way to keep track of its customers, so David wrote a program to help her out. It caught on, and a year later a hundred stores around North America were using it.

It didn't make much money, but it was fun.

"Looking back, I can see a clear progression—from doing things because they'll make the world a better place, to doing things because they're satisfying, because they made me feel good. I was becoming more motivated by what made me feel fulfilled."

Is that selfish?

"I understand the word *selfish* to mean that you neglect, or abuse, other people's interests to serve your own interest. So, no. I wasn't doing things at other people's expense. But I was becoming more self-oriented."

People who used his software were calling him, telling him his product was helping them in their daily lives. "That made me feel good. To me, that's not selfish. That's just plain rewarding. You've done something you enjoy doing, and as a bonus, people are grateful."

People were admiring his programs for their grace and intricacy—almost like admiring a piece of art—and that made him proud.

He also enjoyed sitting in a room working out problems on a computer. It was enriching in much the same way teaching was. Many teachers say that to communicate something to others, you have to think it through in a way you never thought it through before.

"The same thing with computer programming," said Davis. "Computers are much dumber than children. There's a tremendous feeling of honing your thinking to such a sharp edge that you're able to make a dumb machine understand you."

But these were also hard years, working seventy hours a week and draining his savings. But people kept calling him and telling him that they loved his work, and that helped keep him going.

One day, he was using a popular Xerox program, which allowed people to produce typeset-quality documents on their personal computer. He noticed a lack in that program, and figured other users would notice it too. He decided to write a sort of add-on to the Xerox program.

It took thirty hours a week for six months, doing it on the side in addition to his other work. But Xerox liked it, and invited him to display it in its booth at computer shows.

In early 1988 he decided to go for broke, spending a lot of his own money on advertising. "I hadn't drawn a salary in three years, and there I was spending huge chunks of my life savings. At this point, for the first time, I was really an entrepreneur, in the sense that I was taking risks."

He experienced the thrill of a high-stakes bet, like a gambler in Las Vegas, but also abject, total fear.

"Since I'm not much of a gambler, the terror outweighed the thrill."

Today the program is doing very well. David's got his savings back up; after never taking a penny out of his company, he's actually seeing a return.

And he discovered a new enjoyment: freedom.

"There's no question that I draw great pleasure from being my own boss. Let's face it, we spend two-thirds of our waking hours at work. Two-thirds of Life-with-a-Capital-L. So to that extent, I've taken control of two-thirds of my life, anyway."

David sometimes thinks back on his earlier goals—wanting to change the world, and wanting to do it through the children—and feels a certain sense of disappointment. But no regrets.

"We often used the words *selling out* in the Us versus Them period. I can remember when I was beginning grad school, and somebody finishing up their doctorate accepted a position with Quaker Oats. We smirked and chuckled amongst ourselves that he sold out. I think that wasn't true. I think that was unfair.

"It seems to me that selling out means betraying what you believe in for personal gain. I really don't feel I've betrayed anything I believed in. What I'm doing now isn't in conflict with the goals I had as a young man. They're different goals; but they're not conflicting goals. If I were involved in the madness of Saturday-morning commercial television for children, where the programming is just a four-hour commercial for war toys—if I were doing that, I could be fairly accused of selling out. What I'm doing now may or may not be making the world a better place, but it's not in conflict with the goals I had before."

Some who tried to take control of their lives, however, felt not that sense of liberation, but a sense of isolation. Some simply shut the world out. Cocooning would come full force in the late 80s.

The toys for the home, the CDs and stereo TVs and designer sheets and designer food, formed a comfortable pillow. They were not the labor-saving devices our parents craved. Most meant more work, not less—making pasta is a lot harder than buying it in a box. They were life-sweetening devices.

By the late 80s you could come home from the office and have your evening delivered—from the Domino's pizza to the video cassette. By this time there was no need to leave the home at all, and many didn't, physically or emotionally.

This growing sense of isolation also showed up in the way the generation talked to its children. Children of the late 80s were given many frightening messages. Stay away from drugs because they'll kill you. Don't smoke cigarettes because they can kill you. Don't talk to strangers because you could become a missing child with your face on a milk carton.

Certainly these are all sane messages, but their cumulative effect was fear. The children of the Woodstock generation would live in a world of fear much broader than their parents did. Whereas the Woodstock generation grew up with the specific, real fear of death from the atom bomb and the Vietnam War, their children faced a world of death around every corner.

Death also came to a few old friends in 1985. These were not the heroes of the 60s, and the generation watched their passing as one watches his parents' friends, with a mixture of sad longing and curious detachment: Desi Arnaz, Fred Astaire, Ray Bolger, Jackie Gleason, Cary Grant, Danny Kaye, Robert Preston, David Susskind.

But one other death, a short time later, had much more impact.

Rock Hudson died on the morning of October 5, 1985, and for millions of everyday people across the nation AIDS was suddenly no longer some perverted, get-what-they-deserve disease for people they didn't know and didn't care to.

More than twelve thousand were already dead or dying of AIDS and not many apart from the victims' friends or family seemed to notice. But Rock Hudson's death changed that; he was a hero of the straight world—for God's sake, he romanced Doris Day in all those movies! But his death somehow made it more acceptable for ordinary people to be concerned about AIDS.

In a survey conducted shortly after Hudson's death, Americans ranked AIDS as the second most serious health threat facing the nation. Only cancer ranked higher. And overwhelmingly, the country felt more resources were needed to fight it.

Acquired Immune Deficiency Syndrome doesn't usually kill its victims. It simply allows them to be killed.

The AIDS virus looks like a wheel with spokes sticking out of the rim. This bumpy wheel grabs a healthy cell and destroys its ability to reproduce and to make white cells, the body's protection against infection.

The AIDS virus does, however, reproduce infected cells at an accelerated rate, many times faster than other genes. That's why its victims die so quickly.

Without white cells, the body becomes a fragile shell, unable to defend itself against attack, an open path to what doctors call "opportunistic" diseases—lung infections, skin cancer, meningitis, liver disease, prolonged diarrhea, and a parasite that steals sight.

AIDS is an agonizing way to die, full of pain and false hope. It's progressive; a victim can fight off one infection, only to expend in the process his precious, diminishing supply of white cells. The next infection is worse, and the one after that more dangerous still, until pretty soon the body has no more defenses left and the victim dies—always.

Betty Holloran didn't have a technical knowledge of AIDS in December 1984, when the telephone rang and her husband, Jim, picked up the receiver. But she sensed it was a death sentence.

Their second oldest son, Michael, was calling from Colorado.

"Dad, get mom on the phone, too, so that I can tell you both something together." They listened on the two phones in the house.

"Jimmy has AIDS."

Betty Holloran screamed.

The conversation became frantic.

"We're taking the next plane out to San Francisco," Betty said.

"No, Jimmy doesn't want that," Michael said. "He doesn't even want you to call, right away."

Betty called Jimmy's doctor. An hour and a half later she called her son. Jimmy Holloran's voice was weak over the phone, his words were coming in gasps.

"Mom," he said, "what took you so long?"

Tears welled in her eyes. Once again, Jimmy was her son. "Your father and I are coming right out," she told him.

Once again, Jimmy said no.

He was in a clear plastic oxygen tent. He was in bad shape, much worse than they knew. And if mom and dad came out, Jimmy thought, it might be the end for him.

Jimmy had known for months that he had the disease. He started feeling ill in the spring, just after completing what would be an award-winning documentary film on AIDS. He was losing weight, was tired, short of breath, and developing a hoarseness and soreness in his chest and throat. A fungal condition, candidiasis, frequently affects the mouth and esophagus of AIDS victims. Jimmy knew all the symptoms.

He had been feeling okay back in November when he came home to Washington, D.C., to celebrate the twenty-fifth anniversary of Gonzaga High's city championship football team, his team. It was time, friends urged him, to make peace with his mother and father.

Jimmy argued at first, but relented and went to see his mother and father. Before he left they cried, and hugged.

Jimmy began to feel worse, quickly, but still continued to deny his illness, making excuses to himself for feeling so tired, so washed out, for the hacking cough that signaled pneumonia—textbook symptoms. He refused even to see his own doctor until he could only crawl up the steps of his own home. When finally he did seek help, Jimmy was hospitalized immediately.

Jimmy's brothers Bob, Johnny, and Michael flew out to see their brother. The medication he was on helped and by Christmas, when Jim and Betty Holloran arrived to visit their son, he was up and walking.

Christmas that year was a mixture of emotions. One day his parents arrived at a hospital to find Jimmy gone. Frightened, they found a nurse who told them that he was meeting with a support group.

The group was made up of AIDS patients. Many hadn't told their families they were sick; or if they did, probably didn't reveal they had AIDS. AIDS patients were being disowned by their families, and papers carried stories of whole towns forcing children with AIDS out of elementary schools. Some of the dead were being buried in cemeteries for the destitute—potter's fields.

Jimmy returned from his group, happy to see his parents, but upset that so many of his fellow patients were being rejected. "I was embarrassed to tell them that my dad and mom would be waiting for me back in my hospital room," he said.

Jimmy also told his parents to be honest about his illness. He had lived in the shadows long enough.

"I don't want any lies about me when you go home," he told them. "I don't want you to tell people that I have cancer or anything else. I want them to know who I am and I want the truth told about me."

One night, not long afterward, when they were back home, Jim and Betty were playing bridge with some friends from the neighborhood. Betty stopped for a moment and said she had something to share with them:

Jimmy was gay. And Jimmy had AIDS.

"Betty, why are you telling that to people?" said one of her friends, horrified. "Don't tell anybody that."

"My God, this is our son!" she cried in frustration. "He's sick, and he's going to die!"

In February Jimmy moved to Paris for an experimental treatment at the Pasteur Institute. The drugs stopped the progress of the disease, and he sometimes felt good enough to run or sightsee.

He took an apartment, up four flights of steps, and kept his illness a secret. Five days a week he got on a bus and rode to the institute to get his shot of the experimental drug HPA-23.

As a doctor, he knew AIDS was a terminal disease. Like anyone, however, he hoped for a miracle. But the hope collapsed with a sudden, black, cold, crash. Jimmy began fading again.

The experimental drug was working against the AIDS virus. But pneumonia was killing him. His friends convinced him to come home.

Back in San Francisco Jimmy started getting stronger again, but he knew it was only a matter of time before another infection struck.

"The numbers are clearly not on my side," he told the *American Medical News* in October 1985, just days after Rock Hudson's death.

Jimmy returned to Paris for more treatments. His parents followed a few weeks later. Jimmy was forty-three, yet he climbed the steps to his apartment like an old man.

Within a few weeks, he was unable to feed himself. Betty Holloran would buy food and make dinner. Jimmy grew weaker and weaker, until one day he told them, "I'll never get back to the States if I don't leave now."

This time he returned home to Washington.

His parents moved him into their front upstairs bedroom in the house in northwest Washington, D.C. It had a hospital bed, a TV, and a telephone. There was a black leather reclining chair in the room, so that he could sit and watch television.

His friends Dean Bauer and Tom Huster from California came to visit. Others followed.

His high school girlfriend, Mary Flynn, a nurse, stopped by frequently to look after him.

One afternoon, Jimmy went to George Washington Hospital for some tests, and found out that the virus was affecting his sight. A rage built up in him.

He went home and kicked the black leather chair in his bedroom. It was one of the few times that Jimmy showed the frustration, the futility of his illness.

Finally, a new doctor suggested still another experimental treatment, another last chance. This time Jimmy shook his head. Enough. There would be no miracle.

Jim and Betty Holloran stayed with their son night and day. They gave Jimmy intravenous treatments and injections. They shaved him. They fed him. They read to him.

One night, Betty went up to Jimmy's room.

"I'm dying, mom."

"Jim, we're right here with you," she told him. "We love you and we're going to do everything in the world for you. But please, find it in your heart to talk to God."

She prayed for Jimmy that night, as she did every night; not for a miracle—she knew better than that. She prayed that Jimmy Holloran would return to his faith.

John was walking past his brother's room a few nights later. He heard Jimmy's voice, and then realized Jimmy was alone in the room. Slowly, he went in.

"Jimmy, who are you talking to?" John asked.

"I am talking with God."

John had a Bible and at nights would sit by the hospital bed and read passages to his brother. And then on April 17, 1986 Jimmy Holloran slipped into a coma on a quiet Sunday night and died.

A few weeks later Jim and Betty Holloran went to San Francisco. Friends of their son had a party for them. There were doctors Jimmy had worked with, friends he had played tennis and baseball with, and people who had worked on his films.

"We saw all these people and I realized we've been dealing with gay people all our life and didn't know it," Betty said. "They were wonderful people. And they were wonderful to Jimmy."

Traveling home on the plane, Jim and Betty Holloran talked about how wrong they had been. They sat down and wrote a letter to their son, which was published in a magazine.

They wrote about his triumphs as a child and about his victories as a young adult. They wrote about how he must have agonized over his homosexuality so much that he was forced to move away. They also wrote about how, after Jimmy's death, relatives argued about whether to mention AIDS in his obituary.

"But this was no time to shy away from what others might think." AIDS was mentioned in the very first paragraph of Jimmy's obituary in the *Washington Post*.

"Your sickness taught us . . . about who we are and what we really believe," they wrote in the letter. "At some point along the way we stopped praying you'd become straight and started praying simply that God would take care of you.

"We were grateful that in having you at home we'd been given a second chance. Many families don't get that chance with their kids, gay or straight."

The letter was just signed, "Love, Mom and Dad."

Most straight members of the Woodstock generation did not undergo the cathartic experience that Jimmy's mom and dad did. AIDS remained a distant concern for a while. But little by little its reality infiltrated the generation's consciousness, and produced a fear that spread as rapidly as the virus itself.

The Woodstock generation had already been through one sexual revolution. Its fear of AIDS now drove it toward a second—from free sex, to safe sex, to, in some cases, no sex.

Commonly, people now asked potential sex partners if they had a sexual disease and, even, if they would be willing to take an AIDS test. AIDS took much of the spontaneity out of sex. Surveys showed that people in the late 1980s began taking fewer sexual partners. The main reason: the fear of AIDS.

Fear of AIDS provided one more reason for people to settle into their cocoons. But another kind of fear impelled Bernhard Goetz to pull out a gun and shoot four youths who were threatening him on a New York City subway train.

Goetz was indicted for the shootings in January 1985. The outpouring of sympathy for him was as surprising as it was widespread. The details of the case would become more complicated but the public support for Goetz showed a different side of the Woodstock generation; many were thrilled to see someone fight back against crime, to take control of the circumstances around him.

But the argument over Bernie Goetz also had a racist hue—Goetz is white, the four youths are black. An underlying hint of racism was the first ugly sign of trouble the generation would grapple with.

The "new racism" became evident on college campuses. At Columbia University, in a haunting echo of the riots of 1968, students, teachers, and community activists clashed with police on a chilly February morning. Two months later protesters barricaded an administration building and fifty were arrested. The next night a thousand students demonstrated in front of the library.

The issues were the way the university handled a racial fight among students and its position as a major landlord on the edge of Harlem.

Other racial incidents followed. A fistfight broke out between black Mets fans and white Red Sox fans at the University of Massachusetts at Amherst after a World Series game. Racial tensions exploded at Wellesley, the Citadel, the University of Texas at Austin.

"We are getting to the point where things are potentially explosive," Kuumba Kazi-Ferrouillet, managing editor of the *Black Collegian*, told *Ms.* magazine. "It seems to be all over the country. In the South there was a resurgence of the Confederate days with cross burnings and white fraternities doing things in blackface."

Off campus, the new racism showed itself in more terrifying ways. Whites chased blacks onto a busy expressway in the Howard Beach neighborhood of New York and a black man was hit by a car and killed. The workplace witnessed a shift away from affirmative action and a quiet return of ethnic and racial jokes.

The skinheads, groups of white-supremacist youths, exchanged the closet for virulent racist demonstrations.

Twenty years after the Kerner Commission's landmark report warned that America was splitting into two societies, separate and unequal, that split was continuing, and accelerating.

Some rose up in protest. Blacks and whites were arrested together at Columbia University. A larger protest began with a lobbying group, Trans-Africa, which held daily antiapartheid demonstrations near the South African embassy in Washington. The protests ended in November 1985 and were followed by a call for companies nationwide to divest themselves of holdings in South Africa. On college campuses, "shantytowns" sprang up; students lived in shacks to protest the conditions of blacks in South Africa.

But much of the Woodstock generation remained cynical about these protests, arguing they were merely a chic thing to do. Some took delight in noting that famous stars arrived at the South African embassy protests in limousines, and that the student rallies seemed to coincide with good weather.

Stuart Emeny-Smith was not cynical about the protests. For him, they signaled a rebirth of something important.

Stuart was born in London. What he remembers most about the Woodstock years was the Beatles. At the movies on Saturday mornings, Beatles songs were played between the films. He remembers singing "I Want to Hold Your Hand" while holding hands with those around him.

"My family didn't know how to show love and didn't want to show love," he recalled. "And here were these people singing 'All you need is love.' What was important wasn't necessarily the music; it was the people making the music and the people taking notice of what the music had to say."

On a snowy November day in 1980 Stuart took off for what he believed was a warm, southern part of America—San Francisco, which he thought was south of Los Angeles. It was a fortunate error, because he wound up someplace he'd fit in better: the twenty-four-year-old new-wave "squatter" with green hair from London landed smack-dab in the middle of Berkeley.

"It totally blew my mind. It was like walking into the 60s. No one had changed."

And indeed, sitting by a window of a Telegraph Avenue café in the heart of Berkeley even eight years later, with integrated couples strolling by hand in hand, with young women setting up tables to sell tie-dyed T-shirts and peace-symbol earrings, one was tempted to suggest that the hippie movement had never died, but only moved to Berkeley.

As the years went by, Stuart continued to live just the kind of life he wanted. He taught guitar, went to Grateful Dead concerts, and worked for a program that took city kids to the country.

He found that Berkeley not only was supportive of living the way he wanted to, but seemed downright insistent on it. "In Berkeley, it's very easy to step outside of social norms. In fact, if you become a social norm, that's the worst thing you can do in Berkeley. That's when people begin pointing at you."

Students built shanties on campus to protest the university's investment in companies that did business in South Africa, and Stuart found this very uplifting. "It was really gratifying to see a group of younger people, eighteen- and nineteen-year-old students, get together and be very active against apartheid."

Stuart takes pride in the generation that he sees protesting now—and pride in his own generation for changing society.

"Hippie values of sharing, of racial equality, of personal freedom are incorporated throughout society, and not just in Berkeley. I grew up as a kid in a racist, sexist, disgusting example of how humans can get together, and it was generally like that throughout the Western world. And look how it's changed.

"And why has it changed? It certainly hasn't changed because of governments. It didn't change because of Chuck Berry. It changed because of what people did in the 60s."

Some things did not change.

In June 1985 the world watched another hostage drama. Muslim Shiite terrorists hijacked TWA Flight 847. At first, the Beirut airport refused to allow the plane to land—until pilot John Testrake yelled over the radio, "They are beating the passengers. They are threatening to kill them. I want to land now!"

The plane did land, and almost immediately a passenger, U.S. Navy diver Robert Stethem, was beaten, shot in the head, and pushed out the door. The rest of the passengers were held hostage in the hot, uncomfortable plane for seventeen days. The nation, once more, saw the tragedy on its TV sets, and was outraged.

Four months later another American was killed. Leon Klinghoffer, a retired, crippled New Yorker, was shot by Palestinian terrorists as he sat on the Italian cruise ship *Achille Lauro* in his wheelchair. The terrorists dumped his body and the chair into the Mediterranean.

The ship was held for seven days, until the Egyptian government promised the terrorists safe passage. What happened next clearly showed the United States was losing patience and this time Ronald Reagan was going to do something about it.

At Reagan's order, U.S. fighter planes intercepted the Egyptian flight carrying the terrorists to freedom and diverted it to Italy to bring the killers to trial. The leader, Mohammed Abbas, escaped.

Attacks against Americans continued into the next spring. In April 1986, terrorists planted a bomb in a West German disco frequented by American servicemen. Several Americans were killed; sixty were injured.

This time the anger boiled over. Reagan blamed the attacks on Libya, and promised to punish that nation for its "international reign of terror." Punishment soon came.

On April 15, U.S. bombers struck several places in Libya, including military targets and the home of its dictator, Moammar Qaddafi. The U.S. attack was criticized throughout the world, but back home, people applauded. In a *USA Today* poll shortly after the raid, more than three of four Americans supported the attack.

Reagan did not have such widespread support for other issues. During a trip to Europe in May 1985 he planned a visit to Bitburg, West Germany, site of a World War II military cemetery where Nazi SS troops were buried. The visit became a great embarrassment, sparking worldwide outrage. It was seen as a slight to Nazi victims. There were waves of protest and calls for Reagan to cancel the trip. He didn't.

This was an example of what came to be called the Teflon Presidency—outrage didn't stick to the president. Whom did Americans blame for the incident? Not Reagan. Two of three Americans blamed his aides for "poor planning."

About the same time, a new trend in music started in England. Top artists joined together as Band Aid to record "Do They Know It's Christmas?" to raise money for African famine relief. It spread to the USA, where American artists got together to record "We Are the World."

As always, with this generation, the music paralleled its changing course. Some saw this as another example of 60s values like peace and sharing and helping others being played out in 80s style and joined in. Others thought it was a joke.

Once again, the Woodstock generation simultaneously embraced a movement for social change and cynically derided it as merely a chic thing to do—rich folk thinking that by buying an album they will save the world.

Live Aid followed in July 1985, with over a billion people worldwide watching simultaneous concerts in London and Philadelphia. More than sixty pop stars performed to raise money for the starving people in drought-stricken Africa. Joan Baez greeted the Philadelphia crowd: "Good morning, children of the 80s. This is your Woodstock, and it's long overdue."

But she was wrong.

Author Pete Hamill pointed out the many differences between Woodstock and Live Aid, but admitted it revived memories of the 60s:

"The Woodstock generation defined itself by what it was against. The American Live Aid audience was part of the new American generation that thinks Ronald Reagan is a wonderful president, Rambo a wonderful role model, and Grenada a wonderful war . . . one must note that at Philadelphia, the American flag was waved tirelessly . . . and the whole show was sponsored on TV by Pepsi, AT&T, Eastman Kodak, and Chevrolet."

But, he added, "For that single day, at least, the Live Aid concerts welded together popular art and humane politics, using the power, energy, and invention of rock and roll to accomplish something of practical social value. For that single day, a group of the richest, most spoiled, and safest human beings on the planet assembled in concert to try to feed another group of human beings. . . . This is no small thing. . . . Live Aid was a gigantic act of will, and that's why it stirred some flame in the ashes of my own guttering optimism."

Farm Aid followed, as did Comic Relief, and Hands Across America, all efforts to unite people in working for social change. For the first time in almost two decades, since Vietnam and the antidraft movement, and artists like Country Joe McDonald and Joan Baez, the music was coming with a message.

Some would lend their hands to causes like feeding the starving children in Africa, and helping the farmers here in the United States.

National rock critic Edna Gundersen followed these attempts to build, once again, social conscience through music. For her, as for so many in her generation, the magic in the message of the music began twenty years earlier.

The weekend of Woodstock, Edna was seventeen years old. A strong hippie contingent resided in El Paso, Texas, and all were terribly unhappy.

"I remember being with friends, and we were all basically pining that we couldn't be there. For the first time there seemed to be a center of the universe for our generation, and being in El Paso, we felt like we were on Pluto. All through my teenage years, I felt frustrated at the isolation, at being in a city that far from L.A. and New York and places where It Was Happening."

Edna was a student at the University of Texas at El Paso, and she remembers attending love-ins at a park near the university. There people milled around in tie-dyes and fringe jackets, while frat boys stood at the perimeter with signs reading Don't Feed the Animals.

Edna began working on her college newspaper, and wrote about rock and roll whenever she could. The joy of attending a Jimi Hendrix concert was shattered two months later when Hendrix died. "There was that period in the 60s where everybody felt so invincible, and that was so liberating in so many ways. There was free love and drugs and there was such a sense of power. And then when these rock stars started dying, to me it was just so frightening and disheartening, that there was a crack in the cosmic egg."

At some point in the early 70s Edna, like many others, realized it was about time to get a real job and get serious. But over the years she continued to write about rock and roll whenever she could.

Working as a newspaper reporter, her job began taking her to the new social-consciousness concerts of the mid-80s. Most at those events were very young, but Edna did see the Woodstock generation take part in one huge event.

Hands Across America represented an attempt to form a human chain acorss the United States on Memorial Day weekend of 1986. It was "the biggest crock, the biggest fiasco ever constructed," said Edna. "I think it was one of the worst things ever done in the name of charity. It did nothing for nobody. You took your dollars and filled your car tank and stood somewhere. Why not give that money to the people who are hungry? It was a way for people to appease their conscience."

But the Woodstock spirit did live on in some of these events, and continued through the 1988 Amnesty International tour. The tour, which included Bruce Springsteen, Sting, and Tracy Chapman, was held to raise money for, and awareness of, political prisoners around the world.

"I saw three of the shows," Edna said. "I really felt moved by them, stirred by them. I really felt like here's something that has that sort of power that we saw in the 60s, uniting people into action. In this case the action was not demonstrating in the streets, it was sitting down and writing a letter to presidents of governments that were holding political prisoners. I think they really did it, and they did it with the music.

"And people in the audience were holding up matches and lighters, and for once it wasn't just 'Oh, aren't we hip.' You could see in their faces that the message was really reaching them and making them feel something. I think the artists involved in that tour were much more committed than the group that was rounded up to do the media splash of 'We Are the World.'"

One of those artists was Tracy Chapman, whose debut album shook the record industry and stirred memories of the 60s, when music was written to convey a message. She sang of people in welfare lines, the unemployed, the impoverished of body and spirit. Her rich images were played against sparse instrumentation. The album became immensely popular, particularly with the Woodstock generation, who played it over and over again, just as they had with albums twenty years earlier.

U2, and Springsteen, and Suzanne Vega, and a number of others were also singing songs both deeply personal and socially conscious.

Edna felt a mixture of hope and cynicism about where the message music was headed. "I would love for it to succeed. I think there's a genuine building in that direction. I think Tracy Chapman is sincere. However, knowing what record companies do, knowing what unscrupulous business managers might make of things like this, it's a little scary to think that a year or two down the road a group of multimillionaire heavy-metal long-haired boys with their Ferraris and mansions will get together in a room and try to concoct a winning antiwar chant with no other purpose in mind than to make money. That could just render all the messages flat and meaningless. The only way that kind of music works is when it's heartfelt.

"There are some really good bands that have managed to be both commercially successful and retain their integrity. Springsteen is the shining example. But it's much, much harder than it used to be. Record companies watch the bottom line. They will put Saint Bernards in Girl Scout uniforms on stage if they think people will pay money to see it."

The other alternative for the Woodstock generation, musically, was nostalgia. And if Tracy Chapman was the first new album they had bought in a while, there seemed to be no limit to their ability to listen to the music they had grown up with.

Partly because of the media's love affair with twentieth-anniversary stories, the nation had been reliving the 60s for a while. It started in 1983 with the twentieth-anniversary stories about the Beatles' first trip to America and came full force in 1987 with the twentieth anniversary of the Summer of Love. The fortunate coincidence of the compact-disc-player boom made for a perfect marketing match: the twentieth-anniversary release of "Sergeant Pepper" and then the release of the entire Beatles' canon on compact disc.

The nostalgia explosion made for some sad moments, also.

Simon and Garfunkel were one of beloved groups of the 60s. Relying just on their beautiful harmonies and Simon's fascinating lyrics, they created songs that became anthems for the generation. They sang "Sounds of Silence," and the generation meditated. They sang "Bridge over Troubled Water," and the generation felt consoled in its troubles. They sang the Fifty-ninth Street Bridge song, "Feeling Groovy," and it did.

Then, in the late 80s they were to reunite, and Edna Gundersen saw them on stage in Central Park.

"That was a sad, melancholy moment," says Edna. "These two men on stage obviously couldn't stand each other. They wouldn't look at each other.

There was no rapport whatsoever. They left the concert in separate limousines. It was one of the most heartbreaking things I had ever watched. It was obvious they were doing it for the money and there was no passion in the music. And these were the people who in the 60s had made my heart flutter. It was wonderful the excitement they generated, and it was gone.

"It represents a lot of what happened to this so-called Woodstock generation: you can't hang on to the past; you can't go home again. They tried to re-create something that had already died, that was gone.

"I think we are this generation that keeps going to its own funeral—I know people my age who can't let go of the 60s. I feel that friends my age are far more sentimental and nostalgic than our parents ever dreamed of being."

Another friend from the 60s, Ricky Nelson, died on the last day of 1985, when his plane crashed in Texas. Many in the Woodstock generation grew up with Ricky Nelson, and his parents, the ultimate 50s family, on "The Adventures of Ozzie and Harriet." Ricky had forged a career as a singer, having got his start on his parents' show. The nostalgia boom sparked a resurgence of his career in the 80s. In one of his most poignant songs about that boom, "Garden Party," he sang of his desire to move on musically and the public's desire to keep him in the past.

There were signs that the worst in East-West relations was past. The new Soviet leader, Mikhail Gorbachev, hinted at better relations between the United States and the Soviet Union, and President Reagan stopped referring to the Soviet Union as "the evil empire."

Reagan and Gorbachev held four summit meetings, starting in 1985. Gorbachev stressed economic improvement and social reform over military might in the Soviet Union. The summits resulted in a nuclear arms treaty that would, at least to a degree, lessen the threat of nuclear devastation.

But a different hostility captured America's attention. The Vietnam War had been over for more than a decade, but the nation still couldn't cut it loose.

It all started in a courtroom, during a libel suit filed by a retired army general, William Westmoreland, against CBS over the documentary "The Uncounted Enemy: A Vietnam Deception." The documentary charged that Westmoreland, commander of United States ground forces in Vietnam from 1964 to 1968, misrepresented enemy troop figures to his superiors, including President Johnson.

Westmoreland eventually dropped the suit; in exchange, CBS issued a statement that Westmoreland said amounted to an apology.

But the effect of the Westmoreland case on the Woodstock generation was the reliving of the war. Again. As the long, bitter battle between Westmoreland and CBS continued, the evening news once more was filled nightly with accounts of arguments over "body counts" and "Vietnamiza-tion" and "friendly fire" and the like.

In a way, this was the time that America finally confronted Vietnam, a process that had begun a few years earlier with the opening of the Vietnam Memorial.

Gardens of Stone and *Platoon*, two films released in the late 80s, helped the Woodstock generation redefine its sense of the war.

In contrast to the we-cudda-won-it mentality of Rambo, these films symbolized attempts to apologize to those who had fought the war.

In *Gardens of Stone,* rock promoter extraordinaire Bill Graham has a cameo part as a white-turtlenecked, Nehru-jacketed peacenik lawyer. He calls seasoned war veteran James Caan a "baby killer"—and gets socked in the mouth for it—but later apologizes because "that's what decent people do."

These Hollywood productions reflect a real attitude in the late 80s: those who protested the war and those who fought it needed to come together. They would never agree about the war. But the protesters needed to be honorable and just toward those who fought it.

This change was stated bluntly at the beginning of the home video version of *Platoon*. Tacked on is a message from Chrysler Chairman Lee Iacocca, who is walking through a field and discovers a jeep, a "relic of war": "This film *Platoon* is a memorial—not to war but to all the men and women who fought it, in a time and place nobody really understood; who knew only one thing, they were called and they went.

"It was the same from the first musket fired at Concord to the rice paddies of the Mekong Delta. They were called and they went. That in the truest sense is the spirit of America. The more we understand it the more we honor those who kept it alive."

The separation of the man from the war, and the apology to him, were the missing link in the reconciliation of America. But a few movies and apologies, however heartfelt, did not cure suffering.

Jim Marlow of Big Spring, Texas, was in Vietnam in 1970–71. He didn't exactly hate the war protesters; it even occurred to him that he might be doing the same thing under different circumstances.

But years later he still spoke with anger of his return from Vietnam: "They called us baby killers and spit on us and threw bags of dogshit on us at the airport. That's when my outlook changed. They done what they done, we done what we done. But they had no right in the world to do that to us."

His friend and fellow Vietnam veteran Bob Bolan saw the "apology" showing up in some ways; yet, he felt Vietnam veterans still faced some prejudice. "You pick up a newspaper, and you kinda get a little nervous before you start to read it; you know, where's there going to be a story about a Nam vet screwing up. But anytime we do something good, you never hear about it; it's on some back page in a little bitty column. Something goes wrong, it's a big headline, 'VIETNAM VET GOES CRAZY.' So we still have that. "We don't want an apology. It's not an apology we're looking for. We're just looking for respect."

In January 1986, the space shuttle *Challenger* exploded seventy-two seconds after liftoff from Kennedy Space Center, killing the seven astronauts aboard, including teacher Christa McAuliffe. Because the first teacher in space was aboard, children across the country were watching the launch live in their classrooms, and witnessed the tragedy. The immediacy of the disaster created by television made the nation feel part of the tragedy. Even Christa's parents' reactions, as they saw the shuttle explode, were carried live on television and then played over and over on the evening news. For weeks afterward, news focused on U.S. Navy and Coast Guard boats returning to the spaceport with tons of *Challenger* debris.

But even this tragedy did not diminish the nation's interest in the space program. In a poll taken a week after the explosion, three of four people said the nation should not curtail the space program, but find the problem, fix it, and move ahead as soon as possible. And it was Woodstock generation members who were most determined that the United States get back into space as soon as possible.

On July 4, 1986, the nation gathered for another big patriotic party. It was perhaps the summit of the Woodstock generation's love affair with Ronald Reagan and his new patriotism: the 100th anniversary of the Statue of Liberty.

Peter Max was still painting the Statue of Liberty each Fourth of July. Now, however, he had something more to celebrate.

Hundreds of ships, from rowboats to the battleship *Iowa*, crowded New York Harbor. Many were owned or rented by corporations and featured lavish spreads to entertain and impress important customers. Others were manned by everyday families. Millions more watched on shore in New York and New Jersey and celebrated in their town squares and backyards across America.

The Statue of Liberty had been restored at a cost of millions of dollars, raised through a combination of corporate gifts and private donations from people nationwide, including dimes and pennies collected by school-children.

Although few in the crowd knew it, it was Peter Max who had started the ball rolling.

In 1981, two days after helping the Reagans celebrate their first Fourth of July in the White House. Peter was at home painting when a man named Bob Grace showed up at his door with a scrapbook filled with closeup photos of the Statue of Liberty. They showed rust and decay from years of corrosion.

"Please, can you help do something about this?" Grace asked.

Max hesitated, thinking of the magnitude of the project. Then he got an idea: Air France. France gave the statue to America; maybe Air France would help restore it.

He called a friend from the advertising agency that handled the Air France account and arranged an appointment. Hanging in a hallway when Peter arrived at the ad agency was a large photo of Lee Iacocca. When he greeted his friend, Max had changed his mind about Air France.

"I want to talk to you about Lee Iacocca," he said.

Iacocca did head the committee to restore the Statue of Liberty and got most of the credit. But Max helped raise several million dollars.

"It doesn't matter to me who got the credit; I was just happy that it was happening," he said. "Besides, there's still so much more to do for this country."

The death of another artist the following year silenced an important voice for the generation. Andy Warhol's paintings—from the famous Campbell Soup cans to the Marilyn Monroe studies—were an essential part of the 60s. Peter Max's art captured the spirit of the generation. Warhol, with his eye for seeing art in the commonplace and his ability to create magic from the mundane, helped define it.

The public began learning in late 1986 of a secret White House plan to sell arms to Iran in exchange for the release of American hostages held in Lebanon. The profits from the arms sales were then used to help the contras fighting the Sandinista government in Nicaragua.

The Iran-contra affair consumed the country for much of the next year. The man in the middle was a White House aide and a marine, Lt. Col. Oliver North. North was tall and handsome, and stood up straight. Never mind that Congress had banned aid to the contras, or that President Reagan's oft-stated policy was not to trade arms for hostages. North had tried to free captive Americans and he tried to help the contras fighting communism and America loved him.

His nationally televised appearance before a congressional committee riveted the nation. His most explosive testimony came on July 8, when

North drew several top Reagan aides into the scandal, saying they were aware of his actions. Several were forced to resign.

Irangate, as it came to be known, was the most difficult period of the Reagan presidency. One of his shining moments came on December 8, 1987. That day Reagan and Soviet leader Mikhail Gorbachev signed an historic treaty eliminating an entire class of nuclear missiles—midrange missiles. Their vow to make progress toward another treaty was hailed as equally historic, and could be one key to reaching the Woodstock generation. If it does rally behind one issue again, this may well be the one. Polls showed that no other age group more deeply questioned the nuclear arms race or was more firmly convinced that the money could be better used elsewhere. At least on this one issue, Reagan gave it reason to feel hopeful.

The history made on October 19, 1987, had a more immediate impact on generation members' lives. The stock market was devastated by the worst one-day crash in history—the Dow Jones Industrial Average dropped 508 points.

It caused them to question what *Newsweek* had dubbed "the new avarice"; speculation in the stock market in the quest for riches had, in one day, dashed dreams and ruined careers.

By strange coincidence, a film came out shortly afterward, *Wall Street*, about the hidden dangers of living a life guided by greed. It too raised questions about, and pointed a finger at, the Woodstock generation.

The stock market crash helped push the generation beyond simply searching for "influence and affluence." The lesson: what was gained so easily was lost just as easily. The crash helped turn up the heat under those bubbling, simmering Woodstock values.

An incident that occurred in 1988, seemingly innocuous on its surface, turned up the heat even higher, and caused the generation to ask some searching questions about its priorities.

For three weeks the world watched a multi-million-dollar international struggle to free three California gray whales stuck in the ice off Barrow, Alaska. More than a few people wondered, Why is this nation so easily moved by the plight of a few whales, and so stoic about long-standing problems like homelessness in America?

Mitch Snyder wondered too. Snyder showed by example that you could take your 60s ideals and use them to change the 80s world. Or at least a small corner of it.

Snyder became involved in the issue of homelessness after a wave of changes in his own life. The waves began with one sudden splash, a few months after Woodstock weekend. Snyder, then twenty-six and working on Madison Avenue, woke up one morning in a cold sweat.

What am I doing? he thought. This is a crazy way to live.

The thought of getting up every morning for the rest of his life, and going to Madison Avenue to work, terrified him. What made him wake up in that cold sweat? "A lot of luck," Snyder said. "Grace or luck, depending on your perspective."

Leaving his wife and two children behind, Snyder did a Kerouac, traveling around the country for a few months, until 1970, when he was arrested in California. Snyder said he was a passenger in a car that had been rented in one state and driven to another, breaking a law that no longer exists. The police, however, charged him with car theft.

Whatever the specifics, jail became another touch of grace, or luck, or both.

"At the time I wasn't really thrilled, but in hindsight I realize that was a really fortunate accident," Snyder said. "It gave me a couple of years in a very monastic-type setting. Prisons aren't meant to be monasteries but they can be. I was able to read a book a day and met some very fine people."

Among those people were Phillip and Daniel Berrigan, two Catholic priests who had been arrested protesting the Vietnam War.

At about this time, in Washington, D.C., a group was forming called the Community for Creative Non-Violence. CCNV began originally as an antiwar organization and was referred to as part of the "Catholic left." Within a year or two, members decided that the domestic counterpart to violence in Southeast Asia was the hungry and homeless people they saw living a few blocks from the White House. So, in 1972 CCNV opened a soup kitchen not far from the Oval Office.

Snyder, meanwhile, was reading voraciously: a book a day, of history, philosophy, theology. A lot of theology, and Gandhi. Snyder's mother was Jewish, his father Catholic, but both were devout atheists. Snyder developed a deep spiritual belief, if not an adherence to any religion, as the days in prison dragged on.

As prisoners, he and his fellow inmates could sympathize with the POWs forced to squat in tiger cages in Vietnam. As a war protester, he was outraged that these cages were made by a firm in Texas. In protest, he and a few other inmates began to fast.

The next fast was more serious, lasting forty days after the Berrigans were denied parole. This was followed by still another fast, by which Snyder protested his transfer to another prison.

When Synder got out of prison, he went back to his wife and children. His wife has said that she resented his fasts. She felt they were the reason he kept being denied parole, keeping him from his children, who needed him. But Snyder couldn't return to the life he had with them anyway. He left again, and this time the separation was permanent.

He went to New York City, got involved with CCNV's antiwar activities, and soon moved to Washington. Working with the homeless, creating "communities" such as homeless shelters, seemed like a natural progression. Both movements involved trying to get people to live together peacefully.

Snyder became a leader of the CCNV and helped to create the nation's largest and most well known homeless shelter. And he waged one of the most publicized battles in behalf of the homeless.

Just before Reagan's second election, Snyder went on a fast to force the administration to appropriate money to repair his rundown 1,000-bed shelter. Snyder promised to starve himself to death, and fasted for fifty-one days before Reagan relented.

It was this fast that brought Snyder to "60 Minutes" and "Nightline" and into the public eye. Stories in the popular press suggested Snyder was trying to create a "Holiday Inn for the homeless" and questioned his motivation and his methods.

His method was the fast. "Self-immolation is the most powerful manifestation and expression of nonviolence," Snyder said, "whether it's pouring gasoline on yourself and setting yourself on fire, or fasting."

Though at the brink of death during the fast, Snyder remembered a feeling of clarity: "Your mind gets sharper as you go forward. Emotionally it's a roller-coaster ride. Your body deteriorates. But your thought processes and clarity don't diminish; they grow, as does your spirit.

"The inside of you is a battleground in which good and evil are fighting it out."

As the fast wore on, reporters and others asked Snyder if he realized he might die.

"There's also the possibility that you're going to die if you're not fasting," Snyder responded. "What about the person who comes home and finds their house on fire and someone they love at risk? The odds are they would risk themselves to save someone they love.

"Fasting is exactly the same kind of thing, no more, no less."

As Snyder's fame grew, and as he became more successful in focusing the nation's attention on the homeless, Snyder-bashing grew as well. No story was complete without someone calling him egotistical or questioning his motives or mentioning that he had left his wife and children. Rumors circulated that he didn't even live in the shelter but had a beautiful home and a Mercedes in the Washington suburbs.

It was this cynical voice of the Woodstock generation that hurt, at first. "I used to find that more disturbing than I do now," Snyder said.

Then he decided that this cynicism was really a defense mechanism, a way for people to deal with issues they don't understand or don't want to face.

But Snyder also began to see blips of change on the horizon. In the late 1980s thousands began showing up at the CCNV protests. At one, more than four hundred sat in the middle of a street and were arrested, more than had been arrested in Washington since May Day protests of the early 70s. In a six-week whirlwind tour, Snyder visited seventy communities that were working on the homeless issue.

"The country ain't the same as it was ten years ago or eight years ago or five years ago," Snyder said. "There's things happening out there. It's bubbling."

It reminded Snyder of the early days of Students for a Democratic Society, so much so that activists from around the country planned a national organizing meeting.

Snyder, in fact, expects a true social upheaval in the 90s.

"We'll see large numbers of people joining in that struggle for the pursuit of truth and community, and a more positive set of values that embrace 'we' instead of 'me.' Once again we'll be dealing with a large number of people whose depth of involvement is not great, but whose lives will probably never be quite the same.

"We'll always look back with nostalgia to the times we all went skinny-dipping and all got stoned. It was a freer, easier time. But getting involved again in some way, and beginning to expend some time and energy on efforts that are intended to make the world a better place to be, will begin to give us the sense of fulfillment that many of us experienced in the 60s."

CHAPTER TEN

Keep Hope Alive

By the second half of the 1980s the energies Ken Kesey had been gathering on the farm were beginning to bear fruit. In 1986 *Demon Box,* an assortment of previously published magazine articles, with some retouching, was released. It drew mixed reviews at best, but for Kesey it felt good—"I felt I had made a little cage to put my gonzo in."

At the same time it was a bad period for the Kesey family. A bus carrying the University of Oregon wrestling team to a match in Takoma went over a cliff, and his son Jed, a wrestler like his father, was killed. "That kicked the props out from under me," Ken said.

Kesey got through it, in part because of the letters he got from fathers who had also lost children. He was surprised at how much they meant to him. The letters would start, "I really don't know the words to say this," and then they went on and found the words, clear, simple, and heartfelt. He and the other grieving fathers exchanged many letters.

As time went by, Kesey found himself a little broke and hungry, and took a job here or there. In the fall of 1987 he took a job at the University of Oregon, teaching a graduate writing class. It was rewarding to him, although more so spiritually than financially. He and Faye moved into town for the first time in their lives. The students yipped and howled at night, brakes squealed, and the evenings were filled with strange rumblings. For a couple of country folk, it was exhausting.

But the class was invigorating. There were twelve students; together they wrote a novel, *Caverns.* It was set in 1934 and concerned the search for secret pictographs in a cave. The class started from scratch, dreaming up characters, putting them in the story, and letting the tale build from there.

The author was "O.U. Levon," which was "Novel U. [of] O." spelled backward. It was like a wrestling match for the teacher, grappling with the students to get the novel ready and send it off. But one sunny day came the happy news: Viking wanted to publish *Caverns.*

Kesey felt he worked as hard in that class as he would on his own writing. But he had put off his own writing for too long. Two decades of gathering one's energy were long enough.

Kesey had been going to Alaska off and on since 1983, collecting material for what would be his next major novel, maybe the toughest of them all. Set in Alaska, *Sailor's Song* heaps howling cold, danger, and misery upon the characters and the author.

And the hardest part, the reason it took years to gain and regain the momentum? *Sailor's Song* would not be about him or his family or friends. Kesey had to create it out of people and experiences on those fishing boats.

"But I think this is the year I'm going to do it," he said in the summer of 1988, twenty years after prison and heartbreak.

Dust and pollen, backlit by the afternoon sun, seemed to be pouring out of an ancient cottonwood tree toward Kesey and his afternoon perch. He still carried a big plastic cup of rum-and-something. He mopped his sweat-beaded brow. Behind him were two great novels, *Cuckoo's Nest* and *Sometimes a Great Notion;* ahead of him lay the future, full of possibilities.

"If I could retire with four Super Bowl rings I'd be happy," he said. "And I feel like I got two. I feel like I got at least one more good season."

And, perhaps, so does the Woodstock generation. As it passes the twentieth anniversary of its naming and moves into the next decade, it is not stuck paddling against the current, being borne back ceaselessly toward the past. Instead, it is starting clear-eyed into the future.

The generation has two Super Bowl rings—it helped end a war and depose a president. And it has spent twenty years gathering its energies. Perhaps, as with Ken Kesey, two decades of gathering its energies will be enough.

And perhaps, like Kesey, it has another great work or two left in it. Perhaps, this time, that great work will be born—not of its past, of the friends and connections it left behind, but of some new challenge, something as new and difficult to conquer as a fishing boat in Alaska. Perhaps it will be filled with howling cold, danger, and misery, and challenge and excitement and adventure.

The signposts are all there.

Members of the Woodstock generation have lived half their lives after Woodstock. Having spent those twenty years doing the things they needed to do—building careers, starting families, paying the rent, buying homes, and coming down off their 60s high—they are now ready to claim their legacy; they are poised to change the world.

Certainly they have changed the world in many ways over the last twenty years. The sheer size of the generation ensured it would have an impact. But mostly those changes came through happenstance, not intent.

After two decades of playing follow the leader, through the Me years of the 70s and the yuppie days of the 80s, people in the Woodstock generation are finally emerging as individuals—making independent decisions. Now they have the self-confidence and maturity to say: "This is what's right for me; maybe it's not right for the guy at the next desk, but it's right for me."

If Woodstock and the 60s were about anything, they were about the freedom to be what you want. "It's your own trip, man," said the voice from the Woodstock stage warning about the bad brown acid.

The generation hasn't rededicated itself to righting society's wrongs, but it is no longer comfortable ignoring them or mindlessly falling into line.

It's a feeling of: I've done the house and I've done the kids and yes I like money and I want more, but something is missing. And it's this search for something more that is changing the way the generation will live in the 90s.

It's why the *Fortune* 500 business executive in Los Angeles wore a Jesse Jackson button on his suit and didn't mind the scoffing of his colleagues.

"It's your trip, man."

It's why people like David Ransen and Lois Kaufman continue dropping out of secure jobs to create lifestyles that give them more satisfaction and independence.

It's more and more people standing up for what they believe is right, from the thousands who marched in October 1988 in a protest to help the homeless, to the Washington, D.C., businessman who went to court for the first time to fight a traffic ticket he felt was unjust.

It's even the soaring number of people who are no longer tolerating shabby service or poor products and are saying "take it back" to makers of everything from cars to charcoal grills. And so customer-satisfaction programs in American companies have increased over 150 percent between 1985 and 1989.

These thousands of little individual actions are collectively merging to shape the society we'll share in the years ahead. This time experience, maturity, and self-confidence will guide the generation along the way, not the youthful enthusiasm of the 60s. And so these changes are more likely to be permanent.

It's also Ralph Fogel.

Ralph was the Seabee who turned in his bunk and cried in 1970 when he heard about the killings at Kent State. He was a street-wise kid from Brooklyn who had two goals in life: a career in music and making it as a professional basketball player. As he had no musical talent whatever and as he stood only five foot ten, both seemed unlikely.

He was an average student at best. But after high school he enrolled in the twilight program at Brooklyn College, not knowing what he wanted to do with his life except to prove he was not his father's son.

Ralph considered his father a "Russian peasant." He was a man who occasionally beat his son when he was particularly tired or angry, a man who knew little about the world and didn't really care. His mother's side of the family was the "intelligentsia"; she was a teacher, her brothers an accountant, a lawyer, and a businessman—all bright, cultured people. On holidays they would sit around and discuss politics or the world, and Ralph's bored father would often leave the room and go lie down.

"I felt that I had to make up for my father," Ralph said. "I had to prove that the Fogel part of the family was not dimwitted."

After his first year in college Ralph got a summer job earning $39.95 a week as a page on the New York Stock Exchange, running orders to the brokers on the floor.

"The day I walked onto the floor of the New York Stock Exchange was the day that I found that my life had a meaning."

He loved the excitement, the fast-paced atmosphere. He set out to learn everything he could about the stock market and how it works, staying on the floor even during lunch periods and breaks.

He was drawn to a brokerage firm named Spear, Leeds and Kellogg. Unlike some of the stodgy old Wall Street firms, this one had a reputation for giving young people a chance. Ralph got a job there as a clerk, earning $90 a week.

Then came the Vietnam War, and Quang Tri Province, where he was occasionally shelled and where he dreamed about being back in the United States, free to protest the mistake that he considered Vietnam to be.

Ralph came home in October 1970. He married his girlfriend, Rochelle, and returned to Wall Street, working harder than ever. He held down a job at Spear, Leeds and Kellogg during the day and went to school at night. Then in 1976 came the proudest day of his professional life: Ralph bought a seat on the New York Stock Exchange, one of the first members who was not already a partner in a brokerage firm.

He prospered and bought a house, first in Brooklyn and then, like thousands of fellow members of the Woodstock generation, in the suburbs, an upper-middle-class section of New Jersey. Ralph and Rochelle had children and lived a very conventional suburban lifestyle—parties with friends, seeing the neighbors.

But for Ralph, it grew boring. His turn-on was Wall Street, and it was becoming more exciting, more rewarding.

By the late 70s, Wall Street was a changing world and Ralph Fogel was part of it. Older people were leaving, retiring. Younger people, more dynamic and competitive, were moving in. The partners of Spear, Leeds and Kellogg saw the shift and felt the firm should expand and diversify. Ralph Fogel became a key player.

Ralph thrived in the competitive environment; he felt it was a place where good people could move ahead quickly, could be the best that they could be with no barriers but their own personal limitations. And he learned from other people in the firm, about business but also about how to deal with other people. Older partners like Peter Kellogg and Harvey Silberman and Larry Tishman became the role models his father never was.

His life centered around the office. That's where he derived his sense of achievement and sense of self-worth.

Ralph lost touch with his family as he immersed himself more deeply in his quest for financial success. He shielded his children not only from his business life but also from his personal life, and the chore of raising them fell to Rochelle. Then, finally, they were divorced.

Ralph achieved the goals he had set for himself—building his career and becoming wealthy. But he also had a growing feeling that something was missing, a nagging doubt that something wasn't right in his single-minded pursuit of wealth.

Ralph also failed to come to terms with his feelings about his father. And when his father died, Ralph slid slowly into his own emotional quagmire.

He started drinking and experimented with drugs. He became a compulsive overeater and even thought of suicide. He continued to succeed at work, but it became harder for him to connect emotionally with the events of his life outside the office.

Finally, he came to the realization that he needed to do something: either kill himself or get his life back into shape. "Look," Ralph said to himself one day, "either pick up the gun and shoot yourself and they'll bring in the cart and take you away, or get on with your life."

Ralph Fogel chose to get on with his life. He entered therapy and began to see himself in a new light, as a maniacal overachiever whose drive for success was partially born of depression. Slowly, Ralph Fogel began to change, outwardly and inwardly.

He lost eighty pounds and began to reassess his objectives in life.

"Financial security was a very shallow goal; you really have to have balance in your life. My goal now is to make myself a better person. Businesses grow at different rates and so do people."

He started with his children. "I gave them money but I never gave a lot of myself." Now Ralph sees them several times a week and almost every weekend. And they see a different father.

"I would like to be remembered as a good father, at least that I got there at some point. Now, I'm starting to live my life and that's important for my children to see; life is more than a career, life is more than making money.

"I want a good normal life and I want my children to have a good normal healthy life and I want to leave my imprint on society in a positive way."

That imprint includes going to the Veteran's Hospital in Manhattan to work with Vietnam vets of his own age. "I'm giving of my time, my most precious possession." It's one way Ralph Fogel is dealing with Vietnam and the aftermath of the war; but he also feels it's helping to make him a better person.

"I wasn't proud then of what my country had done and my country wasn't proud of me. I did my country well; my country did not do me well."

He met a woman, Kirsten Olsen, with none of the emotional baggage Ralph had carried around all his life. And she, too, helped him sort out his feelings.

Ralph Fogel left for the service in 1968 wearing a business suit. He came back wearing one as well. In 1985, however, he put his uniform back on and marched again with other vets. It was a tickertape parade through lower Manhattan in support of Vietnam vets. There were others from the stock exchange, but most were clerical employees, not members.

Finally, Ralph was proud, not of the war but of the men he served with. He's also proud of the changes he's making in his life and of his country.

"My generation has been greedy. We have allowed things to happen in our country because we have been narrowly focused in our lives. I don't have one black trader working for me and that's disgusting."

So one day in 1989 Ralph walked into the personnel department of his firm and told them to find and hire good minority people. He has helped bring women into the firm and worked with them to get ahead.

"We've been caught up in our own lives. We have been the Me Generation and not put back as much as we've taken out. I know deep in my heart this is something we need to do. It's my job to do it. I've not done a good job, but I plan to."

And this is one of the ways in which the Woodstock generation is changing, not to the sound of a thundering, unified drumbeat as in the 60s, but with thousands of people resolving to make a few changes in their lives, to be better people, to put something back; resolving, like Ralph Fogel, to do a better job.

Sometimes it takes something close to home to push someone over the edge, out of apathy into involvement. That was the case with Mary Mossburger.

Her brother, Jim Copp, had been in Vietnam in 1965. Along with a woman, Donna Long, he returned to Southeast Asia in the fall of 1988. They were trying to distribute a $2.4 million reward, privately collected, for the return of any live prisoner of war or any soldier still missing in action.

Going down the Mekong River, they were captured by Laotians on October 3.

Mary, of Linton, Indiana, began wearing a Vietnam Continues T-shirt. And anger was heard in her voice.

"Our State Department hasn't done a very good job of keeping us informed about what's going on," she said a week after her brother disappeared. She was worried; word had reached her that her brother was sick, and losing weight.

Mary was forty. She had never been involved in a protest, never paid much attention to issues such as the homeless or POWs or MIAs.

"Never before, and I really feel ashamed that I haven't," she confessed. "We've been meeting with different groups of people that are families of POWs and MIAs. I think all American citizens should feel ashamed for not doing more to get them back."

Suddenly, the apathy of the generation had become an integral, personal part of her life. She saw it clearly now. And she didn't like what she saw.

"I mean, they can save the whales and all this, but we have two Americans over there in Laos right now, and it's not getting any national attention. *Newsweek* wants them, 'Good Morning, America' wants them, when and if they get back. But nobody's willing to put them on the national news now. We just don't want them to be forgotten."

Mary's main concerns were POWs and MIAs. But she knew this experience had changed her, taught her something. She could no longer turn her back on other issues. Matters like homelessness in America now caught her eye, an issue she wishes she had paid attention to earlier.

"It's terrible," she said. "I really feel ashamed. People are just sitting back. They complain, but they don't do anything, just like I haven't been doing anything. But I am now, and I'm going to start."

A few weeks later, Jim Copp and Donna Long returned to safety in America.

Mary Mossburger had become involved, but only after being pushed over the edge by a personal issue. Most likely she will become one of those Mitch Snyder talked about: not ready to become deeply committed lifelong activists, but nevertheless unable ever again to wrap themselves in a cloak of apathy.

By the end of the 80s the Woodstock generation was reacting to all sorts of issues, in all sorts of ways.

Cartoonist Berke Breathed, who created the immensely popular "Bloom County," slipped the issue of animal rights into his cartoon in early 1989—and found that the issue had slipped into his own life as well.

The penguin character Opus, in search of his long-lost mother, ventured into an animal-testing laboratory, where cute Disney-like bunnies were strapped to tables.

Before long, Breathed began marching in animal rights protests. "This is the first time I've made the dangerous foray into personal participation," he said. "I believe it's a less transient issue than most, which is why I'm involved."

He wasn't the only cartoonist getting more political. Cathy Guisewite, who creates "Cathy," had her character Andrea commenting harshly just before the 1988 presidential election on the Republicans' poor record on women's issues. A few years earlier people had complained about "Doonesbury" being too political. Now, two of the most popular strips in the country were joining the fray.

Politics and societal concerns were playing a more important role in movies as well. Tom Cruise, for example, went from *Cocktail,* a pointless movie about bartenders, to *Rain Man,* a sensitive film with Dustin Hoffman about autism, and began work on *Born on the Fourth of July,* a biography of Vietnam veteran Ron Kovic.

A curious split occurred in 1988. Once again comedies were king—from Robin Williams' *Good Morning, Vietnam,* which used the war merely as a vehicle for Williams' rapid-fire humor, to *Big,* a boy-in-a-man's-body story, to *Coming to America* and *Three Men and a Baby.* But a new wave of more significant movies appeared at the end of the year. In the Woodstock generation's lifetime, there had never been such a rapid outpouring of serious films. *Running on Empty, The Good Mother, Bird,* and others showed that audiences were getting a little older, and were ready once again for more serious fare.

That fare included the first of what would become a series of movies about the 60s. *Mississippi Burning* tackled the murders of civil rights workers in the South, paralleling the real murders of activists Goodman, Schwerner, and Chaney twenty-five years earlier. Although the film was attacked for telling the story of the civil rights struggle from the white point of view—as *Cry Freedom* did a year earlier—it heralded an onslaught of retrospection about the 60s on film and TV, from the insipid *1969* to the more thoughtful TV shows "The Wonder Years" and "thirtysomething."

The growing change was evident. But there was also an undercurrent of hesitancy. And nowhere else was this more evident than in the election of George Bush.

Bush tried to show a degree of distance from Reagan, but it was the desire to keep the happy Reagan years alive that swept him into power. A turning point came when Bush bet that the Woodstock generation wasn't ready to respond to its old rallying cries. And he was right.

Bush labeled opponent Michael Dukakis a liberal. Dukakis reeled, and denied the charge. The term became known as the L word, so fearful was any candidate of having the label pinned on him.

Abbie Hoffman watched the fight over the L word, and it got his goat. Webster's definition of *liberal* mentions things that the Woodstock generation could respond to: "belonging to the people"; "giving freely, generous"; "tolerant of views differing from one's own." Hoffman tried to advise Dukakis to seize the L word, but Dukakis wasn't taking advice from Abbie Hoffman. Slowly, however, political analysts across the country seized on Dukakis's tactical error. Several weeks later when Dukakis announced that he was not, in fact, embarrassed to be called a liberal, it was too late.

Sitting outside the converted turkey coop in New Hope, Pennsylvania, on a cold but sunny day a few weeks before the election, Abbie Hoffman was in a crummy mood. But not just over what was happening with Dukakis. He had broken his foot in a bad car crash a few weeks earlier. Photos of the crumpled wreck made you wonder how he survived at all. And he had a cold. And he was missing his real passion on Saturday afternoons: watching basketball on television. Especially on Saturdays like this, when he had money on the game.

It was a strange year for Abbie. He was now, to use his own phrase, being "discovered for the third time"—after the 60s, and after his reemergence from hiding. He dabbled with a little standup comedy, but mostly spoke to activist groups and college kids around the country.

Sometimes in his travels he confronted issues that sparked the rebel gene. "Wait. Look at this," he said, pulling out the main tool of his trade, the heavily scrawled legal pad. "This is yesterday's work." The first page was a list of every newspaper in America that required urine testing of its employees. The next contained notes about a water-tower fight in Gettysburg, Pennsylvania.

Earlier in the year his legal pads were filled with notes about Gallaudet University in Washington, D.C.—and the plans for the successful jamming of the university's phone lines through the use of nationwide computer bulletin boards.

The fight at Gallaudet was inspiring. Deaf students, angry over the selection of a hearing president, demanded that a deaf president be hired. They won.

Scribbled in the corner of Abbie's legal pad was a secret university phone number, a key to jamming the university's phone lines. "Only about twelve people outside the university knew this number," he said proudly. "Plus I had to learn how to break through the code breaker. I'm not just a famous person," he said, slightly defensive. "I'm an organizer. I'm making it happen."

The converted turkey coop was musty and cluttered, a blend of high tech and low; photos of a young Abbie on a Greenwich Village street with John and Yoko hung over near the answering machine.

"I have a personal problem, as I become discovered for the third time. I mean, they're cheering me in Boise, Idaho. I sense it'll be more like a Don Quixote, 'Go get 'em, Abbie. Isn't America great. It's such a democracy— we can have somebody like you running around screaming about anything that's wrong and you're allowed to do it.' I can appreciate that, as a personal freedom, but like any American I'm less interested in the words than the actions. And I want to have an impact. And if environmental groups just sell calendars and have rock concerts and the trees keep getting cut down, fuck it."

When Hoffman grew up in Worcester, Massachusetts, he was known in the neighborhood for two reasons. One was his funny first name; you had to get tough if you were a boy named Abbie. The other was that he always fought the schoolyard bully. Anything unjust that he saw—a kid being hazed by some group—would rankle him, and he would stand up for the kid against the group.

But in the 80s when Abbie tried to continue that kind of fight, many in the Woodstock generation would dismiss him, deriding him for showing up at the cause du jour, explaining him away as a selfish publicity hound.

"There is a difference between being self-interested and being selfish," Hoffman responded. "I will never be selfish. I've been through every test. I could have been selfish under one of my twelve identities when I was underground. I could have become a million-dollar-a-year ad executive, cynical about the 60s.

"But I was a fugitive, taking risks with my life. I chose that. I chose to be a volunteer, to go to Guatemala when they were having their earthquake, to help people, with a team of doctors. Under another name, I fought a Free Mary Hartman campaign in Florida because they were censoring it on TV."

Hoffman's eyes blazed when he talked; his smile flashed; his nasal voice, still full of Boston rhythms, drew out the last few words of each sentence for emphasis—mostly when he talked about his battles, like the one against the water tower, symbol of the new development in Bucks County, Pennsylvania.

"Sometimes I say fuck it. Why don't I just go work with other people who appreciate success? It'd be a whole lot easier. I can't tell you how many offers I reject that would bring great amounts of money—but wouldn't challenge me in a way that taking down that ugly fucking tower does."

Walt Disney productions asked him to do an ad for the movie *Ruthless People*. He was to speak in front of the camera about the most ruthless person he had ever met. Hoffman was tempted, partly by the wonderful irony of Walt Disney calling Abbie Hoffman. But he turned it down when the production schedule made it impossible for him to view the film before agreeing to make the commercial.

"You can't imagine how many career offers I've had over the last twenty-eight years. But this is my career. This is why I'm here on the planet: to fight nuclear power, to fight our policy in Central America, to defeat the CIA—this is perfectly legitimate work."

Hoffman in 1988 was a fifty-one-year-old man living in a town that still sells Zap comics and peace buttons, where you can still get macrobiotic wheat meat and a Woodstock pin.

Hoffman understood, in the youth he saw, the fear that you can't change society. He saw it in his own children—he had three, aged twenty-seven, twenty-five, and sixteen, and "no yuppies in the litter." And in the Woodstock generation, he saw something else.

"It's called guilt," he said. "They feel guilty. There's an unfinished revolution."

Hoffman felt ready, if not to finish it, at least to continue it.

"Look, I have to relate to myself as just an average American, which I am too," Hoffman said. "I'm sitting here talking to you and I'm saying why the fuck aren't I watching the basketball game, cause I got money bet on the game."

But he wasn't watching the game. He was out on a blanket, with his foot hurting and his cold bothering him, because "we are out here searching for truth. That's more important.

"Most people in America would rather just watch the parade go by. They'd rather sit in the stands. They're not going to be in the game."

Did that make Abbie Hoffman sad?

"No. It makes the field less crowded. It's easier to do my work. The majority of people were always sitting in the stands. When I find people who are willing to go against the grain, that are willing to make tremendous sacrifices to change an unjust situation—that's what blows my mind out."

There was much to blow Abbie Hoffman's mind out in 1988. The winds of change blew strongest in the campaign of Jesse Jackson. Compared to his historic but unsuccessful run four years earlier, Jackson's presidential campaign touched members of the generation from all walks of life; he began drawing 10 to 20 percent of his vote, in some primaries, from white voters.

Jackson campaigned on the values of the Woodstock generation, equality and justice and caring about the oppressed. When he won a landslide victory in the Michigan Democratic caucuses in March, his candidacy began to be taken seriously.

His speech at the Democratic Convention drew thunderous ovations as he intoned, over and over: "Keep hope alive!"

And though many of the generation could not accept him—because of racial reasons, or personal ones, or political or economic ones—they recognized that, finally, someone was speaking to the issues that stirred the sleeping giant. Jews, for example, stayed away from him, still smarting over a remark four years earlier when he referred to New York as "Hymietown," and distrusting his support for negotiations with the Palestine Liberation Organization. But they understood that he spoke to issues of tolerance and kindness that were part of their political canon.

Perhaps if another black candidate had been saying the same things—someone with less of a reputation as a loose cannon, someone less unpredictable—he could have gained the nomination.

But clearly, Jackson was turning people on. Perhaps not strongly enough to win the nomination, but strongly enough to show that the generation was becoming more thoughtful, more finely attuned to the issues of its youth—and of its future.

The year 1988 saw many symbolic passages for the generation: Superman turned fifty and *Playboy,* once in the forefront of the sexual revolution and now seeming so dated, closed its last American club, banishing its bunnies.

The Olympics again occasioned a mixture of pride and despair. They were marked by the courage of Greg Louganis, who after hitting his head on the board during a dive rebounded to win the gold medal. But they were marred by yet another drug controversy, as Canadian Ben Johnson was stripped of his gold medal after testing positive for steroids.

The death of Andy Warhol on February 22, 1987, sparked a reexamination of 60s art and sensibilities, and the resurrection of Elvis made people wonder if the whole country had gone nuts. For inexplicable reasons, "Elvis sightings" were the rage. He was spotted everywhere, from supermarket checkout lines in California to Texas bars.

Despite the silliness of the Elvis sightings, some serious shifting was under way in the Force. Increasingly, the nation—and particularly the Woodstock generation—was finding that the important issues of the day were becoming impossible to ignore. A CBS–*New York Times* poll showed that environmental issues were high on the minds of Americans; many said they would pay more in taxes or electric bills to help solve the problem.

More personal issues, such as neighborhood watches and anti-drunk-driving crusades, got people out of their homes and into organized campaigns. And broader social issues, such as the continued threat of nuclear war and the growing problem of homelessness in America, began attracting more people.

And, just as Abbie Hoffman predicted, these issues crossed generational, political, and racial lines. It was as though Jesse Jackson's Rainbow Coalition had hit the streets and begun shoveling out the detritus of twenty years of stagnation.

Better Homes and Gardens, a magazine aimed at suburban women, even created a nonprofit foundation to help homeless families across the nation. It followed up in March 1989 with a report to readers explaining how their contributions were used.

Norm Drouhard, of Washington State, took heart in watching others join him in protest, even though not a few thought it strange that he was there himself.

Drouhard was sixty-three years old, a World War II veteran, an air force pilot. He had been homesteading downwind from a nuclear plant, and over the years had begun to worry about possible dangers from radiation emissions. He took part in his first protest over the plant, and got himself arrested on the statehouse lawn.

"I figured they had more to hide than I thought, or I wouldn't have been arrested," Drouhard said. He sold his farm, and began traveling the country, visiting every major nuclear weapons plant in the country.

In the fall of 1988 he took part in a homeless protest in Washington, D.C., and wore a Veterans for Peace T-shirt. He was the oldest protester sitting on the Capitol steps. In the past year, he said, he had begun sensing the winds of change, from the Woodstock generation, and from others as well.

"In the past year, we've had lots of college kids get involved. And there's a lot of grandmothers and grandfathers older than my age. The forties group, the ones that were protesting in the 60s, are not that strong, yet, but a lot of them are coming back.

"My oldest son was a protester in the 60s, and he has two of my grandchildren. He feels as strongly about this as I do, but he's home raising those grandchildren, and I think that's the difference."

Norm said he sees a real change in the college students who have begun appearing at the rallies. "The college kids are very supportive. It gives me a good feeling."

He believes that the Woodstock generation can be inspired by these college kids, just as he has been. "I seem to be more optimistic than most people," he says. "I'm hopeful, yes. I have to have hope. I have seven grandchildren."

Billy Hayes was feeling hopeful too. For the first time, in a long time, he was learning how to deal with his own feelings; to some extent, learning again how to feel.

Prison had created a shell around him that the years of publicity after his escape, promoting the book *Midnight Express* and then the movie, did nothing to dissolve. He wanted to move on to the future, but he was stuck in the past.

"You create a shield to cope with jail," he said. "People get only so far into you, and then that's it."

Finally, he found two things that made his life different. "One opened me up, and the other filled me with love."

He found the first one day in New York when he followed a girl with pretty legs into a building. She walked into a classroom and Billy walked in behind her and sat in the back.

It was an acting class run by Bill Hickey, who would later play the old Mafia don in the hit movie *Prizzi's Honor.*

It wouldn't be the girl, but the class, that would bring Hayes back again. Eventually, Billy began to feel that acting might help him get in touch with himself, to find the pieces of his spirit that he had buried in order to survive prison.

Billy was thinking of taking acting lessons anyway. "I was doing all the publicity and talk shows for the book and the movie, and I enjoyed the energy that was going back and forth with the audience."

He had looked into an acting program but found the curriculum too structured and rigid—too much like school. And school was the last thing he needed after five years in jail and three years on tour.

But he liked Hickey and the freedom of the classes, so he stayed five or six months before moving to Los Angeles to escape "all the Billy Hayes and *Midnight Express* bullshit."

In Los Angeles he found another acting teacher, Eric Morris, who would have a profound effect on Billy Hayes' life. Morris would help him break down many of the barriers that prison life had built up.

"Acting became my salvation. Actors need to touch all parts of their bodies and Eric helped me touch some parts of me that had been hidden for a while."

Billy also got his first acting job—of sorts—through Morris, playing a mutant in a science-fiction movie called *Battle Beyond the Stars,* which starred Richard Thomas, John Saxon, and Robert Vaughn. Morris was also in the film and was able to get some of his students parts playing creatures from outer space.

It took Billy two hours each day to get into makeup; he had to wear a device that made him look like a hunchback. He didn't have any lines, but did get to blow up the spaceship at the end of the film.

The second influence on his life he found at the Cannes Film Festival. A friend mentioned that his cousin, Wendy, would be at Cannes working for one of the movie production studios at the festival: "She's cute and she's blonde and you'll like her," the friend said. Billy was interested.

"We met and danced under a full moon at the gala premiere of *Midnight Express*," Billy said. "And now, it's like I can't remember a time we weren't together."

Billy and Wendy married in 1980. For their honeymoon they went to the Hawaiian island of Kauai. They took one of those famous helicopter trips, and zoomed between mountains while listening to stirring music on headphones. The music they heard, purely by coincidence, was the opening theme from *Midnight Express.*

They bought a house in Los Angeles and Billy set about trying to carve out a career in acting. He appeared in about a dozen plays—including one, *Cage,* in which he played a prison inmate—and "a lot of TV," including brief roles on several soap operas and an appearance on the old series "Stingray," playing a bad guy who gets blown up at the end.

"I want to send out love and light," he says, "and I end up playing bad guys."

He tried to kill the nation's first lady in the movie *Assassination;* he's the blond deckhand who plants plastique explosives on the hull of a yacht and who later empties a machine gun at Charles Bronson—although it is Bronson who fills Hayes full of holes in the end.

Like most struggling actors, he has to read for parts and wishes he had more control over the things he does. He is trying to put together a TV movie which, he hopes, will give him more control.

But Billy is feeling more secure about his work and about himself. He still uses his formal name, William Hayes, on his résumé, something he began doing when he moved to Hollywood as a means of disconnecting himself from the *Midnight Express* Billy Hayes. The only reference to his past is the notation on his résumé that he speaks Turkish.

But if people do make the connection, he'll talk to them about his life and what he learned.

"Prison forced me to take responsibility for myself," he said. "I went around blaming everything on everyone else and suddenly I had no one to blame but myself.

"Before I left the U.S. I protested and bitched about everything that was wrong. There was a lot wrong, and there still is, but losing it made me appreciate how wonderful it really is."

Billy Hayes is even writing a new book, the sequel to *Midnight Express*. It's about what happened to him after prison, about his life back in the United States.

Said Billy, "It's about the really weird years."

For many members of the generation, the really weird years are the ones they remember the best.

A wide-ranging survey of people eighteen to forty-four years old, conducted for *Rolling Stone* in 1988, showed clearly the struggle confronting the Woodstock generation as it, like Billy Hayes, shed its shell and prepared to take on the issues of the 90s.

Asked to name the people they most admired, the respondents named heroes from the generation's past: Dr. Martin Luther King was chosen first, followed by Bobby Kennedy. These men stood for values that, the survey showed, the generation still believed in: peace and justice, tolerance and equality.

Although there was overwhelming support for numerous social issues, the poll showed that only a fraction were active in working on those causes.

Asked how they would like to see the working world change in the next ten years, the respondents chose first comparable-worth pay for women, then employer-provided day care.

Other surveys revealed a similar concern about social issues, as well as a reluctance by people to become involved.

Many believe, however, that the growing concern will overwhelm that reluctance.

Michael Lang, the man who created Woodstock, is one of them.

Michael Lang was busy. The phone rang. It was London calling. It rang again. Artie Kornfeld, who helped Lang plan Woodstock, needed to talk.

For twelve days they had meetings in Lang's sixth-floor loft offices in the Soho section of New York. There were Michael and Artie and Mel Lawrence, who was with Michael when he first met Max Yasgur. There was Stanley Goldstein, who arranged for the campsites at Woodstock and found the Hog Farmers. Even John Roberts and Joel Rosenman were there; they were Lang's original partners, with whom he had split acrimoniously the day after Woodstock ended.

There were others: the people who had planned the festival, who saved the concert when it was thrown out of Woodstock, who made it work.

"I just decided I didn't want to do it without them," Lang said.

Do what?

"We're going to do IT again," he explained. "If we're really going to do it, it wouldn't be right if we didn't do it together."

IT. Another concert for the twentieth anniversary of the festival that gave the generation its name.

Woodstock. Only bigger.

Lang didn't want to get involved in a tenth-anniversary concert in 1979, because he didn't want to produce merely the son of Woodstock. And if he were going to go ahead with this, it would have to be different.

This will be different. It will be international. It will feature four simultaneous festivals. And it will take place on both sides of the Iron Curtain.

Michael planned to announce the festival in April 1989. It was now the end of December, so there was much to do. That's why everyone was so busy. That's why Artie and Joel and John and Mel and everyone else had spent most of the last twelve days in Lang's loft: planning logistics, cash flow, travel; costing out every expense to the smallest detail. The $500,000 budget for the first Woodstock festival was two pages long. This one would take hundreds of pages. "It's a book," Michael said.

Surprisingly, there are relatively few remnants of the first concert around the loft—the home of Better Music, Michael's company. There's a glass copy of the concert poster above an assistant's desk. Some of the original architect's plans, including the stage design, are in frames on a wall.

But there is no blazing neon light announcing "I did Woodstock!" That is not Michael Lang, a man so soft-spoken you have trouble hearing him over the dull hum of traffic outside.

Instead, on the sunlit white walls are posters of his clients—Joe Cocker, Rickie Lee Jones, Billy Joel—and some of the gold records he helped produce. There's an old jukebox in the hallway and an exercise bike in the corner.

Every once in a while someone recognizes Michael, like the woman at the flea market in upstate New York.

"I can't believe it's you," she screamed and then pulled out a copy of *Life* magazine, a special edition produced right after the Woodstock festival. "I'm never without this."

But being recognized is not something Michael enjoys, although it makes him feel good to know that he helped bring some happiness into so many lives.

The idea for the twentieth-anniversary project began more than a year ago and was just "too good a project not to get into," he said. It started when he was in West Berlin touring with Joe Cocker. He simply decided to call up the head of the East German concert bureau to see if he was interested in meeting to talk about a rock-and-roll show.

The head of the concert bureau told him to come on over.

Lang drove through Checkpoint Charlie, a main gate through the Berlin Wall, and took a left.

Recent West German concerts had caused some riots in East Berlin as fans flocked to the wall to listen to the music. He convinced the East Germans to hold a rock-and-roll concert of their own to prevent that from happening again: "The kids won't care what's going on because they'll have their own show."

It worked. Lang helped organize two concerts in East Berlin and they went so well that "they were all knocked out." More than a hundred and twenty thousand fans came to one show alone.

That spawned another idea: Woodstock at the Wall, for summer 1988. The project bogged down in details and bureaucracy and Michael realized in March that it would never be ready on time. And so he and his colleagues decided to shoot for summer 1989 and make it really big. It would be Woodstock Across the Wall, East and West Berlin, with matching concerts in Moscow and New York. Each show would get an international cast of acts.

After more than a dozen trips to Europe, both Germanys signed on. Then the Russians agreed and Michael began negotiating for Lenin Stadium in Moscow and for a stadium in New York. Finally, it looked as if everything were set, save for a few million details.

Then there was a problem. There is always one last problem to solve, just like with the original concert two decades ago.

By May, Michael had still not signed a deal with Warner Bros., which owns the electronic rights to the Woodstock name. Lang had hoped to announce Woodstock around the world in April. That had to be put off.

In 1969, there was no live television of the concert. In 1989, there is no concert without live television; such has life changed.

Television or no television, Michael knows, of course, that *It* will never happen again. Never will there be another Woodstock with the same feeling. This is a different time: The Woodstock generation has matured into different people.

"A lot of the momentum of the 60s just ebbed away in the pursuit of daily life," Lang says. "There was a kind of vacuum but I think people needed a time to decompress."

Michael sees that changing now, as more and more emphasize ecology and making the world a better place to live.

"We're not going anywhere else; this is all we've got. Nobody has been preaching; they're just bringing some of these problems to people's attention."

Peter Max emerged from his "creative retreat" during the 80s. He never really stopped working during his hiatus. He just stopped living such a crazy life.

But unlike some of the old rock stars of the 60s, who made second careers rehashing old material, Max ended the 80s with a newer, a freer, more daring style. His colors were slightly more muted than the Day-Glo of the 60s, but were applied with broader brush strokes, rather than tight lines. It was a more mature style, and a daring one.

He also began exploring new media; computers, for example, using an electronic paint brush.

"I've always fooled around with a computer. If you could go back to Rembrandt or Renoir and tell them there was an art computer, they would die to use it."

And video. Max created a music video for television, which was a wild combination of color, shape, and symbolism. He created some of the logos for MTV and even hosted an MTV show.

Max works on the entire seventh floor of a building in midtown Manhattan. Dozens of paintings adorn walls that cut through the middle of the floor, turning it into a maze of sunsets and colorful ladies. Dozens more are stacked against walls.

One wall is filled with magazine covers featuring Max or his art. They range from *Rolling Stone* to *Business Week*. For *TV Guide*'s 1988 election issue, Peter did a flag surrounded by color.

On one side of the floor two cushioned chairs face a wall of TV monitors—eighteen of them, black Sonys three high and six across, taking up an entire wall. A first-time visitor sits on one of the soft chairs and gets "Maxed" before being admitted to the most private part of the floor.

An assistant starts the tape and suddenly eighteen Peter Maxs appear against the wall. Eighteen visions of him holding the "famous smiling sneaker" that sold a million copies, eighteen images of him watching televisions turned upside down, which he occasionally does when he needs inspiration. The tape is a twenty-minute biography of Peter Max—from China to the White House.

A corner of the floor is walled off—Max's studio. There are no pretty views, no vistas of Manhattan to inspire the artist. The inspiration comes from within.

Peter usually arrives at the studio at 11 A.M. but begins painting and drawing as soon as he wakes up. Some days he spends ten hours at the easel, even taking calls while he paints; he wears a headset connected to the telephone so he can keep his hands free to work.

Sometimes he doesn't paint at all and this makes him unhappy. Other things intrude on his time: gallery openings, and interviews and arrangements for the new line of sportswear he is designing. He is once again putting his designs on items like watches and clothing, but this time Max vows it will never get as big as it was in the early 70s, when he finally had to step away from the crowd.

"I stuck my neck out in the 60s by creating for kids, not for galleries. I will never let it get that big, although it wants to," he says, "but I want to do something for people who can't afford $30,000 for a painting."

Max is also getting renewed respect from the art community. Three separate tours were scheduled for his work in 1989, ten cities each.

On January 20, 1989 Peter was back in Washington at the request of the White House, sitting off to the side of the podium as George Bush was sworn in as the nation's forty-first president. Max was busy sketching. He will do one of the first official portraits of George Bush as the nation's new leader.

The inauguration marked a passage for America, and Max feels that even as he has emerged from his self-imposed retreat, the country has also.

On February 18 thousands of people, many from the Woodstock generation, gathered in New York for a concert to benefit animal rights activists. Peter Max was one of them. He is also active in movements to protect endangered species of animals and to improve the environment, particularly to stop the deterioration of the ozone layer of the atmosphere, a problem which Max feels is one of the most serious facing the world.

"I went on a retreat and it was fantastic," he says. "And then I got a little bored, I needed some excitement. It's like after you work, you need a vacation, but then you need to work again."

For Michael Lang, for Ken Kesey, for Abbie Hoffman, for Billie Hayes, for Peter Max, there is hope.

For the rest of the Woodstock generation, there is also a way to keep hope alive; if it can't get itself back to the garden, then it must create a new garden more suited to a new time.

Through its numbers and its history, through the media's unending focus on it and its own sense of self-importance, the generation has always had the power to change the things it wanted to change. There are signposts everywhere that it is now poised to exercise that power.

In the support for Jesse Jackson from a broadening Rainbow Coalition—from blacks to Hispanics to middle-class whites. In Mary Mossburger's personal pledge to remain involved in national issues. In the thousands suddenly showing up to help Mitch Snyder raise the call to help the nation's homeless.

Signposts everywhere.

In Ralph Fogel's promise to be a better person, to leave his imprint on society.

Signposts everywhere.

In early 1989 it seemed certain that Congress would vote itself a 50 percent pay raise. But the raise was drowned by a tidal wave of massive public protest. Killing a congressional pay raise doesn't approach anything like amassing public support to cure society's ills. But it was the first time in years that the public rose up en masse, and caused Congress to reverse itself on a specific issue. It was the first time in years that the vox populi was heard, and heeded.

Signposts everywhere.

Most important, changes are taking place in the daily lives of the people of the Woodstock generation. They just need a little nudge to cross that line and recapture their former spirit.

The spirit can be an elusive and ephemeral one, even for the staunchest and strongest. The spirit abandoned Abbie Hoffman on April 12, 1989. When his "running mate" Johanna couldn't raise him on the phone, she called their landlord, who found him in his clothes, in bed, under the covers in the converted turkey coop near New Hope, Pennsylvania.

The coroner would find the remnants of 150 phenobarbitol pills in his stomach and would rule that Hoffman had committed suicide. Hoffman's brother Jack would struggle with this idea.

"Maybe he just got tired and rolled over," he said. He talked about the numbing pain that overcomes marathon runners and said, "Maybe Abbie just hit the wall."

All who were close to him struggled to understand. The most obvious answer was the least satisfying. Abbie had been diagnosed as a manic depressive in 1980. It is an illness characterized by a chemical imbalance that creates massive mood swings. Abbie had been taking commonly prescribed drugs such as lithium for many years, to keep that chemical imbalance and those mood swings in check. His car crash in late 1988 added two elements to that equation: a constant pain that exacerbated the mood swings; and pain-killing drugs that disturbed the delicate balance created by the lithium. These factors left him with episodes of deep depression, and one of those was simply too deep to withstand.

It is difficult to accept such a cold answer because Abbie gave off a warmth and exhibited a strength of spirit that no one who knew him had ever experienced before, or is likely to again.

And so they blamed themselves, and the society around them, for neglecting Abbie, for not living up to the Fuck-the-System doctrine he carried with him until the day that he went to sleep and never woke up.

The last time we talked to Abbie was a few weeks before his death; his avid love of sports had brought him to the idea of starting a sports-handicapping business, where people for a fee could call and get hot tips for the weekend's games. He was looking for an advertising company to handle the business, and we offered him a few, but he rejected them: They were too big. He liked to work with the little guys. He was calling collect from an airport, on his way to catch a flight to speak to college students about keeping hope alive. They called his flight and he rang off.

"If I seem depressed it's probably because I hang around with too many young kids," he had said on a quirkily warm February day as we sat on a blanket outside the turkey coop. "Nihilism is very popular among the young. The young in America today are too middle-aged, thery're too grown up. They're not ready to take the courageous steps needed to build massive social movements. It's not necessarily pressure from the outside, they're nervous from the inside."

Pressed on the issue of his own mental health, he said: "You might be looking at someone who's slightly depressed, but don't worry about that. Worry about the country. The country's in worse shape."

But then, as always, he realized he didn't like the negative tone he had reached. He wanted his message to be funny, uplifting, and positive. He wanted to engender hope, not despair.

"I don't think its my role to say hope is naive," he said, the depression suddenly invisible, the smile starting. "I take you back to many dark periods and somehow the world has fought its way out." He was grinning widely now. "It always does, I'm telling you, it always does, and it will again."

The day after his death a memorial service was held in his home town of Worcester, Massachusetts. It was sedate, almost somber, despite everyone's best efforts: They knew Abbie would prefer a party to a wake. There were tie-dyes and Army jackets and business suits, yarmulkes—Hoffman was Jewish—and baseball caps.

Reporters hovered near his mother, Florence Hoffman, who had always made sure Abbie had plenty of dental floss and toothpaste back while he was in hiding. "He was the Jewish road warrior," said son Jack as he escorted her to the waiting limousine. "She was the Jewish road warrior's mama."

The reporters wanted to ask her what Abbie would have thought of the memorial, but couldn't quite bring themselves to ask. But she knew what they were thinking, and smiled at them. "He would have been proud," she said.

Jerry Rubin, dressed in dark pinstripes, was talking about Abbie's sense of humor, and how somber things were this day, how something seemed to be missing, and then he hit on it: "Hey, the service was fine . . . but where's Abbie?"

Rubin walked over to Jack Hoffman, and they embraced. "Still crazy after all these years," said Jack, dressed in Abbie's green and white Boston Celtics jacket. It was one of Abbie's favorite possessions. Abbie loved basketball. And basketball star Bill Walton was there too: He had met Abbie during the underground years, and yet today he said it was hard to think of Abbie as a fugitive from justice. "Justice was always a fugitive from Abbie," he said.

Florence Hoffman liked that. She laughed, and clapped her hands.

And from the crowd of about a thousand people, a crowd spotted with beards and long hair flecked with gray, came a happy sound. Pete Seeger was leading them in song, and had added a lyric for the day:

> Abbie's spirit is living still
> Down by the riverside
> Down by the riverside
> Down by the riverside
> Abbie's spirit is living still
> Down by the riverside.

It is the spirit of hope and belief that We Can Change the World, the spirit that the Woodstock generation is just learning to recapture. It is the spirit that Abbie himself recounted one afternoon when he was tripping his brains out and writing *Woodstock Nation* longhand in his publisher's office the day after that concert in Bethel, New York, twenty years ago:

God, how can you capture the feeling of being with 400,000 people and everyone being stoned on something? Were we pilgrims or lemmings? Was this really the beginning of a new civilization or the symptom of a dying one? Were we establishing a liberated zone or entering a detention camp? . . . You could sure come away pessimistic about the future of the MONSTER. You could sure have legitimate doubts about WOODSTOCK NATION.

But!!! And now I call upon myself to vote and I vote THUMBS UP! Right on! And I'm happy and smilin. Cocksure of the future and rememberin the great scene that Anita told me about how this bus was comin up the Thruway and how it was all freaks and everyone laughin, singin and passin around dope, and the bus stalled in traffic and the kids saw this cat standin in the road and needin a ride and they all started jumpin up and down and yellin "Pick him up!" "Pick him up!" and the bus driver began sweatin all over and shoutin out things about company regulations and other kinds of horseshit. A sort of instant people's militia was formed and they started up the aisle when all of a sudden the bus doors open and this freak with a knapsack on his back came aboard. Everybody was jokin and clownin and even the bus driver felt better.

He didn't accept the joint a cat tried to lay on him but he scratched the guy's shaggy head of hair and smiled.

I ain't never gonna forget that story. No, sir, Flower Power ain't dead at all, brother; all we gotta do is get our shit together . . . and grow some thorns. . . . Power to the People! Power to the Woodstock Nation!

 *Sources and Notes*

The historical information in this book comes from a variety of sources beyond the more than 150 interviews conducted for this book. Much of it the authors lived or reported on themselves during their combined thirty-five years as journalists. For much of the general information, the authors scanned microfilm of the *New York Times,* the *Washington Post,* and *USA Today,* where Tony Casale and Phil Lerman both worked as editors.

The inspiration to include Jimmy Holloran in this book comes from "The All-American Boy Comes Home to Die," a story by John Ed Bradley in the *Washington Post Magazine,* December 7, 1986. All the reporting for this book is fresh, but we are indebted to Bradley for bringing Jimmy Holloran to our attention.

Chapter One

The history of the early years of Woodstock and Bethel is contained in *Woodstock: History of an American Town,* by Alf Evers (Overlook Press, 1976). This formidable work by the Woodstock town historian traces the history of these upstate New York communities from the settlement through the battles Woodstock residents waged against their hippie intruders of the 1960s.

Rolling Stone magazine (September 1969) provided the account of how difficult it was for its staff to reach Woodstock along with recollections of the event from John Fogerty and Peter Townshend (October 1987). *USA Today* (August 15, 1984) provided interviews with Richie Havens and Country Joe McDonald about their remembrances of the festival.

Chapter Two

Some of the details of the meeting between Ken Kesey and Jack Kerouac were taken from Gerald Nicosia's *Memory Babe* (Grove Press, 1983), which examines Kerouac's life and works in immense detail. Although the authors lived through and reported on parts of the Kent State tragedy, William Manchester's *The Glory and the Dream* (Little, Brown, 1973) was a valuable source for the chronology of the events as well as the thoughts of local officials during the tragedy and for some of the events that led up to the riot at the 1968 Democratic convention.

Chapter Three

Richard Reeves's book, *A Ford, Not a Lincoln* (Harcourt Brace Jovanovich, 1975) provided the insight behind Richard Nixon's decision to appoint Gerald Ford as his vice president. The authors spent hours interviewing Billy Hayes developing fresh material for this work. His book, *Midnight Express* (E.P. Dutton, 1977) provided valuable background, all of which was confirmed and discussed with Billy Hayes himself. Some of the events concerning Ken Kesey's life are contained in his autobiographical stories collected in *Demon Box*. He confirmed that each of the events described here did in fact happen to him.

Chapter Four

Some details of Jimmy Carter's long campaign for the presidency are contained in Theodore H. White's *America in Search of Itself* (Harper & Row, 1982). Once again, William Manchester's *The Glory and the Dream* provided a fascinating fact in Herbert Hoover's attempt to have a song written to help people forget the Depression.

Chapter Five

Public opinion polls measuring public confidence in the government during the Carter administration were provided by the Roper Center. The surveys were conducted by Yankelovich, Skelly and White for *Time* (February 1980) and the Roper Organization (February 1979).

The woes of the Carter administration, particularly the problems of Bert Lance, are accounted in great detail in Clark R. Mollenhoff's book, *The President Who Failed* (Macmillan, 1980). Again, Theodore H. White's *America in Search of Itself* (Harper & Row, 1982) was a valuable source in understanding the mood of the administration during this period.

Chapter Six

John Leonard's timely discussion of Abbie Hoffman appeared in the *New York Times* (September 1, 1980). Other historical notes from this period, including quotes from Justice Hugo Black and President Gerald Ford, as well as Leonard's touching discussion of John Lennon's death, were also culled from the *New York Times*.

Chapter Seven

Anecdotal memories of events surrounding the shooting of Ronald Reagan, including his discussion with Labor Secretary Ray Donovan, were taken from *Newsweek*'s special edition (April 3, 1981), an expansive report on all aspects of the incident.

Barbara Garson's essay appeared in the *New York Times* (March 27, 1982). *The New York Times Magazine* (February 13, 1983) not only provided the specifically cited material about new Vietnam scholarship, but aided greatly in understanding America's evolving redefinition of the meaning and substance of the Vietnam War.

Chapter Eight

William Buckley's essay on Grenada appeared in *National Review* (November 25, 1983).

The *Washington Post* provided guideposts to the key events of the period covered in this chapter, as well as the specifically quoted Jesse Jackson speech and the New York City schools memo on "The Day After."

Chapter Nine

The discussion of Garry Trudeau and Doonesbury appeared in the *Washington Post* (August 24, 1986).

Accounts of racist incidents and antiracism activity were catalogued in *Newsweek* (April 6, 1987) and *Ms* magazine (October 1987).

Pete Hamill's essay on Live Aid appeared in *Rolling Stone* (August 29, 1985). The essay, quoted briefly, provided insights into the Woodstock generation's reaction to the new wave of music-and-protest events.

Chapter Ten

The account of Berke Breathed's involvement in protests for animal rights was reported by the Associated Press (January 1988).

 *Acknowledgments*

It is only fitting that a book about the Woodstock generation be a collective effort; and we would not have made it down the long and winding road without a little help from our friends. We offer our thanks to all who took the time to encourage, needle, cajole, prod, nourish, and guide us along the way.

But a special thanks to: Sam Meddis and Paul Clancy, who did interviews for some sections of this book; Lois, Eleanor, Michael, and Haya, for their love and support; Tommy and Amy, two most patient young grownups; Michael Zuckerman, a partner in crime; and Edna Gundersen and David Colton, whose brains we picked and ideas we borrowed.

Index